The Learncurious Companion to the Digital SAT Exam:

VERBAL

2024 Edition

ISBN: 979-8-9888478-0-9

For more information about remote tutoring lessons or personalized test prep plans, please visit www.learncurious.com

For information about LearnCurious' annual scholarship (The Phyliss J. McCarthy Scholarship for Excellence in Writing), please visit www.learncurious.com/scholarship

For bulk print order discount options, please send a request using the contact form found at the bottom of the LearnCurious homepage: www.learncurious.com

2024 Edition | LearnCurious

for Joseph
& Baggletino

The LearnCurious Companion to the Digital SAT Exam
2024 Edition Table of Contents

Part I: Introduction

Part II: Sections & Strategies for the Verbal Modules

Part III: Test-Taking Tips & Appendices

Part I:

Digital
SAT
FAQ

Frequently Asked Questions about the Digital SAT

What is the digital SAT test?

The digital SAT is a standardized test that assesses a student's abilities to complete reading, writing, & math problems under timed circumstances. This test is a college entrance exam administered by The College Board to high school juniors and seniors.

As part of the College Board's "SAT Suite of Assessments," the SAT is required for some college admission applications; however, more and more schools are choosing to be "test optional" and do not include students' test scores as a weighted part of their application screening process.

How is the digital SAT different from the paper-based SAT?

	DIGITAL SAT	PAPER-BASED SAT
Total Time:	134 minutes (*2 hours & 14 minutes*)	180 minutes (*3 hours*)
Score Range:	lower level range = 400 - 1580 higher level score range 400 - 1600	400 - 1600
Verbal Questions:	54 verbal questions total (*27 per module*)	96 verbal questions
Verbal Time:	64 minutes (*= 1 hour & 4 minutes total*) 32 minutes per module	100 minutes
Math Questions:	44 math questions (*22 per module*)	58 math questions
Math Time:	70 minutes (*= 1 hour & 10 minutes total*) 35 minutes per module	80 minutes

New features to expect on the Digital SAT:

- Students will have a highlighting tool to annotate the digital test and a flagging tool to mark questions for later review, as time allows.

- Students will also have access to the Desmos browser-based graphing calculator tool.

    > **STRATEGY NOTE**: *Familiarize yourself with how to use* **Desmos**, *the free online graphing calculator tool that will be included in the resources provided for students to use on the digital SAT.*

- Students will be allowed to write on provided scratch paper. While scrap paper will be taken up after the exam to avoid questions being released, students will be allowed to use pencil or pen to do scratch work by hand.

- Students will also have access to a digital annotation tool that will allow them to make notes in the test application itself.

- Students will be able to view a test-timer at any time during their digital and can hide it until the last five minutes of each stage.

- Students will be able to use a special 'elimination' function to mark answers they have eliminated. This will ~~strikethrough~~ answers that students want to remember are incorrect.

- Students will now have digital access to the same math reference sheet information that is currently available to students taking the paper-based SAT.

Specific, important changes to note from the paper-based SAT:

On the Digital SAT, ...

...reading & writing questions are intermixed and are each now based on one short paragraph instead of grouped with longer passages.

...the 'Global Conversation' passage has been removed

...writing questions will no longer test idioms and commonly-confused words.

...there is no longer a 'NO CHANGE' option on verbal questions.

...students will be able to use a calculator for all math questions.

...imaginary / complex numbers are no longer tested.

...students can input negative responses on fill-in-the-blank style questions.

...math questions will no longer be linked to one another or share common information.

Who can take the digital SAT exam?

11th & 12th grade high school students.

When do students take the digital SAT?

The SAT exams are offered seven times each year, in March, May, June, August, October, November, & December. Registration is required and can be completed at collegeboard.com. Students must bring a government-issued photo ID on test day. Students can take the test as many times as they like, but, to improve control over which scores are submitted to colleges, LearnCurious recommends that students practice with full, timed tests administered at home or at a testing center.

Learncurious encourages students to begin preparing for these exams outside of school as early as possible. The College Board offers formal preparatory practice tests (the PSAT 8/9, PSAT 10, & PSAT NMSQT) to 8th-11th graders that will also be making the switch to a digital version in 2023-2024. Other practice tests are also available, and the SAT itself can be taken more than once.

Juniors have more opportunities to take their SAT tests than seniors do. Starting the college entrance exam process in junior year (or sooner) helps students pace their senior year more comfortably and reduces the stress of their college application season, and can help them score better.

It is often too early in the process for sophomores to consider taking the SAT during the school year, but the summer between sophomore and junior year can be an opportunity for some high-achieving students to complete their first official SAT exam, provided they have taken measures to ensure that they are prepared and are familiar with all of the concepts that appear on the test.

When are the remaining SAT dates for this year?

Upcoming test dates can be found on the College Board's website.

The test is usually administered seven times per year: in <u>March, May, June, August, October, November, & December.</u>

When should students start preparing for the SAT?

With college admissions being so competitive starting formal test prep early is a good idea, especially if students are hoping to be accepted at a T20 or T50 school. Starting early, they get more exposure to the question types, they develop test-taking endurance, they are able to practice strategies they can use on test day, and they feel calmer about the big test when it feels familiar.

Students can now begin taking the PSAT as early as 8th grade, with the addition of the PSAT 8/9 to the College Board's "SAT Suite of Assessments." The PSAT tests have the same types of questions as the SAT, which are different from normal schoolwork. Seeing these question styles earlier and more frequently helps to assure that students have solving systems in place early and aren't scrambling to learn about them later.

If you or your child is in 10th or 11th grade, not to worry, you still have time to prepare with a more compressed approach.

Note that registration windows close about 1 month before each test date. Some test centers fill up quickly. Be sure to register as soon as you know when you'll be ready to take the real thing. If you're not sure when the right time is, consulting a tutor can help.

Taking full-length, timed practice SAT tests outside the house (in a library or at a testing center) and reviewing results with a tutor is an excellent way for students to get practice with SAT question styles in an authentic testing atmosphere. The scores from these practice tests are nearly as valuable as the test-taking time itself, as they yield a ton of data useful to savvy students or tutors, yet they are never sent to colleges.

Will the PSAT be digital as well?

Yes. Students will begin taking the digital PSAT 8/9 and PSAT/NMSQT in autumn of 2023. Students will also be able to take the PSAT digitally starting in the spring of 2024.

Where do students take the digital SAT?

While the digital SAT can be taken on students' personal laptops, it is still necessary for students to take the test in a designated testing facility. More than half of students who take the SAT take it for free on SAT School Day, when the test is hosted during the week by schools. Starting in spring 2024, schools will offer the digital SAT to students on SAT School Day.

Can students take the exam on their computer at home?

No. While a student may use their personal computer to take the test, the digital SAT must be taken at a designated school or testing site. Proctors will be present in each testing room to assist students with setting up the testing software and to ensure that the test is administered and supervised under the SAT's standardization practices. This also ensures that students have knowledgeable help available should they encounter technical difficulties.

Will the paper version of the test still be available to students?

The College Board has announced that they are making a full transition to the digital exam. As of spring 2024, all students in the US who register for the SAT will take the digital SAT; however, some exceptions will be made for students with documented accommodations requiring pencil and paper.

How early in the morning is the SAT?

Most testing centers open at 7:45am local time and close their doors promptly at 8:00am. I recommend that students prepare test materials and plan their outfit and breakfast the night before so that the morning of the test goes as smoothly as possible and arriving early doesn't create stress. Many students are now choosing to meditate on the way to the test to help prepare their concentration for the marathon they're about to run. The test itself will begin between 8:30-9:00 am, after the proctor gives out materials and reads instructions.

How long is the digital SAT & how is it formatted?

The digital SAT exam is 2 hours & 14 minutes long.

It has 2 sections, each with 2 modules: the second module is adapted to fit students' skills based on their performance on the first module of each section.

Reading / Writing
Module 1: 32 minutes, 27 questions
Module 2: 32 minutes, 27 questions

Math
Module 1: 35 minutes, 22 questions
Module 2: 35 minutes, 22 questions

Test-taking endurance is an often-overlooked aspect of test prep. While the digital SAT isn't as lengthy as the paper-based version of the test, students taking the SAT will still be testing for over 2 hours; those with time extension accommodations may not finish their exams for well over 4 hours. It's important to begin training for these mental marathons early and often so that students have the capacity to focus through the entirety of the test comfortably.

What does the SAT actually test?

It's important to understand that the Digital SAT exam is not based on any one school's curriculum standards or teaching approaches; it's designed to test students' knowledge of what The College Board has included on the SAT test.

Let's read that sentence one more time because it's one of the most important things to know about a test like the digital SAT: **it's designed to test students' knowledge of what The College Board has included on the SAT test**.

Even if students have perfect GPAs and straight As, they may be thrown for a loop when first faced with digital SAT questions. This is normal. Students must know how to deal with unique question types and time constraints, preferably well ahead of test day. Advanced familiarity of the test's format and question style for each section makes a huge difference for most students in their ability to score well and feel confident on test day.

<u>In a nutshell, the Digital SAT tests specific skills in 3 subject areas: reading comprehension, writing & language, and mathematics.</u>

Reading Comprehension: active reading, passage analysis & comparison, vocabulary, chart interpretation, & inference-making. Each of the passages will be roughly 50-200 words long. The Digital SAT has been formatted to have only one question related to each passage.

Writing & Language: English grammar, usage rules, rhetoric style, idea expression & analysis, & punctuation.

Mathematics: algebraic & geometric problem solving, data & diagram analysis, and as well as niche topics like trigonometry and pre-calculus, plus some elementary math concepts students that may not have used in a while (like calculating the mean, median, mode, & range of a data set).

> Many parents, after looking at their students' SAT practice math materials, have expressed their alarm to me regarding the difficult wording and advanced concept combination skills required to answer each question in the allotted time, which is usually 1-2 minutes per question. They're right -- these tests *are* challenging, especially with respect to pacing. It's helpful for students to learn when it's strategic to speed up or slow down.

Who gets a time extension?

Allowances of 1.5x time or 2x additional time are available for select students with proper documentation and pre-planning, along with a host of other potential test accommodations. To qualify, a student typically must have a documented history of requiring individual time or special circumstances on assignments in school.

Students with 504 plans or IEPs are more likely to be given a time extension, but it's not guaranteed. **A separate application through the College Board is necessary, and the review process can be lengthy.** Contact The College Board as soon as possible if you or your child would like to apply for a time extension or special accommodations for the Digital SAT.

Is the digital SAT scored the same way as the paper-based test?

The digital SAT is scored using the same overall 200-800 section score scale that the paper-based SAT is, and a section score of 740 on the paper test is reflective of a 740 on the digital test as well.

HOWEVER

The digital SAT is structured using an adaptive system and is scored based on this adaptive model as well. Each section of the test will consist of two modules, and the second module's questions and difficulty level will be based on how well a student does on the first module. So, if a student gets more questions correct in the first module, the second module will include more complex questions and align with a higher overall possible score range relative to a student who performs more poorly in the first part of each section and received second-module questions which are not as complex and do not allow a student to score as highly.

Why are the scores on my digital SAT practice test not precise?

The two dSAT verbal modules modules students take are scored together for a composite in the range of 200-800. The two dSAT math modules are also scored together on a scale of 200-800. A combined perfect score is 800+800=1600.

Please see the section further detailing adaptive scoring starting on page 241.

If a student takes the SAT more than once, do colleges see all of their scores?

The answer depends on the school. Each college or university has its own policy regarding which SAT scores they review with a student's application.

Most fall into three categories:
- *All scores from all tests are required.*
- *Only the highest-scoring sections among all of the tests a student has taken. This policy is called 'superscoring.'*
- *Only the highest-scoring total score among all the tests a student has taken.*

Note that students can find information about a school's SAT score submission preferences on their admissions web pages or by calling the admissions office. (Ideally this call will include a few other well-researched questions that aren't answered on the website. Many schools' admissions faculty keep track of how many times a student reaches out directly).

Do colleges see any PSAT scores?

Most commonly no, unless you do well enough to qualify for a scholarship (and at that point, students likely want them to see). A few secondary schools routinely input PSAT results on student transcripts, but rest easy – a PSAT score is not an admissions criterion.

What about the ACT? Do students have to take both the SAT & ACT? How do SAT scores compare to the ACT scoring scale?

Some schools accept the ACT instead of, or in addition to, the SAT. If your targeted schools are in this category, you have to decide which tests to take and submit.

The ACT is scored on a 1-36 scale. A perfect score is a composite score of 36.

Some students do well on both exams, while others show a performance preference on one or the other. Students' PSAT, SAT, & ACT practice test scores can be helpful predictors when it comes time to decide whether to take both the SAT and ACT or commit to only one of them.

Many factors play into the decision: diagnostic results (SAT vs ACT diagnostic and practice exams are available here) , schedule availability (juggling hectic junior/senior year workloads & extra-curriculars), and even finances (there's a fee for each time a student takes the exam). An experienced tutor can aid this navigation.

Why do students take the SAT?

SAT scores can be required by top-tier universities and colleges as a key component of their application review processes. While many institutions have shifted to being 'test-optional' and no longer require standardized test scores as part of their application package, many students still choose to take these tests and send in their scores to further round out their applications' robustness and provide admissions review personnel with more data demonstrating students' academic performance under pressure.

How can students study well for the digital SAT?

Start early, take practice tests, and work with a tutor! Even a single last-minute session can boost your score on test day.

Working with a tutor is a great way to learn more about designing effective study plans. To contact a LearnCurious tutor, please visit www.learncurious.com/tutoring

Student-Specific FAQ:

*How do I deal with excessive parental pressure?

Resisting parental pressure can be a frustrating experience. It's important to keep in mind that this is *your* life. Make choices that will shape your life the way you want to see it develop. It's okay if others don't understand. That's about them, not you.

Now is the time to forge your own path.

Making mistakes will happen; it's part of the journey. Be kind to yourself and those around you. Express your thoughts and wishes firmly (but respectfully!), and do be willing and open to at least listening to what opportunities or options are being suggested by those that know or care about you. They're telling you for a reason. It's still up to you to decide whether any suggestion seems right for you.

*I bombed the SAT. Now what?

Try again. Create a study plan to target the areas where you can realistically achieve the most improvement; keep to your plan; take practice tests to track your improvement; work with a tutor and take advantage of available resources.

No time to retake it? Don't panic. Many schools are test-optional and will accept applications without SAT/ACT scores. Check out www.fairscore.com to see which schools might be good options for you.

*Are you for real not covering any math in this book?
When's the math companion book coming out?

Just the verbal sections are covered in this book. The math book is coming soon!

BUT, in the meantime, to get you started, the Anxiety-Reducing Techniques section has a segment targeting math anxiety specifically on pages 250-255.

Part II:

Sections & Strategies for the Verbal Modules

Digital SAT Verbal Modules - Quick Facts

Big Picture: Reading (and comprehending) high-level texts is going to be a part of many college courses as well as daily life for a number of people.

Real world connection: We read every day, and it's unlikely to stop anytime in our lifetimes. We'll need to express ourselves in written language for the rest of our lives. Being good at it saves time and avoids headaches. Developing your skills now saves your future self a lot of hassle.

Why though? The better we can understand and think critically about what we're reading, the better we can communicate knowledge we learn from reading to others. Having control over your language means having better control over how you communicate.

Verbal Section Format

Module 1: 32 minutes, 27 questions
Module 2: 32 minutes, 27 questions
Total = 54 passage+question sets; 64 minutes for 2 adaptive modules

Passage Types:

History & Humanities
Natural / Social Sciences
Fiction
Poetry

Reading Comprehension Question Types

Words in Context
Detail
Main Idea
Purpose
Inference
Chart / Graph Interpretation
Support Quotation
Poetic Structure
Paired / Comparison

English Question Types

Punctuation
Tense / Agreement
Special Grammar Rules
Logical Transitions
Notes

Verbal Module Question & Passage Type Frequency

The questions in the verbal modules of the digital SAT fall into four main categories: **Words in Context (WIC), Comprehension, Conventions of Standard English (CSE), and Editing.**

There are also four main types of passages students can expect to see on the digital SAT's verbal modules:

The breakdown of the average frequency of each **question** and **passage** type appearing in the four first released digital SAT tests are detailed below:

Words in Context   **~20%**

Comprehension   **~36%**
Detail, Logical Completion, Chart / Graph Interpretation, Purpose, Support Quotation, Main Idea, Inference / Passage Comparison, & (Poetic) Structure questions*

Conventions of Standard English (CSE)   **~25%**
Punctuation, Tense / Agreement, Miscellaneous Grammar Rules*

Editing   **~19%**
Logical Transitions & Notes questions

* in order of relative frequency of appearance in 324 verbal questions assessed from Digital SAT Tests #1-4

~~~~~~

History & Humanities passages	~47.2%
Natural & Social Sciences passages	~42%
Fiction passages	~7.4%
Poetry passages	~3.4%

*Frequency legend: "mythic" will refer to questions which make up 0-4% of the total question population; "rare" will refer to questions which make up 5-12% of the total question population; "uncommon" will refer to those questions which make up 13-19% of the question population; and "common" will refer to questions which make up 20% or more of test questions.

The questions in the verbal modules of the digital SAT are roughly 20% vocabulary based (testing students' understanding of words in specific contexts) and the remaining 80% of questions test other comprehension skills including identifying passages' purposes, main ideas, and details; making inferences; interpreting charts & graphs; and drawing comparisons between two short passages).

> **STRATEGY:** *If you feel iffy on punctuation, circle any uncommon marks you notice in the passages in the verbal section. You can use these as examples to help remind yourself of the rules surrounding punctuation marks like colons, semicolons, dashes, and apostrophes.*

To study these exams well, it is key to learn which types of questions and passages are your strengths and weaknesses. Using the included diagnostic quizzes and practice tests, keep track of the types of questions / passages you're getting correct and incorrect and focus your study more on the challenge patterns you notice for yourself.

We'll get into the specifics of each question type next…

What Will We Cover?
Reading Comprehension Checklist

Check off which question types you've already learned about.

❑ **Question Types**

- ❑ *Words in Context*
- ❑ *Evidence*
- ❑ *Logical Completion*
- ❑ *Chart / Graph Interpretation*
- ❑ *Support Quotation*
- ❑ *Purpose*
- ❑ *Main Idea*
- ❑ *Passage Comparison*
- ❑ *(Poetic) Structure*

❑ **Example & Practice Question Score Log & Checklist**

❑ Words in Context (pages 26-38)
  ❑ *example questions (score:_____)*
  ❑ *practice questions (score:_____)*

❑ Evidence (pages 39-55)
  ❑ *example questions (score:_____)*
  ❑ *practice questions (score:_____)*

❑ Logical Completion (pages 56-66)
  ❑ *example questions (score:_____)*
  ❑ *practice questions (score:_____)*

❑ Chart / Graph Interpretation (pages 67-82)
  ❑ *example questions (score:_____)*
  ❑ *practice questions (score:_____)*

❑ Support Quotation (pages 83-97)
  ❑ *example questions (score:_____)*
  ❑ *practice questions (score:_____)*

❑ Purpose (pages 98-111)
  ❑ *example questions (score:_____)*
  ❑ *practice questions (score:_____)*

❑ Main Idea (pages 112-123)
  ❑ *example questions (score:_____)*
  ❑ *practice questions (score:_____)*

❑ Passage Comparison (pages 124-132)
  ❑ *example questions (score:_____)*
  ❑ *practice questions (score:_____)*

❑ (Poetic) Structure (pages 133-146)
  ❑ *example questions (score:_____)*
  ❑ *practice questions (score:_____)*

Reading Comprehension Questions

WORDS
IN
CONTEXT

VOCAB IS BACK!

On older versions of the SAT, vocabulary played a more central role in the verbal section(s) of the test, and, after fading from the spotlight on more recent editions of the test, now it's back in focus at the beginning of each digital SAT verbal module.

Here's the breakdown of what LearnCurious calls 'words in context' or WIC questions on the four currently-released digital SAT exams:

	VM1	VM2a	VM2b
Test #1:	2/27 = 7.4%	8/27 = 29.6%	8/27 = 29.6%
Test #2:	4/27 = 14.8%	7/27 = 25.9%	4/27 = 14.8%
Test #3:	5/27 = 18.5%	6/27 = 22.2%	5/27 = 18.5%
Test #4:	6/27 = 22.2%	6/27 = 22.2%	4/27 = 14.8%

To summarize, there are
...between **2-6** 'words in context' (WIC) questions on Verbal Module 1,
...between **6-8** WIC questions on Verbal Module 2a,
...and between **4-8** WIC questions on Verbal Module 2b.

Question frequency: 7.4% - 29.6% == COMMON
Speed rating: quick (usually)

WORDS IN CONTEXT questions appear at the very beginning of each Verbal Module, usually between questions #1-6. They ask students to choose fitting words based on the specific context of a passage. Keep in mind that the words chosen for these questions can often be used in multiple ways, depending on the context; therefore, it's key to **always read the passage to answer these questions correctly.**

How do I identify this type of question?

The 'words in context' questions are the **first** questions in every verbal module that has been released so far. If that pattern continues, students can expect the first **2-8** questions in each verbal module to be vocabulary-focused.

Vocab-centered questions can be identified using these specific question stems:
- *"Which choice completes the text with the most logical and precise word or phrase?"*
- *"As used in the text, what does the word "____" most nearly mean?"*

Look for these words in particular in the question stem to easily identify Words in Context (WIC) questions: *'most nearly means,'* & *'logical and precise word or phrase'*

Here are some examples of what digital SAT 'words in context' questions look like:

1.
You can <u>ensure</u> the safety of your defense if you only hold positions that cannot be attacked.

As used in the text, what does the word "ensure" most nearly mean?

A) guarantee
B) replenish
C) aggravate
D) explain

2.
When a race of plants is once pretty well established, the seed-raisers do not pick out the best plants, but merely go over their seed-beds, and pull up the "rogues," as they call the plants that _____ from the proper standard. With animals this kind of selection is, in fact, also followed; for hardly any one is so careless as to allow his worst animals to breed.

Which choice completes the text with the most logical and precise word or phrase?

A) mimic
B) restore
C) deviate
D) accommodate

3.

Some of the cases of _____ organs are extremely curious; for instance, the presence of teeth in fetal whales, which when grown up have not a tooth in their heads; and the presence of teeth, which never cut through the gums, in the upper jaws of our unborn calves.

Which choice completes the text with the most logical and precise word or phrase?

A) interchangeable
B) unknown
C) rudimentary
D) catastrophic

4.

"Sir," Mr. Wright remarked, "we should reach Giri Bala before the sun sets, to have enough light for photographs." He added with a grin, "The Westerners are a _____ lot; we can't expect them to believe in the lady without any pictures!" This bit of wisdom was indisputable; I turned my back on temptation and reentered the car. "You are right, Dick," I sighed as we sped along, "I sacrifice the mango paradise on the altar of Western realism. Photographs we must have!"

Which choice completes the text with the most logical and precise word or phrase?

A) skeptical
B) offhand
C) satisfactory
D) decisive

Answers on page 373

What are some helpful WIC question strategies?

If you're a flash card and/or checklist fan, **Appendix A** has vocab lists for you!

Even if you're not big on flash cards, consider reviewing the vocabulary words in Appendix A some other way. Digital flash cards are much more portable and sustainable; it's possible someone has already put these lists onto sites like Anki or Quizlet and shared for others to use. If they haven't, you could be the one to help others!

The structure of the digital SAT suggests that questions are pooled in a database and can be re-used. This suggests a higher likelihood that students will see the listed words appear in questions. Of course, there will be new words / questions added to the pool over time, but these lists are a great place to start if you're feeling like bolstering your vocab question scores.

Here are a few strategic questions to ask yourself when faced with vocab questions:

"What other word would fit in the blank?"

This question is best asked before you even look at the answer choice options. It can even be a mini-game you play during the test: hold your hand over the answer bank until you've predicted a synonym.

If you predict an accurate synonym, you give your brain two points of reference to use to match to the correct answer choice instead of one. Then, reveal the answer choices and match both the word in context and your synonym to the most similar word in the answer bank.

Sometimes, before seeing the answer options, you end up choosing one of the answers as your synonym choice. If this happens, you win the mini game and can more confidently choose that answer as being correct.

"Do I want to spend time on this right now?"

If you are low on time or feel time pressure, it makes sense to avoid spending a lot of time on questions that include unfamiliar vocabulary. Make your best guess* and move on.

> *STRATEGY NOTE: If you don't have time to eliminate any answer options and need to make a guess on a question, have a consistent guess letter in mind. There is no truth to the common myth that "C" is the best guess to make. Pick your favorite letter and choose that for any guesses you need to make. By choosing one letter consistently, you are slightly more likely to earn free points by guessing correctly.

"Do I know all of these words?"

There is a broad range of vocabulary tested by the Digital SAT, so being unfamiliar with some of the words on the test is common, even with a stellar vocabulary!

Not to worry - there are a few strategies on the next few pages to add to your vocab question tool belt to bring out when you encounter an unfamiliar word.

"Does this word feel more positive, neutral, or negative?"

&

"Does the context of the passage call for a positive, neutral, or negative word?"

Sometimes, just from the sound of the word, we can glean a bit about its meaning. It's not a perfect system, but it's better than blind guessing.

For example, the sound of the word "abhor" may suggest more of a negative mental image or feeling as compared to the sound of the word "mellifluous" (which may conjure a more positive or calm image/feeling), whereas the word "celery" might sound pretty neutral. Of course, everyone has their subjective experience that may cast a bit of a different slant on a word, so this system isn't perfect but it can be helpful in eliminating some answer choices for a more educated guess.

Do I recognize any prefixes, roots, or suffixes in this word?

We can break down words into their 'affixes' (additions to words like prefixes & suffixes) and roots. Depending on what languages you've studied, you may have more of a database of affix and root knowledge than you think! Many English roots and affixes come from Greek and Latin words and are familiar to us in meaning.

Noticing affixes and roots in less-familiar vocabulary words can be a great help in eliminating potential answer options down to one correct answer.

Prefixes, or additions to the beginning of a word, can give useful information such as number ('mono-' or 'uni-' for one, 'bi-' or 'duo-' for two, etc), time or frequency ('re-' for again, 'pre-' for before (like in prefix!), etc.)

Word roots can sometimes (depending on context & connotation of certain words) give useful information about the core meaning of a word. For example,

Suffixes, or additions to the end of a word, can give useful information about tense ('-ed' for past tense) or part of speech ('-ive' at the end of a word often forms an adjective, such as 'active' or 'passive' — there's a review of active vs passive voice in on pages 197-199, by the way!)

Here's another example with some key affixes and roots you're likely to recognize:

After continually being talked over by her classmates, Luna felt herself grow more _____, choosing to keep her thoughts to herself when previously she'd have chosen to share her opinions.

Which choice completes the text with the most logical and precise word or phrase?

A) introspective
B) inconsiderate
C) indolent
D) timeless

Let's examine our options' affixes and roots before choosing an answer:

introspective
Prefix = 'intro' = Latin prefix meaning 'inside' (think, 'introduce' or 'introvert')
Root = 'spect' = Latin root meaning look or see (think, 'spectacle' or 'inspect')
Suffix = 'ive' = adjective ending

inconsiderate
Prefix = 'in-' = Latin prefix often meaning 'not'
Root = 'consider' = from the Latin *consideratus* meaning 'thoughtful'
Suffix = '-ate' = adjective ending

indolent
Prefix = 'in-' = Latin prefix often meaning 'not'
Root = -dol- = from the Latin *dolens* meaning 'pain' or 'suffering'
Suffix = '-ent' = adjective ending

timeless
Prefix = n/a
Root = 'time' = from Old English *tima* meaning 'season' or 'period'
Suffix = '-less' = adjective ending usually meaning 'without' or 'lacking'

Given the context, answer (A), introspective, makes the most sense.

Let's look at another example with an underlined word of Greek origin:

> Finally, in the year 1645, a settlement was established near the site of the present borough hall, and was called Breuckelen (also spelled Breucklyn, Breuckland, Brucklyn, Broucklyn, Brookland, and Brookline) until about the close of the 18th century, when its ***orthography*** became fixed as Brooklyn.
>
> The name, Breuckelen, meaning marsh land, seems to have been suggested by the resemblance of the situation of the settlement to that of Breuckelen, Holland.
>
> As used in the text, what does the word "orthography" most nearly mean?
>
> A) musicality
> B) spelling
> C) infrastructure
> D) location

Those of us familiar with ORTHO-donture understand that braces and retainers "correct" the position of teeth in the mouth.

An auto-GRAPH is someone's signature. A seismo-GRAPH "writes" out the data generated by earthquakes.

Putting together the clues from potentially more-familiar words can help us build a definition for "orthography" that fits in the context of the passage:

ORTHO- = "correct"
GRAPH = "writing"

We can tell this way that the question is asking about the correct spelling of the word Brooklyn.

B is the correct answer.

Practice WIC Questions:

1.

Chang Yu continues, "High and sunny places are <u>advantageous</u> not only for fighting, but also because they are immune from disastrous floods."

As used in the text, what does the word "advantageous" most nearly mean?

A) deceptive
B) novel
C) innocuous
D) beneficial

2.

So '<u>general</u>' is still the custom of "bidding-weddings" in Wales that printers usually keep the form of invitation in type. Sometimes as many as six hundred couples will walk in the bridal procession.

As used in the text, what does the word "general" most nearly mean?

A) common
B) leader
C) vague
D) nondescript

3.

Wang Hsi explains undefended places as weak points; that is to say, where the general is lacking in capacity, or the soldiers in spirit; where the walls are not strong enough, or the precautions not strict enough; where relief comes too late, or provisions are too _____, or the defenders are variance amongst themselves."

Which choice completes the text with the most logical and precise word or phrase?
A) scanty
B) disputed
C) recognizable
D) mandatory

4.

Neither Alexander nor any of his generals ever crossed the Ganges. Finding determined resistance in the northwest, the Macedonian army refused to penetrate farther; Alexander was forced to leave India and seek his conquests in Persia. From this question we may <u>surmise</u> that the "Son of Zeus" had an occasional doubt that he had already attained perfection.

As used in the text, what does the word "surmise" most nearly mean?

A) foretell
B) recant
C) dispute
D) infer

5.

William Gilpin, who is so admirable in all that <u>relates</u> to landscapes, and usually so correct, stands at the head of Loch Fyne, in Scotland, which he describes as "a bay of salt water, sixty or seventy fathoms deep, four miles in breadth," and about fifty miles long, surrounded by mountains.

As used in the text, what does the word "relates" most nearly mean?

A) fosters
B) interprets
C) pertains
D) accommodates

6.

And in the moment when the sound of "*Om*" touched Siddhartha's ear, his <u>dormant</u> spirit suddenly woke up and realized the foolishness of his actions. Siddhartha was deeply shocked.

As used in the text, what does the word "dormant" most nearly mean?

A) sleeping
B) reciprocal
C) substantial
D) mystifying

7.

There was nothing grand about their enemy; on the contrary, he was a low, mean fellow, whom it was easy to <u>circumvent</u>, and fine fun to play tricks with.

As used in the text, what does the word "circumvent" most nearly mean?

A) originate
B) elude
C) fulfill
D) aggravate

8.

That he had felt this despair, this deep disgust, and that he had not _
_____ it, that the bird, the joyful source and voice in him was still alive after all, this was why he felt joy, this was why he laughed, this was why his face was smiling brightly under his hair which had turned gray.

Which choice completes the text with the most logical and precise word or phrase?

A) compared to
B) surpassed by
C) reacted to
D) succumbed to

9.

We can thus understand the high importance of barriers, whether of land or water, which separate our several zoological and botanical provinces. We can thus understand the _____ of sub-genera, genera, and families.

As used in the text, what does the word "localization" most nearly mean?

A) localization
B) simplicity
C) conceptualization
D) commitment

10.

I awakened the *arriero* to know if there was any danger of bad weather; he said that the peril is <u>imminent</u>, and the difficulty of subsequent escape great to anyone overtaken by bad weather between the two ranges. A certain cave offers the only place of refuge.

As used in the text, what does the word "imminent" most nearly mean?

A) latent
B) impending
C) disputed
D) underscored

CHALLENGE:

Jupiter is a very loosely packed body. Its density is on average only about 1½ times that of water, or about one-fourth the density of the earth. _____ the kinetic theory, we may expect the planet to retain an extensive layer of gases around it; and this is confirmed by the spectroscope, which gives evidence of the presence of a dense atmosphere.

Which choice completes the text with the most logical and precise word or phrase?

A) In accordance by
B) Overshadowed by
C) Irrelevant to
D) In accordance with

Answers on page 373

<u>Recommendations:</u>

If you scored between 0-5, vocab practice is high priority for you.

If you scored between 6-8, vocab practice is medium priority for you.

If you scored between 9-11, vocab practice is low priority for you.

Appendix A has a full list of the vocabulary that has appeared in the WIC questions on the officially-released tests so far. Since vocabulary has been known to repeat and reappear in both other questions' answers and passages, it is a good use of time to ensure that you are familiar with the words in the list in Appendix A.

EVIDENCE

Many of the reading comprehension questions on the digital SAT require students to identify specific details in passages for which there is directly-stated support.

> *STRATEGY: Evidence questions require looking back at the passage, identifying connecting evidence, and matching it to the correct answer choice. There will be direct evidence for these types of questions, meaning the correct answer will contain verbatim or paraphrased evidence directly from the given passage.*

Here's the breakdown of what LearnCurious calls 'evidence' questions on the four currently-released digital SAT exams:

	VM1	VM2a	VM2b
Test #1:	3/27 = 11.1%	1/27 = 3.7%	4/27 = 14.8%
Test #2:	0/27 = 0%	2/27 = 7.4%	4/27 = 14.8%
Test #3:	2/27 = 7.4%	4/27 = 14.8%	3/27 = 11.1%
Test #4:	1/27 = 3.7%	0/27 = 0%	3/27 = 11.1%

To summarize, there are usually
...between **0-3** evidence questions on Verbal Module 1,
...between **0-4** evidence questions on Verbal Module 2a,
...and between **3-4** evidence questions on Verbal Module 2b.

Question frequency: 0 - 14.8% == UNCOMMON
Speed rating: moderate

EVIDENCE questions appear in the early-middle part of Verbal Modules, usually between questions #6 - 16. They ask about specific details from the passage, and students can expect there to be (verbatim or paraphrased) direct evidence from the passage to support the correct answer. **Students must remember to look back at the passage to find directly-stated or paraphrased evidence to support their answers.**

How do I identify evidence questions?

Evidence questions can be identified using these specific question stems:
- *'According to the text, what is true about _____?'*
- *'Based on the text, what is true about _____?'*
- *'Based on the text, how does _____ respond to _____?'*
- *'According to the text, why was _____ significant?'*
- *'Which choice best describes _____, as presented in the text?'*
- *'Based on the text, in what way was _____ LIKE / UNLIKE _____?'*

This last question stem variety is often more complex in nature, so we'll discuss approaches for this question stem type in particular later on:
- *'Which finding from ___, if true, would most directly support the author's claim?*
- *Which finding from ___, if true, would most directly weaken the author's hypothesis?*
- *Which finding from ___, if true, would most directly undermine the author's idea?*

Look for these words in particular in the question stem to easily identify Evidence questions:
- *'according to the passage / text,'*
- *'based on the passage / text,'*
- *'as presented in the text,'*
- *'what is true about'*
- *'the passage states / asserts / makes the claim / indicates'*

Here are several examples of what digital SAT evidence questions look like:

1.
The following is adapted from Frank L. Baum's novel '*The Wonderful Wizard of Oz,*' in which a young girl, Dorothy, is transported to a mysterious, colorful land called Oz where she faces a Wicked Witch.

The Wicked Witch watched Dorothy carefully, to see if she ever took off her shoes, thinking she might steal them. But the child was so proud of her pretty shoes that she never took them off except at night and when she took her bath. The Witch was too much afraid of the dark to dare go in Dorothy's room at night to take the shoes, and her dread of water was greater than her fear of the dark, so she never came near when Dorothy was bathing.

Based on the text, how does the Wicked Witch respond to darkness?

A) With fear
B) With excitement
C) With boredom
D) With flying monkeys

2.

An amulet is a charm, generally, but not invariably, hung from the neck, to protect the wearer against witchcraft, sickness, accidents, etc. Talisman, also from the Arabic, is a word of similar meaning and use, but some distinguish it as importing a more powerful charm. A talisman, whose "virtues are still applied to for stopping blood and in cases of canine madness," figures prominently in one of Sir Walter Scott's novels.

Based on the text, in what way was an amulet unlike a talisman?

A) Amulets have been of many different kinds, and formed of different substances: stones, metals, and strips of parchment are the most common.

B) Amulets may or may not have characters or legends engraved or written on them.

C) Talismans are generally considered as having more mystical power than amulets possess.

D) Talismans are similar to amulets but are generally considered as having less mystical power.

3.

The anchors with two teeth were called *amfiboloi* or *amfistomoi*, and from ancient monuments appear to have resembled generally those used in modern days, except that the stock is absent from them all. Every ship had several anchors; the largest, corresponding to our sheet anchor, was only used in extreme danger.

Which choice best describes when a ship's crew uses a sheet anchor, as presented in the text?

A) In modern days
B) In extreme danger
C) In calm water
D) Near ancient monuments

4.

The following text is from the 1900 poem 'As I Watch'd the Ploughman Ploughing' by Walt Whitman.

"As I watch'd the ploughman ploughing,
Or the sower sowing in the fields—or the harvester harvesting,
I saw there too, O life and death, your analogies:
(Life, life is the tillage, and Death is the harvest according.)"

Based on the text, what is true about life and death?

A) They are unlike the cycles of agricultural work.
B) They are similar to the harvest.
C) They are analogous to the tillage and harvest.
D) They are balanced just like the ploughman and the fields.

5.

In South Africa buffaloes frequent reedy swamps, where they associate in herds of from fifty to a hundred or more individuals. Old bulls may be met with either alone or in small parties of from two or three to eight or ten. This buffalo formerly roamed in herds over the plains of Central and Southern Africa, always in the near vicinity of water, but the numbers are greatly diminished.

Which finding, if true, would most directly weaken the author's claim that the South African buffalo roamed plains "always in the vicinity of water?"

A) Researchers discover evidence of the South African buffalo far from any known bodies of water.

B) Researchers continue to find evidence of the South African buffalo in close proximity to bodies of water.

C) Researchers find no strong evidence of the South African buffalo in the reedy swamps of Central Africa.

D) Researchers discover evidence of the South African buffalo on another continent.

6.

The most ancient anchors consisted of large stones, baskets full of stones, sacks filled with sand, or logs of wood loaded with lead. Such anchors held the vessel merely by their weight and by the friction along the bottom. The anchors of the ancient Greeks, according to Apollonius Rhodius and Stephen of Byzantium, were formed of stone.

Which finding, if true, would most directly weaken the author's claim that the anchors of the ancient Greeks were formed of stone.

A) Athenaeus states that Greek anchors were sometimes made of wood.
B) Iron was afterwards introduced for the construction of anchors.
C) An improvement was made by forming anchors with teeth or ``flukes'' to fasten themselves into the bottom.
D) The words *odontes* and *dentes* are frequently taken for anchors in the Greek and Latin poets.

7.

[The South African buffalo] is relieved of a portion of the parasitic ticks, so common on the hides of thick-skinned animals, by means of the red-beaked rhinoceros birds, *Buphaga erythrorhynca*, a dozen or more of which may be seen partly perched on its horns and partly moving about on its back, and picking up the ticks on which they feed.

Which finding, if true, would most directly undermine the author's claim that parasitic ticks are commonly found on thick-skinned animals' hides?

A) Researchers discover significant evidence that parasitic ticks are found on over 75% of South African buffaloes.

B) Researchers find evidence that only a small percentage of South African buffaloes interact with red-beaked rhinoceros birds.

C) Researchers conclude that parasitic ticks are found only on the hides of red-beaked rhinoceros birds.

D) Researchers find occasional evidence of parasitic ticks on a population of elephants that live in the same region of South Africa.

8.

The following is adapted from Sir Henry Wotton's poem 'The Character of a Happy Life.'

How happy is he born and taught
That serveth not another's will;
Whose armour is his honest thought,
And simple truth his utmost skill!

Whose passions not his masters are;
Whose soul is still prepared for death,
Untied unto the world by care
Of public fame or private breath;
…
—This man is freed from servile bands
Of hope to rise or fear to fall:
Lord of himself, though not of lands,
And having nothing, yet hath all.

Which finding, if true, would most directly undermine the speaker's claim that someone who is free and humble may live a happy life?

A) Significant evidence is shown to indicate a causal relationship between being unprepared for death and happiness.

B) Significant evidence is shown to indicate a strong connection between working toward others' goals and individual happiness.

C) Evidence is shown to indicate a significant positive relationship between personal freedom and possessing material wealth.

D) Evidence is shown to indicate a significant negative relationship between fear of loss and honest thought.

Answers on page 373

What are some helpful evidence question strategies?

Here are a few strategic questions to ask yourself when faced with evidence questions:

"Do I have time for this?"

It will be important to assess whether you have time to go back and reread the context thoroughly enough to choose the correct answer in the time you have remaining. If it feels like you don't have enough time, or the time you have might be better spent on a different question, make your best guess, flag the question to come back to it if possible, and move on.

Getting these questions correct involves reading the passage, question, and answer choices carefully (and slowly) enough to focus and move through the question efficiently.

"What answer choices can I eliminate?"

A good habit for all of the question types we'll cover in this book is to cross off wrong answers as soon as you spot them, but be sure to *read answer choices completely before eliminating them!* Even if you're making a guess on a question, if you have time to do so, eliminate wrong answers first to improve your odds of guessing correctly.

"What key words are available to help me connect to evidence in the passage?"

Identify one or two unique key words in the question to focus on when you look back at the passage to find directly-stated or paraphrased evidence to support your answer choice.

"Did I annotate anything related to this question?"

Remember to use the included annotation tool provided in the testing suite's app.

EVIDENCE questions appear in the early-middle part of Verbal Modules, usually between questions #6 - 16. They ask about specific details from the passage, and students can expect there to be (verbatim or paraphrased) direct evidence from the passage to support the correct answer. **Students must remember to look back at the passage to find directly-stated or paraphrased evidence to support their answers.**

Practice Evidence Questions:

1.
The four species of indigenous South American wool-bearing animals are the llama, the alpaca, the guanaco, and the vicuna. The llama and the alpaca are domesticated; the guanaco and the vicuna run wild. [Alpacas] are not used as beasts of burden like llamas, but are valued only for their wool, of which blankets and ponchos are made. In stature the alpaca is considerably inferior to the llama, but has the same unpleasant habit of spitting.

Based on the text, in what way are llamas unlike alpacas?

A) Llamas are domesticated while alpacas are not.

B) Llamas are used as beasts of burden while alpacas are not.

C) Alpacas are domesticated while llamas are not.

D) Alpacas are used as beasts of burden while llamas are not.

2.
The following is adapted from Mark Twain's novel *The Adventures of Tom Sawyer.*

In one corner they found a closet that promised mystery, but the promise was a fraud—there was nothing in it. Their courage was up now and well in hand. They were about to go down and begin work when—
"Sh!" said Tom.
"What is it?" whispered Huck, blanching with fright.

Based on the text, what is in the closet?

A) Mystery
B) Nothing
C) The promise of fraud
D) A well

3.

The following is adapted from Frank L. Baum's novel '*The Wonderful Wizard of Oz*,' in which a young girl, Dorothy, is transported to a mysterious, colorful land called Oz where she faces a Wicked Witch.

The wicked creature was very cunning, and she finally thought of a trick that would give her what she wanted. She placed a bar of iron in the middle of the kitchen floor, and then by her magic arts made the iron invisible to human eyes. So that when Dorothy walked across the floor she stumbled over the bar, not being able to see it, and fell at full length. She was not much hurt, but in her fall one of the Silver Shoes came off; and before she could reach it, the Witch had snatched it away and put it on her own skinny foot.

Which choice best describes how the Wicked Witch got what she wanted from Dorothy, as presented in the text?

A) Dorothy tricks the Wicked Witch.

B) The Wicked Witch trips Dorothy and steals one of her Silver Shoes.

C) Dorothy escaped before the Wicked Witch could catch her.

D) The Wicked Witch presented a logical argument to Dorothy about why she should hand over the Silver Shoes.

4.

Amber was much valued as an ornamental material in very early times. It has been found in Mycenaean tombs; it is known from lake-dwellings in Switzerland, and it occurs with neolithic remains in Denmark, while in England it is found with interments of the bronze age.

Based on the text, in what way is the amber found in Denmark unlike the amber found in England?

A) Amber found in Denmark was found to be from the bronze age while amber found in England was found to be from the neolithic age.

B) Amber found in Denmark was found to be from the neolithic age while amber found in England was found to be from the bronze age.

C) Amber found in Denmark was found to be from Mycenaean tombs while amber found in England was found to be from the lake-dwellings in Switzerland.

D) Amber found in Denmark was found to be from lake-dwellings while amber found in England was found to be from interments.

5.

The anaconda combines an arboreal with an aquatic life, and feeds chiefly upon birds and mammals, mostly during the night. It lies submerged in the water, with only a small part of its head above the surface, waiting for any suitable prey, or it establishes itself upon the branches of a tree which overhangs the water or the track of game. It is the only large boa which is decidedly ill-tempered.

Which choice best describes the function of the underlined sentence in the text as a whole?

Based on the text, where does the anaconda hunt?

A) In trees
B) In rivers and swamps
C) In trees, rivers, and swamps
D) In the nests and burrows of its prey

6.

The fauna of Brixham cavern closely resembles that of Kent's Hole. It [is] now essentially an animal den, the occasional visits of man being indicated by the rare occurrence of flint-implements. Finally, the cave became a resort of bears; the remains of 334 specimens, in all stages of growth, including even sucking cubs, were discovered.

According to the text, what is true about man's presence in Brixham cavern?

A) Researchers have discovered evidence of bears and humans in both Brixham cavern and Kent's Hole.
B) There is no evidence that early man inhabited the cave.
C) Discovery of man-made tools suggest human presence in Brixham cavern.
D) Evidence of hundreds of bears residing in Brixham cavern suggests that humans have not called the cave home.

7.

The principal timber of commerce is the Douglas fir. The tree is often found 300 feet high and from 8 to 10 feet. in diameter. The wood is tough and strong and highly valued for ships' spars as well as for building purposes. Red or giant cedar, which rivals the Douglas fir in girth, is plentiful, and is used for shingles as well as for interior work. The western white spruce is also much employed for various purposes.

Based on the text, what is true about Douglas fir trees?

A) Douglas fir wood is the only wood used for shingles in the roofing industry.

B) Douglas fir trees grow as tall as western white spruce trees.

C) Douglas fir trees grow as tall as red cedar trees.

D) Douglas fir trees are often seen to grow to 8-10 feet in diameter.

8.

Amethyst is a very widely distributed mineral, but fine clear specimens fit for cutting as ornamental stones are confined to comparatively few localities. Such crystals occur either in cavities in mineral-veins and in granitic rocks, or as a lining in agate geodes.

Which finding, if true, would most directly weaken the author's claim that fine specimens of amethyst are relatively rare?

A) A huge geode, or "amethyst- grotto," from near Santa Cruz in southern Brazil, was exhibited at the Düsseldorf Exhibition of 1902.

B) Many of the hollow agates of Brazil and Uruguay contain a crop of amethyst-crystals in the interior.

C) Much fine amethyst comes from Russia, especially from near Mursinka in the Ekaterinburg district, where it occurs in drusy cavities in granitic rocks.

D) Large deposits of fine grade amethysts have recently been discovered in diverse geologic locations beyond mineral veins and agate geode linings.

9.

In some art, the Amazons approach the model of Artemis, wearing a thin dress, girt high for speed; while on the later painted vases their dress is often peculiarly Persian — that is, close-fitting trousers and a high cap called the *kidaris*.

Based on the text, in what way was the portrayal of Amazons in earlier art unlike that of Amazons in later art?

A) In some early art, the Amazons appear to be influenced more by images with tighter clothing and tall hats, while in later art they were seen wearing *kidaris*.

B) In some early art, the Amazons resembled the Greek Goddess Artemis in dress, while Amazons depicted in later art appear to be influenced more by Persian style.

C) In some early art, the Amazons' appearance appears to be influenced by Persian style, while in some later art, the Amazons resemble the Greek Goddess Artemis in dress.

D) In some early art, the Amazons resembled the *kidaris* in dress, while Amazons depicted in later art appear to be influenced more by images with tighter clothing and tall hats.

10.

The following is adapted from Frank L. Baum's novel '*The Wonderful Wizard of Oz*,' in which a young girl, Dorothy, is transported to a mysterious, colorful land called Oz where she travels to The Emerald City.

Even with eyes protected by the green spectacles, Dorothy and her friends were at first dazzled by the brilliancy of the wonderful City. The streets were lined with beautiful houses all built of green marble and studded everywhere with sparkling emeralds. They walked over a pavement of the same green marble, and where the blocks were joined together were rows of emeralds, set closely, and glittering in the brightness of the sun. The window panes were of green glass; even the sky above the City had a green tint, and the rays of the sun were green.

Which finding, if true, would most directly undermine the passage's claim that everything in the Emerald City appeared green?

A) Green candy and green pop corn were offered for sale, as well as green shoes, green hats, and green clothes of all sorts.

B) At one place a man was selling green lemonade, and when the children bought it Dorothy could see that they paid for it with green pennies.

C) There seemed to be no horses nor animals of any kind; the men carried things around in little green carts, which they pushed before them.

D) Many shops stood in the street, and Dorothy saw that not everything in them was green.

CHALLENGE:

[The South African buffalo] is relieved of a portion of the parasitic ticks, so common on the hides of thick-skinned animals, by means of the red-beaked rhinoceros birds, *Buphaga erythrorhynca*, a dozen or more of which may be seen partly perched on its horns and partly moving about on its back, and picking up the ticks on which they feed.

Which choice best describes the relationship between the South African buffalo and the red-beaked rhinoceros birds, as presented in the text?

A) The South African buffalo and the red-beaked rhinoceros bird have a symbiotic relationship in that the bird relieves the buffalo of parasitic ticks and receives food in return.

B) The South African buffalo and the red-beaked rhinoceros bird have an imbalanced relationship in that the birds receive food from being near the buffalo, but the buffaloes do not receive any benefit from the birds.

C) The South African buffalo and the red-beaked rhinoceros bird compete with each other as the food source of the parasitic ticks.

D) The South African buffalo and the red-beaked rhinoceros bird are both plagued by the problem of parasitic ticks.

Answers on page 373

Recommendations & Tips:

If you scored between 0-5, evidence question practice is **<u>high</u>** priority for you.

If you scored between 6-8, evidence question practice is **<u>medium</u>** priority for you.

If you scored between 9-11, evidence question practice is **<u>low</u>** priority for you.

If you felt uneasy choosing answer letter B for four answers in a row at the beginning of this section, this strategy is especially for you: avoid trying to 'game the test.'

In other words, never change your answer simply because it feels like there have already been 'too many' of that letter. While many tests are fairly evenly distributed in answer options, this is not a guarantee and shouldn't be expected to always be the case. Therefore, only change an answer if you find that there is an option more correct in the context than yours. Do NOT change answers because of how many of that answer you've already marked as correct.

LOGICAL COMPLETION

Here's the breakdown of what LearnCurious calls 'Logical Completion' (LC) questions on the four currently-released digital SAT exams:

	VM1	VM2a	VM2b
Test #1:	1/27 = 3.7%	4/27 = 14.8%	3/27 = 11.1%
Test #2:	1/27 = 3.7%	2/27 = 7.4%	3/27 = 11.1%
Test #3:	3/27 = 11.1%	0/27 = 0%	1/27 = 3.7%
Test #4:	2/27 = 7.4%	2/27 = 7.4%	2/27 = 7.4%

To summarize, there are
...between **1-3** LC questions on Verbal Module 1,
...between **0-4** LC questions on Verbal Module 2a,
...and between **1-3** LC questions on Verbal Module 2b.

Question frequency: 0 - 14.8% == UNCOMMON
Speed rating: moderate

LOGICAL COMPLETION questions appear toward the late-middle of Verbal Modules, usually between questions #13-16. They ask students to note the context of the passage and complete a paragraph or sentence with the most logical answer option. **Students must pay attention to what is happening in the passage, make inferences, and anticipate answer choices having less direct evidence to support correct answer choices than the more direct evidence which is seen in other types of questions.**

How do I identify Logical Completion questions?

Logical Completion questions can be identified using this specific question stem:
- *"Which choice most logically completes the text?"*

Look for these words in particular in the question stem to easily identify Logical Completion questions: *"most logically completes"*

Here are a few examples of what digital SAT Logical Completion questions look like:

1.
Brooklyn is connected with Manhattan by three bridges across the East river—the lowest, known as the Brooklyn, opened in 1883; another, known as the Williamsburg or East River bridge, opened in 1903; and _____.

Which choice most logically completes the text?

A) And a tunnel directly across from the south terminus of Manhattan was completed in 1907.

B) a third, the Manhattan, was opened in 1909.

C) Ferries ply at frequent intervals between numerous points on its west water-front and points in Manhattan.

D) There is also ferry connexion with Jersey City.

2.

The following is adapted from Lewis Carroll's novel *Alice's Adventures in Wonderland,* in which a young girl, Alice, falls down a rabbit hole into a confusing world of colorful characters.

Alice had been looking over his shoulder with some curiosity. "What a funny watch!" she remarked. "It tells the day of the month, and doesn't tell _____."

Which choice most logically completes the text?

A) what year it is!"
B) what season it is!"
C) what temperature it is!"
D) what o'clock it is!"

3.

The following is adapted from Frank L. Baum's novel 'The Wonderful Wizard of Oz,' in which a young girl, Dorothy, is transported by a cyclone from her home in rural Kansas to a mysterious, colorful land called Oz.

After a few hours the road began to be rough, and the walking grew so difficult that the Scarecrow often stumbled over the yellow bricks, which were here very uneven. Sometimes, indeed, they were broken or missing altogether, leaving holes that Toto jumped across and Dorothy walked around. As for the Scarecrow, having no brains, he walked straight ahead, and so stepped into the holes and fell at full length on the hard bricks. It never hurt him, however, _____.

Which choice most logically completes the text?

A) and Dorothy would pick him up and set him upon his feet again, while he joined her in laughing merrily at his own mishap.
B) when Dorothy awoke the sun was shining through the trees and Toto had long been out chasing birds around him and squirrels.
C) she sat up and looked around her.
D) banks of gorgeous flowers were on every hand, and birds with rare and brilliant plumage sang and fluttered in the trees and bushes.

Answers on page 373

What are some helpful Logical Completion question strategies?

Here are a few strategic questions to ask yourself when faced with Logical Completion questions:

"What is happening in the passage?"

Remember, since these are questions that ask students to make predictions, we need to know enough about what is happening in the passage to understand what answer option most logically comes next in the given context.

Students will need to use context clues to make an inference about what most logically comes next to fill in the blank. An inference is an idea based on indirect (implicit) clues or hints instead of direct (explicit) statements. For example, my friend could hint at what they want for their birthday, and I could infer from their clues what to get them as a present.

Thus, students must **pay attention to what is happening in the passage and anticipate answer choices having less direct evidence to support correct answer choices** than the more direct evidence which is seen in other types of questions.

"Do I have time for this?"

It will be important to assess whether you have time to go back and reread the context thoroughly enough to choose the correct answer in the time you have remaining. If it feels like you don't have enough time, or the time you have might be better spent on a different question, make your best guess, flag the question to come back to it if possible, and move on.

Getting these questions correct involves reading the passage, question, and answer choices carefully (and slowly) enough to focus and move through the question efficiently.

LOGICAL COMPLETION questions appear toward the late-middle of Verbal Modules, usually between questions #13-16. They ask students to note the context of the passage and complete a paragraph or sentence with the most logical answer option. **Students must pay attention to what is happening in the passage, make inferences, and anticipate answer choices having less direct evidence to support correct answer choices than the more direct evidence which is seen in other types of questions.**

Practice Logical Completion Questions:

1.

One of the most attractive features of Brooklyn is Prospect Park, occupying about 516 acres of high ground. Its large variety of trees and shrubs, including oak, hickory, elm, maple, chestnut, birch, ash, cedar, pine, larch and sumac _____.

Which choice most logically completes the text?

A) its flower gardens, a palm house, ponds.

B) are among its objects of interest or beauty.

C) a lake of 61 acres for boating, skating and curling.

D) a parade ground of 40 acres for other athletic sports, a menagerie, and numerous pieces of statuary.

2.

The following is adapted from Lewis Carroll's novel 'Alice's Adventures in Wonderland,' in which a young girl, Alice, falls down a rabbit hole into a confusing world of colorful characters.

"They were obliged to have him with them," the Mock Turtle said: "no wise fish would go anywhere without a porpoise."

"Wouldn't it really?" said Alice in a tone of great surprise.

"Of course not," said the Mock Turtle: "why, if a fish came to me, and told me he was going a journey, I should say 'With what porpoise?'"

"Don't you mean 'purpose'?" said Alice.

_____.

Which choice most logically completes the text?

A) "I mean what I say," the Mock Turtle replied in an offended tone.

B) "I couldn't afford to learn it." said the Mock Turtle with a sigh. "I only took the regular course."

C) "Reeling and Writhing, of course, to begin with," the Mock Turtle replied.

D) The Gryphon lifted up both its paws in surprise. "What!" it exclaimed. "You know what to beautify is, I suppose?"

3.

The word Acropolis, though Greek in origin and associated primarily with Greek towns (Athens, Argos, Thebes, Corinth), may be applied generically to all such citadels (Rome, Jerusalem, many in Asia Minor, or even Castle Hill at Edinburgh). The most famous is that of Athens, which, by reason of its historical associations and the famous buildings erected upon it, is generally known without qualification as _____.

Which choice most logically completes the text?

A) the Acropolis.
B) Castle Hill.
C) Edinburgh.
D) Asia Minor.

4.

The following is adapted from Mark Twain's novel 'The Adventures of Tom Sawyer."

Saturday morning was come, and all the summer world was bright and fresh, and brimming with life. There was a song in every heart; and if the heart was young the music issued at the lips. There was cheer in every face and a spring in every step. The locust-trees were in bloom and the fragrance of the blossoms filled the air. Cardiff Hill, beyond the village and above it, was _____.

Which choice most logically completes the text?

A) on the sidewalk with a bucket of whitewash and a long-handled brush.

B) green with vegetation and it lay just far enough away to seem a Delectable Land, dreamy, reposeful, and inviting.

C) a deep melancholy settled down upon his spirit. Life to him seemed hollow, and existence but a burden.

D) thirty yards of board fence nine feet high.

5.

A still more complicated variety of anagram is the ``logogram'' (from the Greek, *logos*, meaning 'word'), a versified puzzle containing several words derived from recombining the letters of the original word, the difficulty lying in the fact that synonyms of the derived words may be used. Thus, _____.

Which choice most logically completes the text?

A) if the original word be ``curtain,'' the word ``dog'' may be used instead of ``cur.''

B) there is another species of anagram, called ``palindrome''

C) it is a word or sentence which may be read backwards as well as forwards

D) for example, the words ``Anna,'' ``noon,'' ``tenet,''

6.

The name Alhambra, meaning in Arabic 'the red,' is probably derived from the color of the sun-dried *tapia*, or bricks, made of fine gravel and clay, _____.

Which choice most logically completes the text?

A) an ancient palace and fortress of the Moorish monarchs of Granada

B) in southern Spain

C) occupying a hilly terrace on the south-eastern border of the city of Granada.

D) of which the outer walls of the structure are built.

7.

The following is adapted from Frank L. Baum's novel 'The Wonderful Wizard of Oz.'

It was Toto that made Dorothy laugh and saved her from growing as gray as her other surroundings. Toto was not gray; he was a little black dog, with long silky hair and small black eyes that twinkled merrily on either side of his funny, wee nose. Toto played all day long, and Dorothy played with him and loved him dearly. Today, however, they were not playing. Uncle Henry sat upon the doorstep and looked anxiously at the sky, which was even grayer than usual. Dorothy _____.

A) stood in the door with Toto in her arms, and looked at the sky too.

B) jumped across and walked around.

C) stepped into the holes and fell at full length on the hard bricks.

D) picked him up and set him upon his feet again, while he joined her in laughing merrily at his own mishap.

8.

The word anchor is derived from the Greek *agkura*, is from *ogke*, a crook or hook and is an instrument of iron or other heavy material used for holding ships or boats in any locality required, thus _____.

Which choice most logically completes the text?

A) after it is let go from the ship by means of the cable, fixes itself in the ground and there holds the vessel fast.

B) the word ``anchor'' is also used figuratively for anything which gives security.

C) preventing them from drifting by winds, tides, currents or other causes.

D) too much care cannot be expended on its manufacture and proper construction.

9.

The pseudonyms adopted by authors are often rearranged forms, more or less exact, of their names; thus _____.

Which choice most logically completes the text?

A) 'Calvinus' becomes 'Alcvinus;' ``Francois Rabelais' becomes 'Alcofribas Nasier;' 'Bryan Waller Proctor' becomes 'Barry Cornwall, poet;' 'Henry Rogers' becomes 'R. E. H. Greyson.'

B) It is to be noted that the last two are impure anagrams, an ``r'' being left out in both cases.

C) Eleanor Audeley,'' wife of Sir John Davies, is said to have been brought before the High Commission in 1634 for extravagances, stimulated by the discovery that her name could be transposed to 'Reveale, O Daniel.'

D) It is to be noted that 'Bryan Waller Proctor' becoming 'Barry Cornwall, poet' and 'Henry Rogers' becoming ``R. E. H. Greyson,'' are impure anagrams because an ``r'' is left out in both cases.

10.

The beginning, the prevalence and duration of the Bronze Age in each country would have been ordered by the accessibility of the metals which form the alloy. Thus, _____.

Which choice most logically completes the text?

A) in some lands bronze may have continued to be a substance of extreme value until the Iron Age was reached.

B) in *tumuli,* in which more than one body was interred.

C) it would only be with the remains of the richer tenants of the tomb that the more valuable objects would be placed.

D) in such a practice would be found a simple explanation of the mixing of implements.

CHALLENGE:

In working amber, it is turned on the lathe and polished with whitening and water or with rotten stone and oil, the final lustre being given by friction with flannel. Therefore, _____.

Which choice most logically completes the text?

A) by gradually heating amber in an oil-bath it becomes soft and flexible.

B) two pieces of amber may be united by smearing the surfaces with linseed oil, heating them, and then pressing them together while hot.

C) during the working much electricity is developed.

D) cloudy amber may be clarified in an oil-bath, as the oil fills the numerous pores to which the turbidity is due.

Answers on page 373

Recommendations:

If you scored between 0-5, logical completion question practice is **high** priority for you.

If you scored between 6-8, logical completion question practice is **medium** priority for you.

If you scored between 9-11, logical completion question practice is **low** priority for you.

CHART / GRAPH INTERPRETATION

Here's the breakdown of what LearnCurious calls 'Chart / Graph Interpretation' (CGI) questions on the four currently-released digital SAT exams:

	VM1	VM2a	VM2b
Test #1:	4/27 = 14.8%	0/27 = 0%	0/27 = 0%
Test #2:	2/27 = 7.4%	1/27 = 3.7%	1/27 = 3.7%
Test #3:	0/27 = 0%	1/27 = 3.7%	3/27 = 11.1%
Test #4:	1/27 = 3.7%	2/27 = 7.4%	2/27 = 7.4%

To summarize, there are
...between **0-4** CGI questions on Verbal Module 1,
...between **0-2** CGI questions on Verbal Module 2a,
...and between **0-3** CGI questions on Verbal Module 2b.

Question frequency: 0 - 14.8% == UNCOMMON
Speed rating: time-consuming

CHART / GRAPH INTERPRETATION questions appear in the early-middle part of Verbal Modules, usually between questions #6 - 16. They ask students to interpret a chart, table, or graph and complete a statement or example.

How do I identify Chart Interpretation questions?

Chart Interpretation questions can be identified using these specific question stems:
- *'Which choice most effectively uses information from the table to complete the example?'*
- *'Which choice most effectively uses information from the graph to illustrate the claim? '*
- *'Which choice best describes data from the table that (support / weaken / undermine) (the author's / researcher's) (claim / hypothesis / idea)*
- *'Which choice most effectively uses data from the table to complete the (statement / text / example)?*

Look for these words in particular in the question stem to easily identify Chart / Graph Interpretation questions: *'information from the table/graph,' 'data from the table,' or 'researcher's claim'*

Here are three examples *(basic (1), medium (2), & advanced (3) difficulty levels)* of what digital SAT Chart Interpretation questions look like:

Note, all three examples pertain to the chart below.

Name	Anagram
Bryan Waller Proctor	Barry Cornwall, poet*
Calvinus	Alcvinus
Dame Eleanor Davies	Never soe mad a ladie
Eleanor Audeley	Reveale, O Daniel
Francois Rabelais	Alcofribas Nasier
Henry Rogers	R. E. H. Greyson*

It is to be noted that the two of these are impure anagrams, an ``r'' being left out in both cases.

1.

An anagram is the result of rearranging the letters of a word or words in such a manner as to produce other words that possess meaning. The construction of anagrams is an amusement of great antiquity. Researchers also have evidence of humorous historic anagrams, such as _____.

Which choice best describes data from the table that supports the researcher's **claim** with an example.

A) "Voltaire," which the celebrated philosopher assumed instead of his family name .

B) Eleanor Audeley being laughed out of court by another anagram submitted by the dean of the Arches: 'Dame Eleanor Davies' became 'Never soe mad a ladie.'

C) 'Calvinus' becoming 'Alcvinus' and 'Francois Rabelais' becoming 'Alcofribas Nasier.'

D) Eleanor Audeley, wife of Sir John Davies, being brought before the High Commission in 1634 for extravagances.

2.

An anagram is the result of transposing the letters of a word or words in such a manner as to produce other words that possess meaning. An anagram is considered to be impure if _____.

Which choice most effectively uses information from the chart to **complete the statement**?

A) any letters are left out from the original word or phrase, such as Henry Rogers' pseudonym becoming Barry Cornwall, poet.

B) an 'r' is left out from the original word or phrase.

C) it can be read backwards as well as forwards, letter by letter, while preserving the same meaning.

D) they have brought before the High Commission for extravagances.

3.

An anagram is the result of rearranging the letters of a word or words in such a manner as to produce other words that possess meaning. Another species of anagram, called a palindrome, is a word or sentence which may be read backwards as well as forwards, letter by letter, while preserving the same meaning.

Which choice most effectively uses information from the chart to illustrate the **claim** made in the passage?

A) Eleanor Audeley's name is an example of a palindrome, as it can be rearranged to spell 'Reveale, O Daniel.'

B) Calvinus' name is an example of an anagram, as it can be rearranged to spell Alcofribas Nasier.

C) Eleanor Audeley's name is an example of an anagram, as it can be rearranged to spell 'Reveale, O Daniel.'

D) Calvinus' name is an example of a palindrome, as it can spelled the same way forwards and backwards.

Answers on page 373

What are some helpful Chart Interpretation question strategies?

If the graph, chart, or table in the question you're given has a title or axis labels, be sure to read them and note any specific units given, as they could be helpful in answering the question as well.

Here are a few strategic questions to ask yourself when faced with Chart Interpretation questions:

"What is the 'claim?'"

> **STRATEGY**: Chart/Graph Interpretation (and Support Quotation) questions usually refer to a "claim" or "hypothesis" stated in the passage. Usually, the passage will directly use the those exact words, so it can be helpful to **get in the habit of annotating the words "claim" and "hypothesis" as soon as you see them in a passage. Chances are, you'll need to spot them easily later.**

"How are these similar to Logical Completion questions?"

Chart and graph interpretation questions ask students to complete the text with the most logical answer choice, based on the information provided in the graph and in the passage.

While the evidence to support the correct answer to Chart / Graph Interpretation questions is often more clear and direct than the evidence to support Logical Completion questions, it is usually hidden among other irrelevant chart data. Expect the process of reading the answer choices and comparing chart data to require both focus and time.

"Do I have time for this?"

Maintaining focus and taking the time to analyze the relevant part(s) of the graph or chart is essential for getting these questions correct. For many, Chart / Graph Interpretation questions are among the most time-consuming of the dSAT's verbal questions. Know in advance of your official test(s) whether this type of question takes you a long time. If it does, be willing to guess on it, skip it, and come back to it if you have time left over once you've finished the other verbal questions.

"Are the answer choices true or false?"

Some of the answer choices will mix and match data from the table and/or passage; eliminate these answers as well as any that offer different data than that which you see in the chart or graph. Eliminate any answers that come back as "false" on the true/false test.

CHART / GRAPH INTERPRETATION questions appear in the early-middle part of Verbal Modules, usually between questions #6 - 16. They ask students to interpret a chart, table, or graph and complete a statement or example.

Practice Chart / Graph Interpretation Questions:

1.

Navigable mileage (Alabama river)	2000 miles
Muscle shoals (in Tennessee river)	38 miles
Amount spent on removal of impediments (to river travel)	$12 million
Duration (of removal projects)	1870-1904; 34 years

The navigable mileage of the Alabama rivers is 2000 m., but obstructions often prevent the formation of a continuous route, notably the ``Muscle Shoals'' of the Tennessee, extending from a point 10 m. below Decatur to Florence, a distance of 38 m. To remove or circumvent these impediments, and to improve the Mobile harbor, the United States government spent, between 1870 and 1904, approximately _____.

Which choice most effectively uses information from the graph to illustrate the claim?

A) $2000
B) $38
C) $12,000,000
D) $34

2.

Year	Event
560	Aethelbert took the throne and became King of Kent.
568	Aethelbert married Berhta.
597	The mission of Augustine landed in Thanet and was received at first with some hesitation by the King.
603	Christ Church was consecrated.
604	Justus became first bishop of Rochester.
616	Aethelberht died and was succeeded by his son Eadbald.

A code of laws issued by Aethelberht, king of Kent, which is still extant, is probably the oldest document in the English language and contains a list of money fines for various crimes. Towards the close of his reign his pre-eminence as Bretwalda was disturbed by the increasing power of Raedwald of East Anglia. Aethelberht died in _____.

Which choice most effectively uses information from the table to complete the example?

A) 560

B) 597

C) 604

D) 616

3.

Navigable mileage (Alabama river)	2000 miles
Muscle shoals (in Tennessee river)	38 miles
Amount spent on removal of impediments (to river travel)	$12 million
Duration (of removal projects)	1870-1904; 34 years

The navigable mileage of the Alabama rivers is 2000 miles, but obstructions often prevent the formation of a continuous route; for example, the the ``Muscle Shoals'' of the Tennessee rivers, extend from a point 10 miles below Decatur to Florence, obstructing a distance of 38 miles. To remove or circumvent these impediments, and to improve the Mobile harbor, the United States government spent, over 34 years, approximately $12,000,000.

Which choice most effectively uses information from the graph to illustrate the passage's claim that the river improvement projects happened over three decades?

A) The United States government spent approximately $12,000,000 on river improvement projects.

B) The United States government spent approximately $18,000,000 on river improvement projects.

C) The United States government spent, between 1870 and 1904, approximately $12,000,000 on river improvement projects.

D) The United States government spent, between 1890 and 1904, approximately $18,000,000 on river improvement projects.

4.

Year	Event
560	Aethelbert took the throne and became King of Kent.
568	Aethelbert married Berhta.
597	The mission of Augustine landed in Thanet and was received at first with some hesitation by the King.
603	Christ Church was consecrated.
604	Justus became first bishop of Rochester.
616	Aethelberht died and was succeeded by his son Eadbald.

Aethelberht, king of Kent, son of Eormenric, came to the throne in the year 560 CE. The first recorded event of his reign, in the year 568, Aethelberht married Berhta, daughter of Charihert, king of Paris, who brought over Bishop Liudhard as her private confessor. In 597, _____ .

Which choice most effectively uses data from the table to complete the text?

A) the mission of Augustine landed in Thanet and was received at first with some hesitation by the king.

B) according to Bede, Aethelberht's supremacy stretched over all the English kingdoms as far as the Humber.

C) Aethelberht's supremacy was been much disputed, but it was at any rate sufficient to guarantee the safety of Augustine in his conference with the British bishops.

D) Aethelberht exercised a stricter sway over Essex, where his nephew Saberht was king.

5.

The amount of timber cut on Dominion government lands in 1904 was 22,760,222 ft., and the amount cut on provincial lands was 325,271,568 ft., giving a total of 348,031,790 ft.

In 1905 the cut on dominion lands exceeded that in 1904, while the amount cut on provincial lands reached 450,385,554 ft.

Cargo shipments of British Columbia lumber, in feet, for the years 1904 and 1905

Location	1904 feet	1905 feet
United Kingdom	7,498,301	13,690,869
South America	15,647,808	13.332,993
Australia	10,045,094	11,596,482
South Africa	2,517,154	7,093,681
China and Japan	4,802,426	4,787,784

This data has led the author to claim that there is a very large market for British Columbia lumber in _____.

Which choice most effectively uses information from the table to complete the author's claim?

A) South America in 1904

B) South Africa in 1904

C) South America in 1905

D) South Africa in 1905

6.

Name	Anagram
Bryan Waller Proctor	Barry Cornwall, poet*
Calvinus	Alcvinus
Dame Eleanor Davies	Never soe mad a ladie
Eleanor Audeley	Reveale, O Daniel
Francois Rabelais	Alcofribas Nasier
Henry Rogers	R. E. H. Greyson*

It is to be noted that the two of these are impure anagrams, an ``r'' being left out in both cases.

An anagram is the result of rearranging the letters of a word or words in such a manner as to produce other words that possess meaning. The construction of anagrams is an amusement of great antiquity. The pseudonyms adopted by authors are often transposed forms, more or less exact, of their names; for example, _____.

Which choice most effectively uses data from the table to complete the example?

A) it is to be noted that the last two are impure anagrams, an ``r'' being left out in both cases.

B) Eleanor Audeley, wife of Sir John Davies, is said to have been brought before the High Commission in 1634 for extravagances, stimulated by the discovery that her name could be transposed to 'Reveale, O Daniel.'

C) another species of anagram, called 'palindrome,' is a word or sentence which may be read backwards as well as forwards, letter by letter, while preserving the same meaning.

D) 'Calvinus' becomes 'Alcvinus;' ``Francois Rabelais' becomes 'Alcofribas Nasier;' 'Bryan Waller Proctor' becomes 'Barry Cornwall, poet;' 'Henry Rogers' becomes 'R. E. H. Greyson.'

7.

Navigable mileage (Alabama river)	2000 miles
Muscle shoals (in Tennessee river)	38 miles
Amount spent on removal of impediments (to river travel)	$12 million
Duration (of removal projects)	1870-1904; 34 years

The navigable mileage of the Alabama rivers is 2000 miles, but obstructions often prevent the formation of a continuous route, notably the ``Muscle Shoals'' of the Tennessee, extending from a point 10 m. below Decatur to Florence, a distance of 38 miles.

Which choice best describes data from the table that weaken the passage's claim about the navigable mileage of the Alabama rivers.

A) The navigable mileage of the Alabama rivers is actually 1904 miles.

B) The navigable mileage of the Alabama rivers is actually 38 miles.

C) The navigable mileage of the Alabama rivers is actually 2500 miles.

D) The navigable mileage of the Alabama rivers is actually 1870 miles.

8.

The figures relating to temperature and precipitation are from a table prepared by Mr R.F. Stupart, director of the meteorological service. The station at Victoria may be taken as representing the conditions of the southern part of the coast of British Columbia, although the rainfall is much greater on exposed parts of the outer coast.

Location	Mean Temperature (in Fahrenheit)			Absolute Temperature		Rainfall (in inches)		
	Coldest Month	Warmest Month	Average Annual Temp.	Highest	Lowest	Wettest Month	Driest Month	Average Annual
Victoria	January 37.5°	July 60.3°	48.8°	90°	-1°	December 7.98	July .4	37.77
Agassiz	January 33.0°	Aug. 64.7°	48.9°	97°	-13°	December 9.43	July 1.55	66.85
Kamloops	January 24.2°	Aug. 68.5°	47.1°	101°	-27°	July 1.61	April .37	11.46
Port Simpson	January 34.9°	Aug. 56.9°	45.1°	88°	-10°	October 12.42	June 4.37	94.63

A researcher interprets the data and concludes that rainfall in Victoria _____ from December to July.

Which choice most effectively uses data from the table and text to complete the researcher's statement?

A) decreases

B) increases

C) stays the same

D) inclines

78

9.

Name	Anagram
Bryan Waller Proctor	Barry Cornwall, poet*
Calvinus	Alcvinus
Dame Eleanor Davies	Never soe mad a ladie
Eleanor Audeley	Reveale, O Daniel
Francois Rabelais	Alcofribas Nasier
Henry Rogers	R. E. H. Greyson*

*It is to be noted that the two of these are impure anagrams, an ``r'' being left out in both cases.

An anagram is the result of rearranging the letters of a word or words in such a manner as to produce other words that possess meaning. The construction of anagrams is an amusement of great antiquity. Another species of anagram, called a palindrome, is a word or sentence which may be read backwards as well as forwards, letter by letter, while preserving the same meaning; for example, _____.

Which choice most effectively uses data from the table to complete the example?

A) 'Alcvinus' is an anagram of the name 'Calvinus' while the words 'Anna,' 'noon,' and 'tenet' are palindromes.

B) the sentence with which Adam is humorously supposed to have greeted Eve: ``Madam, I'm Adam!''

C) the pseudonyms adopted by authors are often transposed forms, more or less exact, of their names;

D) it is to be noted that the last two are impure anagrams, an ``r'' being left out in both cases.

10.

The figures relating to temperature and precipitation are from a table prepared by Mr R.F. Stupart, director of the meteorological service. The
station at Victoria may be taken as representing the conditions of the
southern part of the coast of British Columbia, although the rainfall is
much greater on exposed parts of the outer coast.

Location	Mean Temperature (in Fahrenheit)			Absolute Temperature		Rainfall (in inches)		
	Coldest Month	Warmest Month	Average Annual Temp.	Highest	Lowest	Wettest Month	Driest Month	Average Annual
Victoria	January 37.5°	July 60.3°	48.8°	90°	-1°	December 7.98	July .4	37.77
Agassiz	January 33.0°	Aug. 64.7°	48.9°	97°	-13°	December 9.43	July 1.55	66.85
Kamloops	January 24.2°	Aug. 68.5°	47.1°	101°	-27°	July 1.61	April .37	11.46
Port Simpson	January 34.9°	Aug. 56.9°	45.1°	88°	-10°	October 12.42	June 4.37	94.63

A researcher interprets the data and concludes that _____.

A) the driest month in Victoria sees more rain than the wettest month in
Kamloops.

B) the driest month in Agassiz sees more rain than the wettest month in
Port Simpson.

C) the wettest month in Kamloops sees less rain than the driest month in
Agassiz.

D) the wettest month in Port Simpson sees less rain than the driest month
in Kamloops.

CHALLENGE:

Navigable mileage (Alabama river)	2000 miles
Muscle shoals (in Tennessee river)	38 miles
Amount spent on removal of impediments (to river travel)	$12 million
Duration (of removal projects)	1870-1904; 34 years

The navigable mileage of the Alabama rivers is 2000 miles, but obstructions often prevent the formation of a continuous route, notably the "Muscle Shoals" of the Tennessee, extending from a point 10 m. below Decatur to Florence, a distance of 38 miles.

Which choice best describes data from the table that undermine the passage's claim about the navigable mileage of the Alabama rivers.

A) To remove or circumvent these impediments, and to improve the Mobile harbor, the United States government spent, between 1870 and 1904, approximately $12,000,000.

B) As the streams in the mineral region are not navigable, the railways are the carriers of its products.

C) The navigable mileage of the Alabama rivers is actually 2500 miles, and, to remove impediments, the United States government spent $18,000,000.

D) An increasing amount of Alabama cotton is sent to New Orleans for shipment, and Pensacola, Florida, receives much of the lumber.

Answers on page 373

Recommendations:

If you scored between 0-3, chart/graph interpretation question practice is **<u>high</u>** priority for you.

If you scored between 4-8, chart/graph interpretation question practice is **<u>medium</u>** priority for you.

If you scored between 9-11, chart/graph interpretation question practice is **<u>low</u>** priority for you.

Did you notice that there were no letter 'B' answers in this question bank? If you did, and if it made you feel uneasy, perhaps more inclined to choose answer letter B, simply because it hasn't yet shown up, this message is for YOU!

Don't change your answers, or prioritize answer letter options due to their frequency of appearance. It's tempting to do, but it's not only a waste of time but also a common reason that some students have changed their correct answer choice to an incorrect one.

While many tests are fairly evenly distributed in answer options, this is not a guarantee and shouldn't be expected to always be the case. Therefore, only change an answer if you find that there is an option more correct in the context than yours.

SUPPORT QUOTATION

Here's the breakdown of what LearnCurious calls 'Support Quotation' (SQ) questions on the four currently-released digital SAT exams:

	VM1	VM2a	VM2b
Test #1:	0/27 = 0%	3/27 = 11.1%	1/27 = 3.7%
Test #2:	1/27 = 3.7%	2/27 = 7.4%	1/27 = 3.7%
Test #3:	1/27 = 3.7%	1/27 = 3.7%	1/27 = 3.7%
Test #4:	1/27 = 3.7%	3/27 = 11.1%	0/27 = 0%

To summarize, there are
...between **0-1** SQ questions on Verbal Module 1,
...between **1-3** SQ questions on Verbal Module 2a,
...and between **0-1** SQ questions on Verbal Module 2b.

Question frequency: 0-11.1% == RARE
Speed rating: moderate/time-consuming

SUPPORT QUOTATION questions appear in the early-middle part of Verbal Modules, usually between questions #6 - 16. They ask students to support a specific claim from the passage, often fiction or poetry; the College Board refers to these as 'Textual Evidence' questions. Support Quotation) questions usually refer to a "claim" or "hypothesis" stated in the passage. Usually, the passage will directly use the those exact words, so it can be helpful to **get in the habit of annotating the words "claim" and "hypothesis" as soon as you see them in a passage. Chances are, you'll need to spot them easily later.**

How do I identify Support Quotation questions?

Support Quotation questions can be identified using these specific question stems:
- 'Which quotation from _____ most effectively illustrates the claim?'
- 'Which quotation from _____ best illustrates the (_____'s) claim?'

Look for these words in particular in the question stem to easily identify Support Quotation (SQ) questions: 'which quotation'

Here are two examples of what digital SAT Support Quotation questions look like:

1.
The following is adapted from Frank L. Baum's novel 'The Wonderful Wizard of Oz.'

They soon they found themselves in the midst of a great meadow of scarlet poppies. Now, it is well known that when there are many of these flowers together their odor is so powerful that anyone who breathes it falls asleep, and if the sleeper is not carried away from the scent of the flowers, he sleeps on and on forever. But Dorothy did not know this, nor could she get away from the bright red flowers that were everywhere about; so presently her eyes grew heavy and she felt she must sit down to rest and to sleep, but the Tin Woodman would not let her do this.

Which quotation most effectively illustrates the **claim** that anyone who breathes the scent of the poppy field falls asleep?

A) "We must hurry and get back to the road of yellow brick before dark," he said; and the Scarecrow agreed with him."

B) "So they kept walking until Dorothy could stand no longer."

C) "Dorothy's eyes closed in spite of herself and she forgot where she was and fell among the poppies, fast asleep."

D) "What shall we do?" asked the Tin Woodman.

2.

'The Rainbow' is a poem by William Wordsworth. The poem conveys the perpetual joy the speaker feels upon seeing a rainbow.

My heart leaps up when I behold
A rainbow in the sky:
So was it when my life began;
So is it now I am a man;
So be it when I shall grow old,
    Or let me die!
The Child is father of the Man;
I could wish my days to be
Bound each to each by natural piety.

Which quotation from 'The Rainbow' most effectively illustrates the intensity of the speaker's claims?

A) "So was it when my life began;"

B) "Or let me die!"

C) "The Child is father of the Man;"

D) "I could wish my days to be"

Answers on page 373

What are some helpful Support Quotation question strategies?

Here are a few strategic questions to ask yourself when faced with Support Quotation questions:

"Is the passage a poem or prose (non-poem, fiction or non-fiction) text?"

If you are someone who enjoys analyzing poetry quickly, these questions are likely to be up your alley.

If not, these are questions to assess quickly using this initial question. If poetry isn't your thing and/or you haven't studied it much, consider guessing on, skipping, and coming back to these questions as time allows. It can be time-consuming to try to make sense of a poem that you've never seen before.

"Is there citation information?"

The citation information (title of work, author's name, date of publication) at the very beginning of every fiction and poetry passage on the dSAT can be key to answering the questions.

> **STRATEGY**: If you're not already doing so, develop the habit of reading and annotating the citation information that is found at the very beginning of every fiction and poetry passage on the dSAT.

"What is the 'claim?'"

> **STRATEGY**: Chart/Graph Interpretation (and Support Quotation) questions usually refer to a "claim" or "hypothesis" stated in the passage. Usually, the passage will directly use the those exact words, so it can be helpful to **get in the habit of annotating the words "claim" and "hypothesis" as soon as you see them in a passage. Chances are, you'll need to spot them easily later.**

"How are these similar to Logical Completion questions?"

Chart and graph interpretation questions ask students to complete the text with the most logical answer choice, based on the information provided in the graph and in the passage.

While the evidence to support the correct answer to Chart / Graph Interpretation questions is often more clear and direct than the evidence to support Logical Completion questions, it is usually hidden among other irrelevant chart data. Expect the process of reading the answer choices and comparing chart data to require both focus and time.

SUPPORT QUOTATION questions appear in the early-middle part of Verbal Modules, usually between questions #6 - 16. They ask students to support a specific claim from the passage, often fiction or poetry; the College Board refers to these as 'Textual Evidence' questions. Support Quotation) questions usually refer to a "claim" or "hypothesis" stated in the passage. Usually, the passage will directly use the those exact words, so it can be helpful to **get in the habit of annotating the words "claim" and "hypothesis" as soon as you see them in a passage. Chances are, you'll need to spot them easily later.**

Practice Support Quotation (SQ) Questions:

1.
The following text is adapted from Lewis Carroll's *Alice in Wonderland*.

"Would you tell me," said Alice, a little timidly, "why you are painting those roses?"

Which quotation best answers Alice's question?

A) "Five and Seven said nothing, but looked at Two."
B) "Two began in a low voice, "Why the fact is, you see, Miss, this here ought to have been a red rose-tree."
C) "We put a white one in by mistake, and if the Queen was to find it out, we should all have our heads cut off, you know."
D) "So you see, Miss, we're doing our best, afore she comes, to—"

2.

The following is adapted from Mark Twain's novel 'The Adventures of Tom Sawyer."

Tom resumed his whitewashing, and said carelessly:
"Well, maybe it is, and maybe it ain't. All I know, is, it suits Tom Sawyer."
"Oh come, now, you don't mean to let on that you like it?" Ben asked.
The brush continued to move.
"Like it? Well, I don't see why I oughtn't to like it. Does a boy get a chance to whitewash a fence every day?"
That put the thing in a new light.

Which quotation from the story best illustrates that Ben has begun thinking differently about the task of whitewashing?

A) Tom considered and said, "You see, Aunt Polly's awful particular about this fence — right here on the street."

B) Ben watching every move and getting more and more interested, more and more absorbed. Presently he said, "Say, Tom, let me whitewash a little."

C) Ben stopped nibbling his apple.

D) Tom swept his brush daintily back and forth — stepped back to note the effect — added a touch here and there — and criticized the effect again.

3.

The following is adapted from Frank L. Baum's novel 'The Wonderful Wizard of Oz,' in which a young girl, Dorothy, is transported to a mysterious, colorful land called Oz where she travels to The Emerald City.

"Because if you did not wear spectacles the brightness and glory of the Emerald City would blind you. Even those who live in the City must wear spectacles night and day. They are all locked on, for Oz so ordered it when the City was first built, and I have the only key that will unlock them."

Which quotation best illustrates the Guardian of the Gates' claim that the glasses that the citizens of Emerald City wear cannot be removed?

A) "The Guardian of the Gates found a pair of glasses that would just fit Dorothy and put them over her eyes."

B) "There were two golden bands fastened to them that passed around the back of her head."

C) "The glasses were locked together by a little key that was at the end of a chain the Guardian of the Gates wore around his neck. When they were on, Dorothy could not take them off had she wished."

D) "Of course, Dorothy did not wish to be blinded by the glare of the Emerald City, so she said nothing."

4.

'The Unfading Beauty' is a poem by Thomas Carew. The speaker of the poem claims that physical attractiveness and attraction fades over time.

He that loves a rosy cheek,
  Or a coral lip admires,
Or from star-like eyes doth seek
  Fuel to maintain his fires:
As old Time makes these decay,
So his flames must waste away.

But a smooth and steadfast mind,
  Gentle thoughts and calm desires,
Hearts with equal love combined,
  Kindle never-dying fires.
Where these are not, I despise
Lovely cheeks or lips or eyes.

Which quotation from 'The Unfading Beauty' most effectively illustrates the claim?

A) "He that loves a rosy cheek,
  Or a coral lip admires,"

B) "As old Time makes these decay,
So his flames must waste away."

C) "But a smooth and steadfast mind,
  Gentle thoughts and calm desires,"

D) "Where these are not, I despise
Lovely cheeks or lips or eyes."

5.

The following is adapted from Mark Twain's novel 'The Adventures of Tom Sawyer."

"Treasure's hid in mighty particular places, Huck — sometimes on islands, sometimes in rotten chests under the end of a limb of an old dead tree, just where the shadow falls at midnight; but mostly under the floor in ha'nted houses."
"Who hides it?"
"Why, robbers, of course—who'd you reckon? Sunday-school sup'rintendents?"

Which quotation from the text most effectively illustrates the claim that treasure can be found in unusual places?

A) "Who hides it?"

B) sup'rintendents?"

C) "Sometimes in rotten chests under the end of a limb of an old dead tree, just where the shadow falls at midnight."

D) "So would I. But robbers don't do that way. They always hide it and leave it there."

6.

"To Amarantha, that she would dishevel her Hair" is a poem by Richard Lovelace. The poem conveys the speaker's desire for Amarantha to wear her hair loose and unbraided.

Amarantha sweet and fair,
Ah, braid no more that shining hair!
As my curious hand or eye
Hovering round thee, let it fly!

Let it fly as unconfined
As its calm ravisher the wind,
Who hath left his darling, th' East,
To wanton o'er that spicy nest.

Every tress must be confest,
But neatly tangled at the best;
Like a clew of golden thread
Most excellently ravellèd.

Do not then wind up that light
In ribbands, and o'ercloud in night,
Like the Sun in 's early ray;
But shake your head, and scatter day!

Which quotation from the poem most effectively illustrates the speaker's desire?

A) "Ah, braid no more that shining hair!"

B) "Every tress must be confest,"

C) "In ribbands, and o'ercloud in night,"

D) "But shake your head, and scatter day!"

7.

The following is adapted from Mark Twain's novel *'The Adventures of Tom Sawyer."*

There comes a time in every rightly-constructed boy's life when he has a raging desire to go somewhere and dig for hidden treasure. This desire suddenly came upon Tom one day. He sallied out to find Joe Harper, but failed of success. Next he sought Ben Rogers; he had gone fishing. Presently he stumbled upon Huck Finn the Red-Handed. Huck would answer. Tom took him to a private place and opened the matter to him confidentially. Huck was willing.

A) Which quotation from the story most effectively illustrates the claim that Huck was willing to help Tom?
B) "Why, is it hid all around?"
C) Huck had a troublesome superabundance of that sort of time which is not money.
D) "Where'll we dig?" said Huck.

8.

The following is adapted from Frank L. Baum's novel *'The Wonderful Wizard of Oz,'* in which a young girl, Dorothy, is transported to a mysterious, colorful land called Oz where she faces a Wicked Witch.

"You are a wicked creature!" cried Dorothy. "You have no right to take my shoe from me."
Dorothy was so very angry that she picked up the bucket of water that stood near and dashed it over the Witch, wetting her from head to foot. Instantly the wicked woman gave a loud cry of fear, and then, as Dorothy looked at her in wonder, the Witch began to shrink and fall away."
"See what you have done!" she screamed. "In a minute I shall melt away."

Which quotation from the story best illustrates the Wicked Witch's claim that she will melt away?

A) "I will not," retorted the Witch, "for it is now my shoe, and not yours."
B) "I'm very sorry, indeed," said Dorothy, who was truly frightened to see the Witch actually melting away like brown sugar before her very eyes.
C) "Of course not," answered Dorothy. "How should I?"
D) "Well, in a few minutes you will have the castle to yourself"

9.

The following is adapted from Ben Jonson's poem 'Hymn to Diana.' The speaker asks Diana, Roman Goddess of the Moon, to shine brightly enough to see at night.

Queen and huntress, chaste and fair,
  Now the sun is laid to sleep,
Seated in thy silver chair,
  State in wonted manner keep:
    Hesperus entreats thy light,
    Goddess excellently bright.

Earth, let not thy envious shade
  Dare itself to interpose;
Cynthia's shining orb was made
  Heaven to clear when day did close:
    Bless us then with wishèd sight,
    Goddess excellently bright.

Lay thy bow of pearl apart,
  And thy crystal-shining quiver;
Give unto the flying hart
  Space to breathe, how short soever:
    Thou that mak'st a day of night—
    Goddess excellently bright.

Which quotation from the poem most effectively illustrates the speaker's request?

A) Now the sun is laid to sleep,

B) Earth, let not thy envious shade

C) Bless us then with wishèd sight,

D) Lay thy bow of pearl apart,

10.
The following is adapted from Walt Whitman's 1900 poem 'As I Watch'd the Ploughman Ploughing,' in which Whitman claims that certain types of farm labor are comparable to life and death.

As I watch'd the ploughman ploughing,
Or the sower sowing in the fields—or the harvester harvesting,
I saw there too, O life and death, your analogies:
(Life, life is the tillage, and Death is the harvest according.)

Which quotation from the poem most effectively illustrates the claim?

A) "As I watch'd the ploughman ploughing,"

B) "Or the sower sowing in the fields—or the harvester harvesting,"

C) "I saw there too, O life and death, your analogies:"

D) "(Life, life is the tillage, and Death is the harvest according.)"

CHALLENGE:

Amaranth, from the Greek *amarantos*, meaning unwithering, is a name chiefly used in poetry and applied to certain plants which typified immortality.

Which quote from Milton's 'Paradise Lost' best supports the claim that amaranth typified immortality?

A) "In paradise, fast by the tree of life,
Began to bloom; but soon for man's offence"

B) "To heaven removed, where first it grew, there grows,
And flowers aloft, shading the fount of life,"

C) "And where the river of bliss through midst of heaven
Rolls o'er elysian flowers her amber stream:"

D) "With these that never fade the spirits elect
Bind their resplendent locks."

Answers on page 374

Recommendations:

If you scored between 0-3, support quotation question practice is **high** priority for you.

If you scored between 4-8, support quotation question practice is **medium** priority for you.

If you scored between 9-11, support quotation question practice is **low** priority for you.

PURPOSE

Here's the breakdown of what LearnCurious calls 'Purpose' questions on the four currently-released digital SAT exams:

	VM1	VM2a	VM2b
Test #1:	2/27 = 7.4%	0/27 = 0%	0/27 = 0%
Test #2:	3/27 = 11.1%	0/27 = 0%	0/27 = 0%
Test #3:	0/27 = 0%	2/27 = 7.4%	3/27 = 11.1%
Test #4:	2/27 = 7.4%	0/27 = 0%	3/27 = 11.1%

To summarize, there are
...between **0-3** purpose questions on Verbal Module 1,
...between **0-2** purpose questions on Verbal Module 2a,
...and between **0-3** purpose questions on Verbal Module 2b.

Question frequency: 0-11.1% == RARE
Speed rating: moderate

PURPOSE questions appear in the early-middle part of Verbal Modules, usually between questions #6 - 16. They ask students to assess how a piece of text is functioning within the passage. To answer Purpose questions more easily, **put yourself in the author's shoes & ask yourself "If I were the author of this text, why would I have bothered writing it?" and "What would be the goal I'd be hoping to achieve in writing this piece?"**

How do I identify purpose questions?

Purpose questions can be identified using these specific question stems:
- *'Which choice best describes the function of the underlined portion in the text as a whole?'*
- *'Which choice best describes the function of the _____ sentence in the overall structure of the text?'*
- *'Which choice best describes the function of the underlined sentence in the text as a whole?'*
- *'Which choice best states the main purpose of the text?'*

Look for these words in particular in the question stem to easily identify Purpose questions: *'purpose,' 'main purpose,' 'function' / 'function as,' 'in order to,' 'to illustrate,' 'serves to,' 'so that,' 'because.'*

Here are a few examples of what digital SAT 'purpose' questions look like:

1.
'As I Watch'd the Ploughman Ploughing' is a 1900 poem by Walt Whitman.

"As I watch'd the ploughman ploughing,
Or the sower sowing in the fields—or the harvester harvesting,
I saw there too, O life and death, your analogies:
(Life, life is the tillage, and Death is the harvest according.)"

Which choice best states the **main purpose** of the text?

A) To identify a key difference between types of agricultural work and laborers

B) To note a observed relationship between the cycle of farm labor and that of life and death

C) To observe a similarity between sowing seeds and harvesting crops

D) To recollect a daydream the author had while on a farm

2.

The color of amethyst is usually attributed to the presence of manganese, but as it is capable of being much altered and even discharged by heat it has been referred by some authorities to an organic source. On exposure to heat, amethyst generally becomes yellow, and much of the *cairngorm* or yellow quartz of jewelry is said to be merely "burnt amethyst." Veins of amethystine quartz are apt to lose their color on the exposed outcrop.

Which choice best states the **main purpose** of the text?

A) To describe the color properties of amethyst
B) To postulate that the change in color in amethyst is due to human interference
C) To reiterate the properties of amethyst that make it especially valuable
D) To pose a rhetorical question about "burnt amethyst"

3.

The following text is from the poem 'The Rainbow' by William Wordsworth.

My heart leaps up when I behold
A rainbow in the sky:
So was it when my life began;
So is it now I am a man;
So be it when I shall grow old,
   Or let me die!
The Child is father of the Man;
I could wish my days to be
Bound each to each by natural piety.

Which choice best describes the **function of the underlined portion** in the text as a whole?

A) It brings to light a concern of the speaker.
B) It elaborates on an example given earlier in the poem.
C) It reflects the speaker's feelings about growing old.
D) It serves to convey the strength of the speaker's feelings.

4.

The following is adapted from Lewis Carroll's novel *Alice's Adventures in Wonderland,* in which a young girl, Alice, falls down a rabbit hole into a confusing world of colorful characters.

"They were obliged to have him with them," the Mock Turtle said: "no wise fish would go anywhere without a porpoise."

"Wouldn't it really?" said Alice in a tone of great surprise.

"Of course not," said the Mock Turtle: "why, if a fish came to me, and told me he was going a journey, I should say 'With what porpoise?'"

"Don't you mean 'purpose'?" said Alice.

"I mean what I say," the Mock Turtle replied in an offended tone.

Which choice best describes the function of the underlined portion in the text as a whole?

A) It indicates that the Mock Turtle knows information that Alice does not.

B) It portrays the Mock Turtle as rude and unflappable.

C) It describes the symbiotic relationship between fish and porpoises.

D) It simultaneously serves to amuse the reader with a humorous pun and confuse Alice.

Answers on page 374

What are some helpful Purpose question strategies?

Here are a few strategic questions to ask yourself when faced with Purpose questions:

What is the difference between the main idea and the main purpose of a text?

Main idea = WHAT the passage is mostly about

Main purpose = WHY the passage exists / what goal its author had in mind

The difference is a matter of asking yourself

"WHAT?" for Main Idea Questions
and
"WHY?" for Purpose Questions.

To find the purpose of a paragraph or line of text, pretend you are the one who wrote the piece of text. Ask yourself:

"If I were the author of this text, why would I have bothered writing it?"

and

"What would be the goal I'd be hoping to achieve in writing this piece?"

PURPOSE questions appear in the early-middle part of Verbal Modules, usually between questions #6 - 16. They ask students to assess how a piece of text is functioning within the passage. To answer Purpose questions more easily, **put yourself in the author's shoes & ask yourself "If I were the author of this text, why would I have bothered writing it?" and "What would be the goal I'd be hoping to achieve in writing this piece?"**

Practice Purpose Questions:

1.

The first brick buildings in America were erected on Manhattan Island in the year 1633 by a governor of the Dutch West India Company. These bricks were made in Holland, where the industry had long reached great excellence; <u>for many years bricks were imported into America from Holland and from England.</u>

Which choice best describes the function of the underlined sentence in the text as a whole?

A) It provides information about the number of bricks imported from Holland.

B) It provides information about the countries from which Holland imports bricks.

C) It provides information about the number of bricks imported from England.

D) It provides information about the countries from which America imported bricks.

2.

The Canadian Pacific Railway Company has two lines of mail steamer running from Vancouver and Victoria: the Empress line, which runs to Japan and China once in three weeks and the Australian line to Honolulu, Fiji and Sydney, once a month. The same company also has a line of steamers running to Alaska, as well as a fleet of coasting steamers.

Which choice best states the main purpose of the text?

A) To describe the most popular route offered by the Canadian Pacific Railway Company.

B) To support a popular hypothesis about the Canadian Pacific Railway Company.

C) To underscore the importance of the Empress line to the economy of Vancouver.

D) To provide basic details about the transportation types and routes offered by the Canadian Pacific Railway Company.

3.

The four species of indigenous South American wool-bearing animals are the llama, the alpaca, the guanaco, and the vicuna. The llama and the alpaca are domesticated; the guanaco and the vicuna run wild.[Alpacas] are not used as beasts of burden like llamas, but are valued only for their wool, of which blankets and ponchos are made. In stature the alpaca is considerably inferior to the llama, but has the same unpleasant habit of spitting.

Which choice best describes the function of the underlined portion in the text as a whole?

A) To give details about why alpacas are considered domesticated while llamas are not.
B) To compare and contrast the guanaco and the vicuna.
C) To compare and contrast alpacas and llamas.
D) To indicate the differences in value between the llama and the vicuna.

4.
The following text is from the poem 'Hymn to Diana' by Ben Jonson. In the poem, Jonson describes the moon using allusions to Roman mythology.

Queen and huntress, chaste and fair,
  Now the sun is laid to sleep,
Seated in thy silver chair,
  State in wonted manner keep:
    Hesperus entreats thy light,
    Goddess excellently bright.

Earth, let not thy envious shade
  Dare itself to interpose;
Cynthia's shining orb was made
  Heaven to clear when day did close:
    Bless us then with wishèd sight,
    Goddess excellently bright.

Lay thy bow of pearl apart,
  And thy crystal-shining quiver;
Give unto the flying hart
  Space to breathe, how short soever:
    Thou that mak'st a day of night—
    Goddess excellently bright.

Which choice best describes the function of the underlined portion in the text as a whole?

A) It serves to emphasize the brightness of the moon.

B) It serves to contrast the moon with the sun.

C) It serves to convey the speaker's preference for the daytime.

D) It serves to warn the audience of the danger of hunting at night.

5.

An immense variety of ornamental paving and walling tiles is now manufactured of different colors, sizes, and shapes, and the use of these for lining sculleries, lavatories, bathrooms, provision shops, etc, makes for cleanliness and improved sanitary conditions. <u>Besides, however, being put to these uses, tiles are often used in the ornamentation of buildings, externally as well as internally.</u>

Which choice best describes the function of the second sentence in the overall structure of the text?

A) It promotes the idea of using tile for decoration over flooring or sanitary surfaces.
B) It gives further examples of how tiles are used for ornamentation.
C) It provides details on where tiles are used for decoration inside of structures.
D) It indicates a shift in a preference for interior ornamentation to exterior ornamentation.

6.

'As I Watch'd the Ploughman Ploughing' is a 1900 poem by Walt Whitman.

As I watch'd the ploughman ploughing,
Or the sower sowing in the fields—or the harvester harvesting,
I saw there too, O life and death, your analogies:
<u>(Life, life is the tillage, and Death is the harvest according.)</u>

Which choice best describes the function of the underlined portion in the text as a whole?

A) To specify the connections noted by the author between farm labor and the life cycle
B) To recommend that others observe farmers at work and appreciate their efforts
C) To acknowledge that death is like tillage and that life is like the harvest
D) To remind the audience that tillage is a type of important work for farmers

7.

The following is adapted from Frank L. Baum's novel *The Wonderful Wizard of Oz*, in which a young girl, Dorothy, is transported by a cyclone from her home in rural Kansas to a mysterious, colorful land called Oz.

When Dorothy awoke, the sun was shining through the trees and Toto had long been out chasing birds around him and squirrels. She sat up and looked around her. There was the Scarecrow, still standing patiently in his corner, waiting for her.

"We must go and search for water," she said to him.

"Why do you want water?" he asked.

"To wash my face clean after the dust of the road, and to drink, so the dry bread will not stick in my throat."

"It must be inconvenient to be made of flesh," said the Scarecrow thoughtfully, "for you must sleep, and eat and drink. However, you have brains, and it is worth a lot of bother to be able to think properly."

Which choice best states the main purpose of the text?

A) To compare the perspectives of Dorothy and the Scarecrow with regard to human basic needs like washing, eating, and sleeping.

B) To indicate that Dorothy is envious of the Scarecrow not needing to wash, eat, or sleep.

C) To describe a problem faced by Dorothy that is solved by the Scarecrow.

D) To examine the relationship between the Scarecrow and fire.

8.

The following text is from the poem 'The Rainbow' by William Wordsworth.

My heart leaps up when I behold
A rainbow in the sky:
So was it when my life began;
So is it now I am a man;
So be it when I shall grow old,
    Or let me die!
The Child is father of the Man;
I could wish my days to be
Bound each to each by natural piety.

Which choice best states the main purpose of the text?

A) The poem conveys the perpetual joy the speaker feels upon seeing a rainbow.
B) The poem denotes the importance of seeing a rainbow and taking time for daily reflection in nature.
C) The poem contrasts the delight the author felt as a child with the dismay he feels as an adult.
D) The poem describes an old man's fond memory of a rainbow.

9.

Upon the death of Mrs Brontë her husband invited his sister-in-law, Elizabeth Branwell, to leave Penzance and to take up her residence with his family at Haworth. Miss Branwell accepted the trust and <u>would seem to have watched over her nephew and five nieces with conscientious care.</u>

Which choice best describes the function of the underlined sentence in the text as a whole?

A) To undermine Miss Branwell's decision to leave Penzance.
B) To describe how Miss Branwell contributed to the household at Haworth.
C) To indicate the high level of mistreatment of the children by Miss Branwell.
D) To validate a previous claim made about Miss Branwell.

10.

Talisman, also from the Arabic, is a word of similar meaning and use to the word 'amulet,' but some distinguish it as importing a more powerful charm. A talisman, whose ``virtues are still applied to for stopping blood and in cases of canine madness," figures prominently in, and gives name to, one of Sir Walter Scott's novels.

Which choice best describes the function of the underlined portion in the text as a whole?

A) To compare the connotations of the words talisman and amulet.

B) To state an observation and follow it with an example from history.

C) To clarify the difference between the word 'talisman' and the word 'charm.'

D) To indicate that the words 'talisman' and 'amulet' are derived from two very different languages of origin.

CHALLENGE:

The following is adapted from Mark Twain's novel *The Adventures of Tom Sawyer.*

Sighing, Tom dipped his brush and passed it along the topmost plank; repeated the operation; did it again; compared the insignificant whitewashed streak with the far-reaching continent of unwhitewashed fence, and sat down on a tree-box discouraged. Jim came skipping out at the gate with a tin pail, and singing Buffalo Gals. Bringing water from the town pump had always been hateful work in Tom's eyes, before, but now it did not strike him so. <u>He remembered that there was company at the pump.</u>

Which choice best describes the function of the underlined portion in the text as a whole?

A) It clarifies why Tom would've preferred whitewashing the fence to fetching the water.
B) It notes that Jim is skipping and singing.
C) It gives an example of the kind of company Tom liked to keep.
D) It indicates the reason that Tom would have preferred fetching water to whitewashing the fence.

Answers on page 374

Recommendations:

If you scored between 0-3, purpose question practice is **high** priority for you.

If you scored between 4-8, purpose question practice is **medium** priority for you.

If you scored between 9-11, purpose question practice is **low** priority for you.

MAIN
IDEA

Here's the breakdown of what LearnCurious calls 'Main Idea' questions on the four currently-released digital SAT exams:

	VM1	VM2a	VM2b
Test #1:	1/27 = 3.7%	0/27 = 0%	0/27 = 0%
Test #2:	2/27 = 7.4%	0/27 = 0%	1/27 = 3.7%
Test #3:	1/27 = 3.7%	0/27 = 0%	0/27 = 0%
Test #4:	2/27 = 7.4%	0/27 = 0%	0/27 = 0%

To summarize, there are
...between **1-2** main idea questions on Verbal Module 1,
... **0** main idea questions on Verbal Module 2a,
...and between **0-1** main idea questions on Verbal Module 2b.

Question frequency: 0-7.4% == RARE
Speed rating: moderate

MAIN IDEA questions appear in the early-middle part of Verbal Modules, usually between questions #6 - 16. They ask students to identify the primary claim or focus of the passage. **To efficiently find the main idea of a passage, write a mini summary by briefly (in one sentence) answering the questions who? what? where? when? how?**

How do I identify Main Idea questions?

Main Idea questions can be identified using these specific question stems:
- *"What is the main idea of the text?"*
- *"Which choice best states the main idea of the text?"*

Look for these words in particular in the question stem to easily identify Main Idea questions: *'main idea,' or 'primary claim'*

Here are three examples of what digital SAT Main Idea questions look like:

1.
The work of laying bricks or tiles as paving falls to the lot of the bricklayer. Paving formed of ordinary bricks laid flat or on their edges was once in general use but is now almost abandoned in favor of floors of special tiles or cement paving, the latter being practically non-porous and therefore more sanitary.

Which choice best states the main idea of the text?

A) The passage compares and contrast bricklayers' work with that of cement pavers.

B) The passage indicates the reason that brick floors are preferred to cement paving.

C) The passage provides information about bricklaying and the shift to tile or cement flooring.

D) The passage makes a claim and then gives an example of a potential reason a bricklayer might choose brick over cement.

2.

If we look either at the shadow of any object in the distance or at a distant landmark over a level plain on a hot day, the effect of an ascending current of heated air is almost always evident: the air in these currents sometimes appears to shimmer.

What is the main idea of the text?

A) To contrast the researcher's theory with that of Mr. Murray.

B) To specify a reason why spiders are able to travel through the air.

C) To describe how to observe a specific natural phenomenon.

D) To compare spider travel to that of soap-bubbles.

3.

The following text is from the 1900 poem 'As I Watch'd the Ploughman Ploughing' by Walt Whitman.

As I watch'd the ploughman ploughing,
Or the sower sowing in the fields—or the harvester harvesting,
I saw there too, O life and death, your analogies:
(Life, life is the tillage, and Death is the harvest according.)

What is the main idea of the text?

A) The narrator describes observing laborers on a farm.

B) The narrator raises concern about the dangers of agricultural equipment.

C) The narrator relays information about harvesting crops.

D) The narrator draws a comparison between the cyclic nature of farm work and life and death.

Answers on page 374

What are some helpful Main Idea question strategies?

Here are a few strategic questions to ask yourself when faced with Main Idea questions:

Remember, there is an important difference between identifying the Main Idea of a passage versus its purpose.

What is the difference between the main idea and the main purpose of a text?

Main idea = WHAT the passage is mostly about

Main purpose = WHY the passage exists / what goal its author had

The difference is a matter of asking yourself

"WHAT?" for Main Idea Questions
and
"WHY?" for Purpose Questions.

To efficiently find the main idea of a passage, write a mini summary by briefly (in one sentence) answering the questions **who? what? where? when? how?**

MAIN IDEA questions appear in the early-middle part of Verbal Modules, usually between questions #6 - 16. They ask students to identify the primary claim or focus of the passage. **To efficiently find the main idea of a passage, briefly (in one sentence) answering the questions who? what? where? when? how?**

Practice Main Idea Questions:

1.

The Bronx, formerly a district comprising several towns in Westchester county, New York, is now (since 1898) the northernmost of the five boroughs of New York City. Several settlements in the Bronx were made by the English and the Dutch between 1640 and 1650.

Which choice best states the main idea of the text?

A) To indicate who first settled The Bronx region of New York.
B) To provide details about why The Bronx is no longer considered part of New York.
C) To briefly describe the history of The Bronx.
D) To provide an example of the items imported to the Bronx in the 1640s and 1650s.

2.

The following is adapted from Frank L. Baum's novel *The Wonderful Wizard of Oz*, in which a young girl, Dorothy, is transported to a mysterious, colorful land called Oz where she travels to The Emerald City.

There were many people — men, women, and children — walking about, and these were all dressed in green clothes and had greenish skins. They looked at Dorothy and her strangely assorted company with wondering eyes, and the children all ran away and hid behind their mothers when they saw the Lion; no one spoke to them. Everyone seemed happy and contented and prosperous.

Which choice best states the main idea of the text?

A) It indicates that not everything in the city was green.
B) It provides reasonable doubt about the green appearance of the city and its inhabitants.
C) It describes the appearances and responses of the citizens of Emerald City to seeing Dorothy and her traveling companions.
D) It relates the green appearance of the city with the queasy feeling the children got when seeing the Lion.

3.

The following is adapted from William Wordsworth's poem 'The Rainbow.'

My heart leaps up when I behold
A rainbow in the sky:
So was it when my life began;
So is it now I am a man;
So be it when I shall grow old,
　　Or let me die!
The Child is father of the Man;
I could wish my days to be
Bound each to each by natural piety.

What is the main idea of the text?

A) The poem reflects the speaker's distaste for rainbows and other natural phenomena.

B) The poem contrasts the speaker's reaction to rainbows as a child and as an adult.

C) The poem describes the speaker's perpetual delight at seeing rainbows.

D) The poem details how parents and children see rainbows differently.

4.

They are beautiful objects in the autumn woods; *Amanita muscaria*, the fly fungus, formerly known as *Agaricus muscarius*, being especially remarkable by its bright red cap covered with white warts. Others are pure white or of varying shades of yellow or green.

What is the main idea of the text?

A) To describe where students of mycology might find specimens of *Amanita muscariu*.
B) To provide an example of dangerous fungi and how to identify them.
C) To provide details about some of the color variations of a certain fungus.
D) To indicate that *Amanita muscaria* is particularly difficult to identify.

5.

'Hymn to Diana' is a poem by Ben Jonson.

Queen and huntress, chaste and fair,
  Now the sun is laid to sleep,
Seated in thy silver chair,
  State in wonted manner keep:
    Hesperus entreats thy light,
    Goddess excellently bright.

Earth, let not thy envious shade
  Dare itself to interpose;
Cynthia's shining orb was made
  Heaven to clear when day did close:
    Bless us then with wishèd sight,
    Goddess excellently bright.

Lay thy bow of pearl apart,
  And thy crystal-shining quiver;
Give unto the flying hart
  Space to breathe, how short soever:
    Thou that mak'st a day of night—
    Goddess excellently bright.

What is the main idea of the text?

A) The speaker asks a huntress to guide him through a sacred forest.

B) The speaker observes a woman seated in a silver chair and asks for her help.

C) The speaker addresses the bright, full moon with admiration and appreciation.

D) The speaker requests help from a deity in his quest to go hunting at night.

6.

The alpaca is one of two domesticated breeds of South American camel-like ungulates descended from the wild huanaco or guanaco. Alpacas are kept in large flocks which graze on the level heights of the Andes of southern Peru and northern Bolivia, at an elevation of from 14,000 to 16,000 feet above the sea-level, throughout the year.

What is the main idea of the text?

A) The text questions whether the alpaca has been fully domesticated.

B) The text indicates that alpacas are rarely found below 14,000 feet in elevation above sea level.

C) The text describes the habitat of the domesticated South American alpaca.

D) The text provides details about the taxonomic family in which a student will find the alpaca.

7.

The following is adapted from Mark Twain's novel *The Adventures of Tom Sawyer.*

When the middle of the afternoon came, from being a poor poverty-stricken boy in the morning, Tom was literally rolling in wealth. He had besides the things before mentioned, twelve marbles, part of a harp, a piece of blue bottle-glass to look through, a spool cannon, a key that wouldn't unlock anything, a fragment of chalk, a glass stopper of a decanter, a tin soldier, a couple of tadpoles, six fire-crackers, a kitten with only one eye, a brass door-knob, a dog-collar—but no dog, the handle of a knife, four pieces of orange-peel, and a dilapidated old window sash.

What is the main idea of the text?

A) The passage describes Tom's favorite childhood possessions in detail.
B) The passage indicates contradictory results Tom's scheme and Ben's.
C) The passage provides details about the items Tom collected in one day.
D) The passage suggests that Tom grew up wealthy and amassed a collection of favorite items.

8.

For the word "billion" runs as glibly off the tongue as "million," and both are so wholly unrealizable by us that the actual difference between them might easily pass unnoticed. What is a million? It is a thousand thousands. But what is a billion? It is a million millions.

What is the main idea of the text?

A) It poses a question and then indicates that the answer is surprising.

B) It makes a claim and supports it by comparing the distance between our sun and planets and our sun and other suns.

C) It suggests numbers in the millions and billions can be difficult to distinguish in magnitude.

D) It poses and answers a rhetorical question then describes a means of comprehending numbers in the millions versus those in the billions.

9.

Observing that the water charged with gelatinous particles is in an impure state, and that the luminous appearance in all common cases is produced by the agitation of the fluid in contact with the atmosphere, I am inclined to consider that the phosphorescence is the result of the decomposition of the organic particles, by which process (one is tempted almost to call it a kind of respiration) the ocean becomes purified.

Which choice best states the main idea of the text?

A) It describes a natural phenomenon that occurs near Fernando Noronha.

B) It suggests that phosphorescence is the result of the decomposition of the organic particles.

C) It summarizes a study conducted in order to assess phosphorescence levels in certain marine particles.

D) It compares theories about the causes of an observed phenomenon in Fernando Noronha.

10.

It might be thought that an ice block had, by the pressure in the mold, been first reduced to powder so fine that it readily penetrated every crevice of the mold, and then that this powdered ice, like snow, was again combined by freezing. Yet the mere aspect of the cylinders pressed from blocks of ice shows us that the it has not been formed in this manner; they are generally clearer than ice which is produced from snow, and the individual larger pieces of ice which have been used to produce them are recognized, though they are somewhat changed and flattened.

What is the main idea of the text?

A) The passage concludes that ice doesn't need to be fully smashed in order to be molded but suggests that further research will be helpful in understanding this finding further.

B) The passage indicates contradictory results in theories surrounding ice block experiments and provides details about the current competing theories.

C) The passage introduces a possible theory about why ice fills molds so precisely then elaborates on why that theory has been observed to not be the case.

D) The passage suggests that more research in compressing ice blocks is needed to understand how it happens.

CHALLENGE:

If we look either at the shadow of any object in the distance or at a distant landmark over a level plain on a hot day, the effect of an ascending current of heated air is almost always evident: the air in these currents sometimes appears to shimmer. Scientists have noted that while soap-bubbles will no rise indoors, they are seen to ascent outdoors in these upward currents of warmer air.

Which choice best states the main idea of the text?

A) To specify a reason why spiders are able to travel through the air.

B) To compare spider travel to that of soap-bubbles.

C) To explain a way scientists know that upward-moving currents of air are present outdoors.

D) To contrast the researcher's theory about spiders' threads with that of Mr. Murray.

Answers on page 374

<u>Recommendations:</u>

If you scored between 0-4, main idea question practice is **<u>high</u>** priority for you.

If you scored between 5-8, main idea question practice is **<u>medium</u>** priority for you.

If you scored between 9-11, main idea question practice is **<u>low</u>** priority for you.

If you were uncomfortable with the long line of "C" answer choices in that exercise, know it was for a reason: to provide another example of the necessity of choosing the answer that is the best fit rather than the answer letter option that seems like it 'should' come next based on what answers have already seemed best on previous questions. Pretend those other questions' answers don't exist.

> STRATEGY: Approach each question as though there's been no discernable answer letter pattern. Don't try to game the test!

PASSAGE COMPARISON

Here's the breakdown of what LearnCurious calls 'Passage Comparison' (PC) questions on the four currently-released digital SAT exams:

	VM1	VM2a	VM2b
Test #1:	1/27 = 3.7%	0/27 = 0%	0/27 = 0%
Test #2:	0/27 = 0%	1/27 = 3.7%	1/27 = 3.7%
Test #3:	0/27 = 0%	1/27 = 3.7%	1/27 = 3.7%
Test #4:	0/27 = 0%	1/27 = 3.7%	1/27 = 3.7%

To summarize, there are
...between **0-1** PC questions on Verbal Module 1,
...between **0-1** PC questions on Verbal Module 2a,
...and between **0-1** PC questions on Verbal Module 2b.

Question frequency: 0 - 3.7% == MYTHIC
Speed rating: TIME-CONSUMING

PASSAGE COMPARISON questions appear in the early-middle part of Verbal Modules, usually between questions #6 - 16. They ask students to compare and contrast authors' or passage characters' views on a claim or topic. **Since Passage Comparison questions are so rare, it's often a good time-management strategy to guess on them, flag them for review, and come back to them if you have time.**

How do I identify Passage Comparison questions?

Passage Comparison questions can be identified using these specific question stems:

- 'Based on the texts, how would (the author of Text 2) most likely respond to ((the claims of) the author of Text 1)?'

- 'Based on the texts, how would (the author of Text 1) most likely respond to (the claims of Text 2)?'

- 'Based on the texts, how would (the author of Text 2) most likely respond to (the _____ discussed in Text 1)?'

- 'Based on the texts, what would (the author of Text 1) most likely say about___(the author of Text 2)?'

Look for these words in particular in the question stem to easily identify Passage Comparison (PC) questions: *'most likely,' 'the author of Text 1 / 2'*

Here are two examples of what digital SAT Passage Comparison questions look like:

1.
The Alhambra was built chiefly between 1248 and 1354, during the reigns of Al Ahmar and his successors. Immediately after the expulsion of the Moors in 1492, their conquerors began, by successive acts of vandalism, to spoil the marvelous beauty of the Alhambra.

Text 1

Charles V. (1516-1556) rebuilt portions of the Alhambra in the modern style of the period and destroyed the greater part of the winter palace to make room for a modern structure which has never been completed.

Text 2

Philip V. (1700-1746) '**Italianized**' the rooms and completed the degradation by running up partitions which blocked up whole apartments.

Based on the texts, how would Charles V most likely respond to the changes made to the Alhambra by Philip V?

A) Charles V would perhaps respond to the changes made by Philip V by suggesting that Philip complete the modern structure that Charles planned and started but never finished.

B) Philip V would perhaps respond to the changes made by Charles V by pointing out that Charles V's unfinished restoration projects are separate from those of his own that were still in progress

C) Charles V would perhaps respond to the changes made by Philip V by protesting the destruction of the winter palace.

D) Philip V would perhaps respond to the changes made by Charles V by rejecting them in favor of a more modern, French design.

2.

The Alhambra was built chiefly between 1248 and 1354, during the reigns of Al Ahmar and his successors. Immediately after the expulsion of the Moors in 1492, their conquerors began, by successive acts of vandalism, to spoil the marvelous beauty of the Alhambra.

Text 1

Charles V. (1516-1556) rebuilt portions of the Alhambra in the modern style of the period and destroyed the greater part of the winter palace to make room for a modern structure which has never been completed.

Text 2

Philip V. (1700-1746) **'Italianized'** the rooms and completed the degradation by running up partitions which blocked up whole apartments.

Based on the texts, how would the leader described in Text 2 most likely respond to the changes made to the Alhambra by the leader of Text 1?

A) Charles V would perhaps respond to the changes made by Philip V by protesting the destruction of the winter palace.

B) Philip V would perhaps respond to the changes made by Charles V by rejecting them in favor of a more modern, French design.

C) Charles V would perhaps respond to the changes made by Philip V by suggesting that Philip complete the modern structure that Charles planned and started but never finished.

D) Philip V would perhaps respond to the changes made by Charles V by pointing out that Charles V's unfinished restoration projects are separate from those of his own that were still in progress.

Answers on page 374

What are some helpful Passage Comparison question strategies?

Here are a few strategic questions to ask yourself when faced with Passage Comparison questions:

"Do I have time for this?"

Passage Comparison questions are not only LONG but also requires more critical thinking skills than many of the other question types. They are often among the most time-consuming to answer for many students.

Since Passage Comparison questions are so rare in the first place, it's often a good time-management strategy to guess on them, flag them for review, and come back to them if you have time. If not, you don't even need to go back to guess.

"How are these similar to Logical Completion or Support Quote questions?"

Chart / Graph Interpretation and Support Quote questions also ask students to complete the text with the most logical answer choice, based on the explicit and implicit evidence provided in graphs and passages. .

While the evidence to support the correct answer to Chart / Graph Interpretation questions is often more clear and direct than the evidence to support Logical Completion questions, when you do tackle a Passage Completion question, remember that they require students to make inferences. Remember, an inference is an idea based on clues or hints instead of direct (explicit) statements; anticipate answer having less direct evidence to support correct answers.

PASSAGE COMPARISON questions appear in the early-middle part of Verbal Modules, usually between questions #6 - 16. They ask students to compare and contrast authors' or passage characters' views on a claim or topic. **Since Passage Comparison questions are so rare, it's often a good time-management strategy to guess on them, flag them for review, and come back to them if you have time.**

Practice Passage Comparison (PC) Questions:

1.

Text 1

According to J. Vurtheim, the Amazons were of Greek origin: "all the Amazons were Dianas, as Diana herself was an Amazon." In works of art, combat between Amazons and Greeks is placed on the same level as and often associated with combat between Greeks and centaurs. Their occupation was hunting and war; their arms were the bow, spear, axe, and a half shield, nearly in the shape of a crescent, called a *pelta*.

Text 2

The history of Bohemia affords a parallel to the Greek Amazons. During the 8th century, a large band of women, under a certain Vlasta, carried on war against the duke of Bohemia and enslaved or put to death all men who fell into their hands. Additionally, the Spanish explorer Orellana asserted that he had come into conflict with fighting women in South America on the river Maranon. The existence of 'Amazons' (in the sense of fighting women) in the army of Dahomey is an undoubted fact, but they are said to have died out during the French protectorate.

Based on the texts, how would Orellana most likely respond to the claims made by Vurtheim about the Amazons' origin?

A) Orellana might point out that the battle between Theseus and the Amazons is a favorite subject on the friezes of temples.

B) Orellana might suggest that there was a battle between Theseus and the Amazons.

C) Orellana might point out that he'd encountered a group of fighting women in South America.

D) Orellana might suggest that Amazons were usually on horseback but sometimes on foot.

2.

The Alhambra was built chiefly between 1248 and 1354, during the reigns of Al Ahmar and his successors. Immediately after the expulsion of the Moors in 1492, their conquerors began, by successive acts of vandalism, to spoil the marvelous beauty of the Alhambra.

Text 1

Charles V. (1516-1556) rebuilt portions of the Alhambra in the modern style of the period and destroyed the greater part of the winter palace to make room for a modern structure which has never been completed.

Text 2

Philip V. (1700-1746) 'Italianized' the rooms and completed the degradation by running up partitions which blocked up whole apartments.

Based on the texts, how would Philip V most likely respond to the changes made to the Alhambra by Charles V?

A) Philip V would perhaps respond to the changes made by Charles V by pointing out that Charles V's unfinished restoration projects are separate from those of his own that were still in progress.

B) Philip V would perhaps respond to the changes made by Charles V by rejecting them in favor of a more modern, French design.

C) Charles V would perhaps respond to the changes made by Philip V by suggesting that Philip complete the modern structure that Charles planned and started but never finished.

D) Charles V would perhaps respond to the changes made by Philip V by protesting the destruction of the winter palace.

CHALLENGE:

Text 1

According to J. Vurtheim, the Amazons were of Greek origin: "all the Amazons were Dianas, as Diana herself was an Amazon." In works of art, combat between Amazons and Greeks is placed on the same level as and often associated with combat between Greeks and centaurs. Their occupation was hunting and war; their arms were the bow, spear, axe, and a half shield, nearly in the shape of a crescent, called a *pelta.*

Text 2

The history of Bohemia affords a parallel to the Greek Amazons. During the 8th century, a large band of women, under a certain Vlasta, carried on war against the duke of Bohemia and enslaved or put to death all men who fell into their hands. Additionally, the Spanish explorer Orellana asserted that he had come into conflict with fighting women in South America on the river Maranon. The existence of 'Amazons' (in the sense of fighting women) in the army of Dahomey is an undoubted fact, but they are said to have died out during the French protectorate.

Based on the texts, how would the author of Text 1 most likely respond to the claims made by the author of Text 2?

A) The author of Text 2 would note that, since these other historic groups of fighting women were not Greek, then they were not Amazons.

B) The author of Text 1 would perhaps concede that Greek Amazons were greatly influenced by the groups of South American Amazons.

C) The author of Text 2 would perhaps concede that Greek Amazons were greatly influenced by the groups of South American Amazons.

D) The author of Text 1 would note that, since these other historic groups of fighting women were not Greek, then they were not Amazons.

Answers on page 374

Recommendations:

If you scored between 0-1, passage comparison question practice is **high** priority for you.

If you scored between 1-2, passage comparison question practice is **medium** priority for you.

If you scored between 2-3, passage comparison question practice is **low** priority for you.

(POETIC)*
STRUCTURE

Here's the breakdown of what LearnCurious calls '(Poetic) Structure' (PS) questions on the four currently-released digital SAT exams:

	VM1	VM2a	VM2b
Test #1:	0/27 = 0%	0/27 = 0%	0/27 = 0%
Test #2:	1/27 = 3.7%	0/27 = 0%	0/27 = 0%
Test #3:	1/27 = 3.7%	0/27 = 0%	0/27 = 0%
Test #4:	0/27 = 0%	0/27 = 0%	1/27 = 3.7%

To summarize, there are
...between **0-1** PS questions on Verbal Module 1,
...**0** PS questions on Verbal Module 2a,
...and between **0-1** PS questions on Verbal Module 2b.

Question frequency: 0 - 3.7% == MYTHIC
Speed rating: MODERATE

*Note: The word 'poetic' is in parentheses in this question type's name because only some of the dSAT's structure questions are have poetry passages; however, since poetry passages are more common on structure (and support quotation) passages, we've included it as a reference here to help ensure readers target poetic structure in particular.

(POETIC) STRUCTURE questions appear in the early-middle part of Verbal Modules, usually between questions #6 - 16. They ask students to assess the how the passage (often poetry or fiction) is structured; these are similar to purpose questions. **Read the passage and citation carefully, noting shifts and transition words, and turn answer choices into TRUE / FALSE questions; eliminate any answers that are FALSE.**

How do I identify (Poetic) Structure questions?

(Poetic) Structure questions can be identified using this specific question stem:
- *Which choice best describes the overall structure of the text?*

Look for these words in particular in the question stem to easily identify (Poetic) Structure (PS) questions: *'overall structure'*

Here are three examples of what digital SAT (Poetic) Structure questions look like:

1.
'To Amarantha, that she would dishevel her Hair' is a poem by Richard Lovelace.

Amarantha sweet and fair,
Ah, braid no more that shining hair!
As my curious hand or eye
Hovering round thee, let it fly!

Let it fly as unconfined
As its calm ravisher the wind,
Who hath left his darling, th' East,
To wanton o'er that spicy nest.

Every tress must be confest,
But neatly tangled at the best;
Like a clew of golden thread
Most excellently ravellèd.

Do not then wind up that light
In ribbands, and o'ercloud in night,
Like the Sun in 's early ray;
But shake your head, and scatter day!

Which choice best describes the overall **structure** of the text?

A) The speaker reminisces about his old friend Amarantha, who has lovely golden hair.

B) The speaker gives examples of women's hairstyles and suggests that Amarantha consider the way she styles her hair.

C) The speaker addresses Amarantha and requests that she wear her hair unbraided and loose before comparing it to golden thread and sunlight.

D) The speaker wonders whether Amarantha has difficulty maintaining her hair and avoiding tangles.

2.

These observations teach, then, that ice need not be completely smashed to fit into the prescribed mold, but that it may give way without losing its coherence. This can be still more completely proved, and we can acquire a still better insight into the cause of the pliability of ice, if we press the ice between two plane wooden boards, instead of in the mold, into which we cannot see.

Which choice best describes the overall **structure** of the text?

A) It introduces an experiment and its methods.

B) It states a conclusion an suggests further research.

C) It contrasts a current theory with past theories.

D) It lists several examples of experimental methods.

3.

'On a Fly drinking out of his Cup' is a poem by William Oldys.

Busy, curious, thirsty fly!
Drink with me and drink as I:
Freely welcome to my cup,
Couldst thou sip and sip it up:
Make the most of life you may,
Life is short and wears away.

Both alike are mine and thine
Hastening quick to their decline:
Thine 's a summer, mine 's no more,
Though repeated to threescore.
Threescore summers, when they're gone,
Will appear as short as one!

Which choice best describes the overall **structure** of the text?

A) The poem's speaker welcomes a fly to enjoy the afternoon with him and then philosophizes about the life cycle of flies.

B) The poem's speaker raises a question about life to a passing fly on a hot afternoon.

C) The poem's speaker addresses a fly, invites it to drink from his cup, draws a comparison between their life spans, and comments on the speed of time's passage.

D) The poem's speaker laments that his life seems as short as that of the fly he found drinking from his cup.

Answers on page 374

What are some helpful (Poetic) Structure question strategies?

Here are a few strategic questions to ask yourself when faced with (Poetic) Structure questions:

"What transition words are present in the passage?"

Transition words are great signals of shifts happening in a passage, and these shifts are often mentioned in the correct answers to (Poetic) Structure questions. Develop the habit of noticing transition words and/or marking them with the annotation tool.

For more information on transition words, see pages 203-217.

"Are the answer choices true or false?

Pay attention to specific verbs in answer choices on Purpose & (Poetic) Structure question types and use them in structuring a TRUE/FALSE question to 'test' the answer choices.

For instance, if an answer choice reads,

- *"It introduces an experiment and its methods."*

rephrase the answer choice as a series of TRUE/FALSE questions:

- *"Does the passage introduce an experiment?*

- *"Does the passage also introduce the experiment's methods?*

Each part of the answer choice must be correct. If an answer gets a FALSE on any of your TRUE / FALSE tests, eliminate that answer.

For more information on verbs, see pages 183-191.

> STRATEGY: If _**even one part**_ of the answer choice is incorrect or doesn't match what you read in the passage, eliminate it.

"Is the passage a poem or prose (non-poem, fiction or non-fiction) text?"

If you are someone who enjoys analyzing poetry quickly, these questions are likely to be up your alley.

If not, these are questions to assess quickly using this initial question. If poetry isn't your thing and/or you haven't studied it much, consider guessing on, skipping, and coming back to these questions as time allows. It can be time-consuming to try to make sense of a poem that you've never seen before.

"Is there citation information?"

The citation information (title of work, author's name, date of publication) at the very beginning of every fiction and poetry passage on the dSAT can be key to answering the questions.

(POETIC) STRUCTURE questions appear in the early-middle part of Verbal Modules, usually between questions #6 - 16. They ask students to assess the how the passage (often poetry or fiction) is structured; these are similar to purpose questions. **Read the passage and citation carefully, noting shifts and transition words, and turn answer choices into TRUE / FALSE questions; eliminate any answers that are FALSE.**

Practice (Poetic) Structure (PS) Questions:

1.
A spider which was about three-tenths of an inch in length emitted four or five threads from its spinners. The spider suddenly let go its hold of the post and was quickly borne out of sight.

Which choice best describes the overall structure of the text?

A) It makes a series of observations about a creature's behavior.

B) It provides detail about how the air in these currents sometimes appears to shimmer.

C) It draws a similarity between the fine lines projected from a spider's spinners and rays of light.

D) It specifies a reason why spiders are able to fly through the air.

2.
This experiment, which was first made by Tyndall, shows that a block of ice may be pressed into any mold just like a piece of wax. Instead of the snow, I take irregular pieces of ice, press them together, add new pieces of ice, press them again, and so on, until the mold is full. After pressure is applied, the mass is taken out, and it forms a compact coherent cylinder of tolerably clear ice, which has a perfectly sharp edge, and is an accurate copy of the mold.

Which choice best describes the overall structure of the text?

A) The text introduces an experiment and its methods.

B) The text compares two types of research.

C) The text contrasts a current theory with past theories.

D) The text lists several examples of experimental methods.

3.

The following is adapted from Frank L. Baum's novel 'The Wonderful Wizard of Oz,' in which a young girl, Dorothy, is transported by a cyclone from her home in rural Kansas to a mysterious, colorful land called Oz.

Toto was not gray; he was a little black dog, with long silky hair and small black eyes that twinkled merrily on either side of his funny, wee nose. Toto played all day long, and Dorothy played with him and loved him dearly. Today, however, they were not playing. Uncle Henry sat upon the door-step and looked anxiously at the sky, which was even grayer than usual. Dorothy stood in the door with Toto in her arms, and looked at the sky too.

Which choice best describes the overall structure of the text?

A) It introduces a non-human character.
B) It contrasts the colors of Toto with the colors of the sky.
C) It details Dorothy's relationship with Toto then shifts to a foreboding tone when characters look at the sky.
D) It describes the type of horse Toto is and how Dorothy plays with him.

4.

The following is adapted from Lewis Carroll's novel 'Alice's Adventures in Wonderland,' in which a young girl, Alice, falls down a rabbit hole into a confusing world of colorful characters.

The Gryphon added "Come, let's hear some of your adventures."
"I could tell you my adventures — beginning from this morning," said Alice a little timidly, "but it's no use going back to yesterday because I was a different person then."

Which choice best describes the overall structure of the text?

A) It introduces a setting and describes the existential quandary of the Gryphon.
B) It notes the request of one character and the response of the other.
C) It contrasts a current character's issue with past characters'.
D) It lists several examples of tea party accessories.

5.

In the spaces beyond the solar system we are faced by a new order of distance. From sun to planets is measured in millions of miles, but from sun to sun is measured in billions.

Which choice best describes the overall structure of the text?

A) It makes a claim and supports it by comparing the distance between our sun and planets and our sun and other suns.
B) It compares the words million and billion and then makes a statement about their magnitude.
C) It poses and answers a rhetorical question then describes a means of comprehending numbers in the millions versus those in the billions.
D) It poses a question and then indicates that the answer is surprising.

6.

The following is adapted from Mark Twain's novel 'The Adventures of Tom Sawyer."

When the middle of the afternoon came, from being a poor poverty-stricken boy in the morning, Tom was literally rolling in wealth. He had besides the things before mentioned, twelve marbles, part of a harp, a piece of blue bottle-glass to look through, a spool cannon, a key that wouldn't unlock anything, a fragment of chalk, a glass stopper of a decanter, a tin soldier, a couple of tadpoles, six fire-crackers, a kitten with only one eye, a brass door-knob, a dog-collar—but no dog, the handle of a knife, four pieces of orange-peel, and a dilapidated old window sash.

Which choice best describes the overall structure of the text?

A) It lists the items that Tom had to trade in order to have his friends whitewash the fence for him.
B) It describes the items that Tom has in his room in increasing detail.
C) It compares the items that Tom collected to those that Ben collected.
D) It indicates the change in Tom's financial state from morning to afternoon and then lists the items he'd collected.

7.

Scientists have noted that while soap-bubbles will not rise indoors, they are seen to ascend outdoors in upward currents of warmer air. Hence, we see the similarity between the way spiders' threads rise through the air and the way soap-bubbles rise outdoors.

Which choice best describes the overall structure of the text?

A) It provides detail about how the air in these currents sometimes appears to shimmer.
B) It draws a similarity between the fine lines projected from a spider's spinners and rays of light.
C) It notes a fact about soap-bubbles and then compares their movement to that of spiders' threads.
D) It specifies a reason why spiders are able to fly through the air.

8.

The following is adapted from Frank L. Baum's novel 'The Wonderful Wizard of Oz,' in which Dorothy, is transported to a mysterious, colorful land where she befriends a Scarecrow, a Tin Woodman, and a Cowardly Lion.

They found the ladder so heavy they could not pull it up, so the Scarecrow fell off the wall and the others jumped down upon him so that the hard floor would not hurt their feet. Of course they took pains not to light on his head and get the pins in their feet. When all were safely down they picked up the Scarecrow, whose body was quite flattened out, and patted his straw into shape again.

"We must cross this strange place in order to get to the other side," said Dorothy, "for it would be unwise for us to go any other way except due South."

Which choice best describes the overall structure of the text?

A) It contrasts a current character's issue with past characters'.
B) It notes the request of one character and the response of the other.
C) It introduces a problem and describes how the group addressed it creatively.
D) It introduces a setting and describes the existential quandary of the Scarecrow.

9.

The following is adapted from Mark Twain's novel 'The Adventures of Tom Sawyer," in which a young boy, Tom, experiences life in a small town along the Mississippi River.

Saturday morning was come, and all the summer world was bright and fresh, and brimming with life. There was a song in every heart; and if the heart was young the music issued at the lips. There was cheer in every face and a spring in every step. The locust-trees were in bloom and the fragrance of the blossoms filled the air. Cardiff Hill, beyond the village and above it, was green with vegetation and it lay just far enough away to seem a Delectable Land, dreamy, reposeful, and inviting.

Which choice best describes the overall structure of the text?

A) The text compares Tom's observations of the landscape to those of Ben.

B) The text describes an idyllic, summer setting in detail.

C) The text introduces a scheme and then details how Tom executed his ploy.

D) The text raises a question and indicates how the Tom answered it.

10.
The following text is from the 1837 poem 'Earliest Spring' by William Dean Howells.

Tossing his mane of snows in wildest eddies and tangles,
  Lion-like March cometh in, hoarse, with tempestuous breath,
Through all the moaning chimneys, and 'thwart all the hollows and angles
  Round the shuddering house, threating of winter and death.

But in my heart I feel the life of the wood and the meadow
  Thrilling the pulses that own kindred with fibres that lift
Bud and blade to the sunward, within the inscrutable shadow,
  Deep in the oak's chill core, under the gathering drift.

Nay, to earth's life in mine some prescience, or dream, or desire
  (How shall I name it aright?) comes for a moment and goes—
Rapture of life ineffable, perfect—as if in the brier,
  Leafless there by my door, trembled a sense of the rose.

Which choice best describes the overall structure of the text?

A) The speaker describes the wintry chill of the month of March while acknowledging subtle hints of springtime emerging as the season changes.

B) The speaker describes experiencing a moment in March that he found perfect.

C) The speaker observes the changing season and the alarming signs of springtime's arrival.

D) The speaker bemoans the arrival of spring and expresses his desire for winter to last longer.

CHALLENGE:

'The Character of a Happy Life' is a poem by Sir Henry Wotton.

How happy is he born and taught
That serveth not another's will;
Whose armour is his honest thought,
And simple truth his utmost skill!

Whose passions not his masters are;
Whose soul is still prepared for death,
Untied unto the world by care
Of public fame or private breath;
…
—This man is freed from servile bands
Of hope to rise or fear to fall:
Lord of himself, though not of lands,
And having nothing, yet hath all.

Which choice best describes the overall structure of the text?

A) The speaker describes the virtues that a person must possess to live a happy life.

B) The speaker praises altruistic acts and then goes on to criticize those who do not own land.

C) The speaker gives examples of people he's known who have claimed to have led happy lives.

D) The speaker wonders how seeking fame affects one's ability to rule over others.

Answers on page 374

Recommendations:

If you scored between 0-4, structure question practice is **high** priority for you.

If you scored between 5-8, structure question practice is **medium** priority for you.

If you scored between 9-11, structure question practice is **low** priority for you.

Reading Comprehension
Question Types Overview, Identification Phrases, & Strategies

WORDS IN CONTEXT questions appear at the very beginning of each Verbal Module, usually between questions #1-6. They ask students to choose fitting words based on the specific context of a passage.

> *Frequency:* common; *Speed rating:* quick (usually)
> *Identifier(s):* 'most nearly means,' & 'logical and precise word or phrase,'
> *Strategies:*
> - come up with a synonym and match it to the answer choices
> - look out for words which can be used multiple ways; consider other connotations
> - use word positivity / negativity & roots/prefixes/suffixes to help break down unfamiliar vocab

EVIDENCE questions appear in the early-middle part of Verbal Modules, usually between questions #6 - 16. They ask about specific details from the passage, and students can expect there to be (verbatim or paraphrased) direct evidence from the passage to support the correct answer.

> *Frequency:* uncommon; *Speed rating:* moderate
> *Identifier(s):* - 'according to the passage / text,' 'based on the passage / text,' 'as presented in the text,' 'what is true about,' or 'the passage states / asserts / makes the claim / indicates'
> *Strategies:*
> - look back at the passage to find directly-stated or paraphrased evidence to support your answer

LOGICAL COMPLETION questions appear toward the late-middle of Verbal Modules, usually between questions #13-16. They ask students to note the context of the passage and complete a paragraph or sentence with the most logical answer option.

> *Frequency:* uncommon; *Speed rating:* moderate
> *Identifier(s):* "most logically completes"
> *Strategies:*
> - pay attention to what is happening in the passage; read closely.
> - anticipate answer having less direct evidence to support correct answers
> - use context clues to make an inference about what comes next.
>   *(inference: an idea based on clues or hints instead of direct (explicit) statements)*

CHART / GRAPH INTERPRETATION questions appear in the early-middle part of Verbal Modules, usually between questions #6 - 16. They ask students to interpret a chart, table, or graph and complete a statement or example.
> *Frequency:* uncommon/rare; *Speed rating:* **time-consuming**
> *Identifier(s):* 'information from the table/graph,' or 'data from the table'
> *Strategies:*
> - annotate the "claim" or "hypothesis" in the passage text!
> - pay attention to how the graph is titled and how axes or tables are labeled
> - ask yourself whether the answer choices are true or false
> - eliminate any false statements that conflict with the data from the chart or passage.

SUPPORT QUOTATION questions appear in the early-middle part of Verbal Modules, usually between questions #6 - 16. They ask students to support a specific claim from the passage, often fiction or poetry; the College Board refers to these as 'Textual Evidence' questions.

Frequency: rare; *Speed rating*: moderate/time-consuming
Identifier(s): 'which quotation'
Strategies:
- note whether the passage is poetry or prose (non-poetry, either fiction or non-fiction)
- read and annotate the citation (title, author, date info) at the beginning of fiction/poetry passages.
- annotate the "claim" or "hypothesis" in the passage text!
- use context clues to make an inference *(an educated guess based on indirect / implicit evidence)*about what comes next for questions that have a blank; anticipate having less direct evidence to support correct answers

PURPOSE questions appear in the early-middle part of Verbal Modules, usually between questions #6 - 16. They ask students to assess how a piece of text is functioning within the passage.

Frequency: rare; *Speed rating*: moderate
Identifier(s): 'purpose,' 'function' / 'function as,' 'in order to,' 'to illustrate,' 'serves to,' 'so that,' 'because.'
Strategies:
- remember to distinguish whether you're looking for the main purpose (ask "why") or the main idea (ask "what?") of the passage
- put yourself in the author's shoes & ask yourself "If I were the author of this text, why would I have bothered writing it?" and "What would be the goal I'd be hoping to achieve in writing this piece?"

MAIN IDEA questions appear in the early-middle part of Verbal Modules, usually between questions #6 - 16. They ask students to identify the primary claim or focus of the passage.

Frequency: rare; *Speed rating*: moderate
Identifier(s): 'main idea,' or 'primary claim'
Strategies:
- ask yourself what the majority of the paragraph is about or what the majority of the sentences have in common.
- write a mini summary by briefly (in one sentence) answering the questions **who? what? where? when? how?**

PASSAGE COMPARISON questions appear in the early-middle part of Verbal Modules, usually between questions #6 - 16. They ask students to compare and contrast authors' or passage characters' views on a claim or topic. Since Passage Comparison questions are so rare, it's often a good time-management strategy to guess on them, flag them for review, and come back to them if you have time.

Frequency: mythic; *Speed rating*: time-consuming
Identifier(s): 'most likely,' 'the author of Text 1 / 2'
Strategies:
- remember that PC questions require students to make inferences: guesses based on clues or hints instead of direct (explicit) statements; anticipate answer having less direct evidence to support correct answers.
- save for last

(POETIC) STRUCTURE questions appear in the early-middle part of Verbal Modules, usually between questions #6 - 16. They ask students to assess the how the passage is structured; these are similar to purpose questions.

Frequency: mythic; *Speed rating*: moderate
Identifiers: 'overall structure'
Strategies:
- read the passage / citation information carefully
- annotate transition words
- turn answer choices into TRUE / FALSE questions; eliminate any answers that are FALSE.

Writing
&
Editing

What Will We Cover?
Writing & Editing Checklist

❑ Punctuation

    ❑ *colons*
    ❑ *semicolons*
    ❑ *commas*
    ❑ *apostrophes*
    ❑ *dashes (single and paired)*
    ❑ *quotation marks*
    ❑ *parentheses, periods, question marks, exclamation marks*

❑ Grammar

    ❑ *parts of speech (nouns, pronouns, verbs, prepositions, conjunctions, adjectives, & adverbs)*
    ❑ *agreement (subject-verb, pronoun-antecedent, verb tense)*
    ❑ *active voice vs. passive voice*
    ❑ *comparatives & superlatives*
    ❑ *obscure but present special grammar rules*

❑ Editing

    ❑ *logical transitions*
    ❑ *notes*

❑ Example Questions & Practice Questions

    ❑ *colon example questions (score:_____) & practice questions (score:_____)*
    ❑ *semicolon example questions (score:_____) & practice questions (score:_____)*
    ❑ *comma example questions (score:_____) & practice questions (score:_____)*
    ❑ *apostrophe example questions (score:_____) & practice questions (score:_____)*
    ❑ *dash example questions (score:_____) & practice questions (score:_____)*
    ❑ *parts of speech: noun practice (score:_____), pronoun practice (score:_____), verb tense practice (score:_____), preposition exercise (score:_____)*
    ❑ *agreement example questions (score:_____) & practice questions (score:_____)*
    ❑ *active vs passive voice practice questions (score:_____)*
    ❑ *comparatives, comparisons, & specificity practice questions (score:_____)*

Must-Know English Punctuation Rules

After reading this chapter you will be able to...
- ❑ *demonstrate understanding of the English punctuation marks tested by the dSAT*
- ❑ *combine sentences in well-informed & stylistically-rich ways*
- ❑ *carry forward your knowledge of advanced English style rules beyond the SAT to enhance your writing skills in college and beyond*

Why didn't we learn this stuff in school?

Students & parents alike often cringe at the topic of English punctuation. Students are frustrated because they simply haven't been taught how & when to properly use less-common punctuation marks like semicolons (;), colons (:), and em-dashes (—). Parents often feel worried for the same reasons — with the added pressure of trying to explain what they don't fully understand.

Strangely, few people are formally taught the rules of punctuation in their grade-school English classes. Some stellar teachers out there make a point to teach these essential tools for expression, but more often it seems like students are expected to just "pick up" on the dozen or so rules that govern when to use a comma. That doesn't really happen unless a student is both a particularly prolific reader and an avid observer of style.

Adding to the challenge, country-dependent rules of style, like those involving quotation marks, simply require prior knowledge, while punctuation on the Internet follows different, often frequently-changing rules, that are different from those expected on the SAT & ACT exams.

Which punctuation marks are tested on the SAT & ACT?

Punctuation is one of three main English sub-areas covered by the dSAT (the other two are grammar & editing, which will be covered later in this section).

Students must know advanced functions of specific punctuation marks: periods, commas, colons, semicolons, dashes, quotation marks, parentheses, question marks, and apostrophes will all usually make at least one appearance per section.

Punctuation Marks to Know:

- ❑ Colon
- ❑ Semicolon
- ❑ Comma
- ❑ Apostrophe
- ❑ Dash (single and double)
- ❑ Quotation marks
- ❑ Period
- ❑ Question mark
- ❑ Exclamation point

Check off which ones you're familiar with already and those you learn in this chapter.

Let's start with the colon. Good colon use doesn't appear forced.

COLONS

One of the most important rules to know when you spot a colon question is that, on the dSAT (and this is true for the ACT, too), **colons must come after a complete sentence or independent clause.***

In other words, a colon can only go where a period can go, but a colon allows us to add information after the colon that is relevant to what precedes it.

The colon is an extremely flexible punctuation mark!

What follows a colon can be
- one word
- a longer dependent clause
- a list
- another complete sentence / independent clause

STRATEGY: In order to use colons well, what follows a colon usually answers the most logical question someone might ask about the complete sentence that precedes the colon (before that question even needs to be asked).

*An independent clause is simply a complete sentence, meaning it has at least a subject (who/what is 'doing' the action in the sentence) and a predicate (description of the subject that is begun by a verb). Fun fact: the shortest English sentence is "I am."

Let's look at a few examples of good colon use...

ONE WORD AFTER COLON

The smell could've only come from one thing: **cheese.**

(Logical question = "Where could the smell have come from?" Answer after colon = cheese.)

DEPENDENT CLAUSE AFTER COLON

Their day went exactly as they'd hoped: **safely and smoothly.**

Logical question = "How did they hope their day would go?"
Answer after colon = safely & smoothly

LIST AFTER COLON

They wanted to purchase a few items at the store: **bananas, spinach, and protein bars.**

Logical question = "What did they want to buy?"
Answer after colon = bananas, spinach & protein bars.

COMPLETE SENTENCE / INDEPENDENT CLAUSE AFTER COLON

It was the first time she'd heard the noise: **the sharp whistling sound seemed come from the basement.**

Logical question = "What noise?'
Answer after colon = sharp whistling coming from the basement.

Let's look through a more examples of common uses of colons...

A colon is often **used to start a list**, even if it's only one item long.

I ate just one thing: a bag of 40 malted milk balls.

"Two possibilities exist: either we are alone in the universe or we are not. Both are equally terrifying." — Arthur C. Clarke

A colon follows a main independent clause* to expand upon or clarify its subject matter by adding either a dependent clause or another independent clause.

His team included his buddies from college: Jason, Matt, & Hassan.

"We must all suffer from one of two pains: the pain of discipline or the pain of regret." — Jim Rohn

A colon **functions the same way as a single dash** (and vice versa):

She only had one thing on her mind: Thanksgiving dinner.
She only had one thing on her mind — Thanksgiving dinner.

They had a family motto — "Only get seconds when you've finish-ed your plate completely."
They had a family motto: "Only get seconds when you've finished your plate completely."

A colon **can express a time or ratio**.

The proportion of flour to sugar should be 3:1.

Class starts at 11:30 AM sharp.

A colon can separate a title from a subtitle.

Star Wars: A New Hope

A colon **can introduce text or dialogue & follow a letter's salutation.**

Yoda: Do* or do not — there is no try.

Capitalize the first word after a colon when it is a proper noun or when it starts a quotation.

To Whom It May Concern:

A colon **does *not* come right after a verb**.

Their team will ~~play: Joey, John, & Jerry~~.
incorrect & awkward

A colon is _**not** **used with the words "including" or "such as" or "like" or**_ _**"the following/as follows"**_ because they duplicate the meaning of the colon, so having both would be redundant.

The colors of the painting are ~~as follows:~~ red, orange, & yellow.
incorrect & wordy

The colors of the rainbow include red, orange, & yellow.
correct & concise

Practice Colon Questions:

Instructions: Place colons in the most logical position in the following sentences. If a sentence does NOT require a colon, mark it as 'correct.'

1. She wanted to visit three places.

2. She wanted to visit three places Greece, Italy, and Spain.

3. They had a family rule always clear your place after dinner.

4. He played two sports volleyball and lacrosse.

5. The team had three main goals have fun, work hard, and win.

6. Twenty things happened today 19 good and 1 bad.

7. I want to learn to play many instruments piano, in particular.

8. "Worrying is like a rocking chair it gives you something to do, but it doesn't get you anywhere." - _National Lampoon's Van Wilder_

9. He only had one thing on his mind after Thanksgiving dinner a nap.

10. They wanted to get a few things from the store camping supplies, a new broom, and heated gloves.

Answers on page 375

SEMICOLONS

A semicolon **functions as a soft period**. It looks like both a period and comma and acts like both, too.

A semicolon **separates two independent clauses* (like a period).**

> *Remember, an independent clause is simply a complete sentence, meaning it has at least a subject (who/what is 'doing' the action in the sentence) and a predicate (description of the subject that is begun by a verb). Fun fact: the shortest English sentence is "I am."*

A semicolon also **creates a shorter visual pause** between related complete thoughts (like a comma) by not capitalizing the first word of the second sentence (unless it meets other capitalization criteria, like being a proper noun).

> Shrek is an ogre; Donkey isn't.

> "Prejudices are rarely overcome by argument; not being founded in reason, they cannot be destroyed by logic." — *Tryon Edwards*

A semicolon **can separate list items** (in what's referred to as a 'complex list') when the list items already contain essential commas.

> He's lived in three cities: Destin, FL; Roanoke, VA; and Portland, OR.

> "To laugh often and much; to win the respect of intelligent people and the affection of children; to earn the appreciation of honest critics and endure the betrayal of false friends; to appreciate beauty; to find the best in others; to leave the world a bit better, whether by a healthy child, a garden patch, or a redeemed social condition; to know even one life has breathed easier because you have lived. This is to have succeeded." — Ralph Waldo Emerson

Practice Semicolon Questions

1. This half starts with a capital letter this half doesn't.

2. This part of the year can be stressful ask for help when you need it.

3. They wanted to visit three places: Jackson Hole, Wyoming Park City, Utah and Aspen, Colorado.

4. They hired the crew: Alex, the videographer Calvin, the producer; and Ernie, the chef.

(This last one is in dSAT style and is longer than the majority of punctuation questions -- don't worry! It also contains a special case use of the semicolon that we covered in this chapter.)

CHALLENGE:

The pseudonyms adopted by authors are often transposed forms, more or less exact, of their names: thus _____. It is to be noted that the last two are impure anagrams because an ``r'' is left out in both cases.

Which choice completes the text so that it conforms to the conventions of standard English?

A) 'Calvinus' becomes 'Alcvinus,' ``Francois Rabelais' becomes 'Alcofribas Nasier;' 'Bryan Waller Proctor' becomes 'Barry Cornwall, poet;' 'Henry Rogers' becomes 'R. E. H. Greyson.'

B) 'Calvinus' becomes 'Alcvinus' ``Francois Rabelais' becomes 'Alcofribas Nasier' 'Bryan Waller Proctor' becomes 'Barry Cornwall, poet' 'Henry Rogers' becomes 'R. E. H. Greyson.'

C) 'Calvinus' becomes 'Alcvinus,' ``Francois Rabelais' becomes 'Alcofribas Nasier;' 'Bryan Waller Proctor' becomes 'Barry Cornwall, poet,' 'Henry Rogers' becomes 'R. E. H. Greyson.'

D) 'Calvinus' becomes 'Alcvinus;' ``Francois Rabelais' becomes 'Alcofribas Nasier;' 'Bryan Waller Proctor' becomes 'Barry Cornwall, poet;' 'Henry Rogers' becomes 'R. E. H. Greyson.'

Answers on page 375

COMMAS

There are 12 comma rules to know for the dSAT:

Comma Rule 1 - A (comma + FANBOYS coordinating conjunction) combo can separate complete sentences and is equivalent to a period or semicolon.

A comma can separate two complete sentences if you pair it with a FANBOYS (for, and, nor, but, or, yet, & so) coordinating conjunction.

For
And
Nor
But
Or
Yet
So

This COMMA + CONJUNCTION combo avoids the dreaded comma splice error.

Examples:
- *She's going, and I'm going with her.*
- *The fish schooled around me, but it wasn't scary.*
- *"Be kind, for everyone you meet is fighting a hard battle."* — *Plato*
- *"Every man die, but not every man truly lives."* — *William Wallace*

> **STRATEGY:** *A comma can separate two complete sentences if you pair it with a FANBOYS (for, and, nor, but, or, yet, & so) coordinating conjunction. Watch out for the word because! It's not the "B" in FANBOYS. For example, there is no comma needed in the sentence, "I'm indoors because it is cold outside."*

All of these are considered grammatically correct:
- *It's snowing today, and I'm glad to be indoors.*
- *It's snowing today. I'm glad to be indoors.*
- *It's snowing today; I'm glad to be indoors.*
- *It's snowing today: I'm glad to be indoors.*

Comma Rule 2 - Two commas can be used like parentheses.

Two commas can be used like parentheses (or double dashes, as we'll see in the coming pages) to surround appositive, or 'non-essential,' clauses that aren't required to complete a sentence. These phrases are also sometimes called 'interrupters.'

Interrupter clauses are phrases that add non-essential, but helpful, relevant detail to sentences; however, they can be removed successfully from a sentence and what remains is complete and coherent.

Examples:
- *You are, without a doubt, the worst pirate I've ever seen.*
- *Twenty ducks waddled, one right after the other, down to the lake.*

Students are also likely to see appositive commas surrounding interrupting words (like 'therefore' or 'however') that both simulate pauses we make when speaking and indicate that the nature of the word between the commas is more emphatic than transitional. In other words, it's there for emphasis rather than as a true, functioning transition word because it can be removed without effect on the overall meaning of the sentence.

Example:
- *He was, therefore, released from custody.*

", however," and ", therefore," function as comma units and, therefore, can't be used to separate two complete sentences unless paired with a FANBOYS conjunction. Note how, in the following example, the word 'therefore' is not needed at all and clutters up the sentence.

Example:
- *We cannot make it, and, therefore, we must cancel and reschedule.*

A pair of commas that surrounds extra information (the way that dash pairs and parentheses do) is called an appositive comma pair. As with double dashes & parentheses, what's between appositive commas can be removed from the sentence without affecting its grammatical correctness or overall meaning.

Expanded Examples:

> - *Some holiday traditions, such as watching beloved movies or spending time with family, are festive rituals that many people look forward to every year.*

Sentence with the interrupter removed =
Some holiday traditions are festive rituals that many people look forward to every year.

> - *Other people — like the fictional character Scrooge — don't enjoy the holidays very much at all.*

Sentence with the interrupter removed =
Other people don't enjoy holidays very much at all.

> **STRATEGY**: *Words between appositive commas can be removed, and the sentence will still make sense. Try removing the appositive phrase that is between the commas (or dashes / parentheses) and reading the sentence again. Many questions on the digital SAT (and ACT) exams contain examples of interrupter or appositive clauses. Remember, Interrupter clauses can be surrounded by pairs of commas, dashes, or parentheses. These must be balanced pairs — no mixing and matching!*

dSAT style example:

Crochet, an art taught to many by their _____ a relaxing and productive form of meditation.

A) grandmothers, is
B) grandmothers is
C) grandmothers — is
D) grandmother is

Answer: A

B is incorrect because we need a balancing punctuation mark to separate the interrupter phrase from the rest of the sentence

C is incorrect because we need the same punctuation mark before and after the interrupter phrase

D is incorrect because grandmother needs to be plural, and we need a balancing punctuation mark to separate the interrupter phrase from the rest of the sentence

STRATEGY: Remember, you can identify a mid-sentence interrupter when you can remove it completely and are left with a sentence that makes sense and is grammatically correct.

Comma Rule 3 - A comma appears after introductory clauses.

A comma follows a dependent clause that begins a sentence.

Examples:
  - *When I graduate, I will do great things.*
  - *First though, I'm going to catch up on sleep.*

Comma Rule 4 - The Oxford Comma is used but not directly tested.

An Oxford comma comes before the "and" in a list (of 3+ items) and prevents confusion. While the Oxford comma is considered optional in some parts of the grammar world, the SAT & ACT both expect its use; however, since there is controversy over this particular comma rule, it is not usually included in or directly tested by SAT or ACT English question answer options.

Examples:
- *The fortune will be split among Ali, Bali, and Cali.*
- *Their favorite authors were Martin, Rothfuss, and Salvatore.*
- *They saw elephants, zebras, and giraffes.*
- *"A satisfied life is better than a successful life because our success is measured by others, but our satisfaction is measured by our own soul, mind, and heart." — Vishnu Bharath*

Comma Rule 5 - Commas are used to separate adjectives that modify the same noun.

A comma can be placed between two coordinate adjectives* where putting "and" would be appropriate.

*A good way to know if you're dealing with coordinate adjectives is to reverse their order. If they carry the same weight and modify the noun in an equal way when reversed, then you have a pair of coordinate adjectives.

Examples:
- *They are a cute, well-suited couple.*
- *It's a beautiful, sunny day outside.*
- *"When I write, I feel like an armless, legless man with a crayon in his mouth." — Kurt Vonnegut*

Comma Rule 6 - Commas are used to set off dates, addresses, & titles.

A comma is used to denote proper format when writing dates, cities/states, & numbers larger than 999.

Examples:
- *May 2nd, 2019*
- *Westchester, NY*
- *Joe Peabody, Esq.*
- *Sal Amander, PhD.*
- *MLK, Jr.*

Comma Rule 7 - A comma is used to separate a direct quotation from the rest of a sentence.

Examples:
- *"Don't spoil it for me," he said.*
- *One of the most famous quotes of all time, "I'll be back," is from which movie?*

Comma Rule 8 - Commas can be used to prevent readers' confusion or to indicate that a clause is non-essential.

Commas can be placed in order to help ensure that readers know what an author intends.

Examples:
- *Did the crocodile eat, Robert? = correct*
- *vs.*
- *Did the crocodile eat Robert?* = incorrect*

- *We're going to learn how to cut and paste, kids! - correct*
- *vs.*
- *We're going to learn how to cut and paste kids!* = incorrect*

(Note: without the comma, these sentences take a dark turn.)

A comma can also be used to add a non-essential dependent clause after an independent clause..

Examples:
> - *He was just going to have one more potato chip, just one more.*
> - *"Some cause happiness wherever they go, others whenever they go."* — *Oscar Wilde*

Comma Rule 9 - Commas are used before/after direct address.

Commas are before (and often after) addressing someone directly by either name or title.

Examples
> - *"Oh, excuse me, Your Honor, the two youths."*
> - *"Frankly, Scarlett, I don't give a damn."*

Comma Rule 10 - A comma is used to separate in-line questions.

A comma is used separate question phrases from other statements.

Examples:
> - *You love her, don't you?*
> - *It's complicated, you know?*

Comma Rule 11 - A comma is used to offset contrasting phrases.

A comma is used to offset contrasting information in a clear way.

Examples:
> - *Everyone cheered, except for Michael.*
> - *Despite booing the actors, he didn't like being booed.*

Comma Rule 12 - A comma is used after introductory words.

Commas are used after conjunctive adverbs, adverbial phrases, and intro words like 'well' and 'yes' at sentences' beginnings.

Examples:

- *A comma is used after conditional clauses & introductory phrases or a conjunctive adverb at the beginning of a sentence.*
- *"If you choose not to find joy in the snow, you will have less joy in your life but the same amount of snow." — Anonymous*
- *"While one person hesitates because he feels inferior, the other is busy making mistakes and becoming superior." — Henry C. Link*

Here's a sample list of conjunctive adverbs and adverbial phrases: *accordingly, however, also, moreover, consequently, on the other hand, for example, otherwise, for instance, similarly, furthermore, therefore, hence, thus.**

Examples:

- *So, I'm not the only one who hears that alarm, right?*
- *Yeah, it's been going off all morning.*
- *Uh, you guys aren't concerned by that?*

*Please note that some of these words can also function as coordinating conjunctions (FANBOYS) and do not require a comma following them when used to separate complete clauses. As we saw back in Rule 1, a comma is required before the FANBOYS conjunction in these cases.

Practice Comma Questions

1. "I award you no points and may God have mercy on your soul." - *Billy Madison*

2. Gentlemen I wash my hands of this weirdness." - *Pirates of the Caribbean*

3. "Keep the change ya filthy animal." - *Home Alone*

4. "Whatever I feel like I wanna do gosh!" - *Napoleon Dynamite*

5. "Yeah well that's just like your opinion, man." - *The Big Lebowski*

6. "So you see my son there is a very fine line between love and nausea." - *Coming to America*

7. "Fish are friends not food." - *Finding Nemo*

8. "Facts can be so misleading, whereas rumors, true or false, are always revealing." - *Inglorious Bast*rds*

9. She wanted to go to the fair for she enjoyed eating funnel cakes.

10. They wanted to go to the festival because they enjoyed the atmosphere.

11. Cookie dough is delicious; therefore I want to eat it all.

12. I do not however like the stomach ache or salmonella risk.

13. Sometimes I take the risk y'all not gonna lie.

14. She was born on September 18th 1959 in Austin Texas.

15. "He looks you know like a man." - *Miss Swan, MAD TV*

16. "Stop looking at me swan!" - *Billy Madison*

Answers (& comma type categories) on page 375

APOSTROPHES

Apostrophes are used to show:

- **Possession** = noun belonging to another noun

    Example: *Shane's skills won him his friends' respect.*
        - the skills belonging to Shane / the respect belonging to his friends

- **Contraction** = shortening words to mimic speech

    Example: *We're going to the same show Jack's going to tonight. Let's get there early.*
        - (we + are) contraction / the show belonging to Jack / (let + us) contraction

Let's go into more detail about these uses...

An apostrophe is used to denote possession for singular and plural nouns.

    Remember:
    singular = just one *(ex. dog)*
    plural = more than one *(ex. dogs)*

For singular nouns & acronyms ending in any letter except "s," add an apostrophe + s

    Examples:
    - *dog's toy*
    - *match's flame*
    - *FDA's ban*

For plural nouns ending in "s" = add only an apostrophe

    Examples:
    - *teachers' bathroom*
    - *students' desks.*

For plural nouns not ending in "s" , add apostrophe + s

Examples:
- *men's clothing*
- *people's court*

STRATEGY: Keep in mind that possessive pronouns *(mine, yours, hers, his, its, ours, & theirs)* & adjectives *(my, your, her, his, its, our, their)* don't require an apostrophe. They by definition are possessive and do not, therefore, require an apostrophe to denote it.

An apostrophe can also be used to denote contraction and take the place of letter(s) in the contracted words.

When do not becomes don't, the space between the two words is eliminated and the apostrophe replaces the o in not.

Examples:
- *do not = don't*
- *let us = let's*
- *you will = you'll*

STRATEGY: Know the difference between its and it's.
  its = possessive pronoun (like your, my, our, his, hers, etc == doesn't need an apostrophe because the definition is possessive already)
  it's = contraction of 'it is,' 'it was,' or 'it has'
  its' = never correct on dSAT

An apostrophe is <u>not</u> used to pluralize singular nouns.

Apostrophes can only used to pluralize numeric digits & single letters for clarity purposes.

Examples:
- *She made sure to cross her t's and dot her i's.*
- *Back in the 90's, he brought home a report card with straight A's.*

A pair of apostrophes can function as single quotation marks to surround titles in headings or quotes within quotes.

Examples:
- *'Twister' premiered this week in 1996.*
- *"For every metric, there should be a 'paired' metric that assesses the adverse consequences of the first." — Andy Grove*

Advanced / Untested (but Potentially Interesting) Apostrophe Use

Apostrophes can be used to mimic speech patterns or accents. Apostrophes begin a word when the first letter or syllable is elided (or skipped) to mimic speech patterns.

Front of word, : *'Til / 'tain't / 'tis / 'twas / 'tisn't*
End of word: *nothin'*
Sentence: *'E's goin' to 'ave tea wiv the Queen, 'e is.*

Double contractions (like I'd've for "I would have" or couldn't've for "could not have") are rare on the SAT & ACT but fairly common in conversation.

Even wilder triple contractions are more commonly found in southern US vernacular:

you'dn't've = you would not have

I'dn't've = I would not have

it'dn't've = it would not have

y'all'd've = you all would have

Practice Apostrophe Questions:

Instructions: add apostrophes to the movie quotes below. If no apostrophes are needed or if they are already correctly-placed, mark the sentence as CORRECT.

1. "Its not a man purse. It's a satchel. Indiana Jones wears one." - *The Hangover*

2. "I'll be back." - *The Terminator*

3. "Im your fathers brothers nephews cousins former roommate." - *Spaceballs*

4. "Yeah, youre a legend in your own mind." - *Dirty Harry*

5. "Sounds like somebodys got a case of the Mondays." - *Office Space*

6. "What did one shepherd say to the other? Lets get the flock outta here." - *Lethal Weapon*

CHALLENGE:
"So youre tellin me theres a chance." - *Dumb & Dumber*

Answers on page 376

DASHES

A single dash functions like a colon to add on a single word, dependent clause, or independent clause.

A dash differs slightly from a colon or comma in that it signals an abrupt interruption and is often a purposeful stylistic choice to set information apart visually for emphasis.

Examples:
- *I ate all of your cookies — nah, just kidding!*
- *"Anybody might be an accuser — a personal enemy, an infamous person, a child, parent, brother, or sister." — John Wilson*

A pair of dashes functions like a pair of appositive commas or parentheses.

What's between two dashes can be removed from the sentence & it will still be grammatically correct. Used twice, exactly like parentheses or appositive commas, to add information.

The three versions of the sentence below are grammatically equivalent:
- The whole class — eight girls and seven boys — will be ready.
- The whole class (eight girls and seven boys) will be ready.
- The whole class, eight girls and seven boys, will be ready.

- Taken out, the sentence still reads correctly: "The whole class will be ready."

Examples:
- *His friend — the one who moved away — writes him letters every so often.*
- *"As human beings, our greatness lies not so much in being able to remake the world — that is the myth of the atomic age — as in being able to remake ourselves." — Mahatma Gandhi*
- *Shaina knew where the house was — Mulberry Street.*

STRATEGY: If you see a single dash or a single quotation mark in the answer options, look for non-underlined partners farther back or ahead in the sentence.

Practice Dash Questions:

Instructions: Place a dash (or pair of dashes) where they fit best in the sentence. If no dash is required, or is already correctly placed, mark the sentence as CORRECT.

1. Everyone showed up to the party except Dave.

2. Joey and Cal — the heads of student government were liked by the majority of the students at the school.

3. Siobhan couldn't believe the judge's sentence life in prison.

4. The pair of friends Dan and Noah had known each other since childhood.

5. After starting a successful toy business, the brothers branched out into a new business — hat sales.

6. Finally after studying and training for years Ben officially became a licensed physical therapist.

Answers on page 376

PARENTHESES

Parentheses are used to add related but unnecessary information, clarify a writer's meaning, or denote a citation.

*See also: dash pairs and/or appositive commas. Which punctuation pair to use depends on author's style choice, but typically parentheses look the most appropriate of the three directly before a period, for example.

QUOTATION MARKS

In **direct quotation**, a comma comes before the first quotation mark, and the end punctuation mark goes inside the quotation marks. It's also helpful to note that a direct quote begins with a capital letter.

Examples:
- *The cow says, "Moo."*
- *Today I asked a kindergartner if Friday was his favorite day of the week, and his response was, "I don't know. I don't know a lot of things. I'm confused all the time."*

In **indirect quotation**, there is no comma required before and no capital letter to begin an embedded quote. Indirect quotation is used to denote a word as a word.

Examples:
- *He said that he'd "get back to me."*
- *I kept repeating the word "small" until it stopped sounding like a word.*

While they work well to denote sarcasm, quotation marks are <u>not</u> used for emphasis.

PERIODS

Periods, also known as full stops, separate two complete sentences (AKA independent clauses), create abbreviations, and denote lower-case acronyms. Independent clauses can be connected by a period, colon, semicolon, question mark, exclamation mark, or comma + FANBOYS* conjunction pair.

FANBOYS = for, and, nor, but, or, yet, & so.

Examples:
- *I'm too hungry to come up with a better example — i.e., I need to take a break.*
- *"Mastery doesn't come from an infographic." — Tony Robbins*

QUESTION MARKS

Question marks are placed in the middle or at the end of a sentence to denote a question.

Examples:
- *I just heard from Andy, and — surely he's kidding? — he says he's on a flight to Timbuktu.*
- *"Whassamatta wit' you?"*

EXCLAMATION POINTS

Exclamation points are used to denote excitement, anger, or emphasis.

Examples:
- *I love it!*
- *"Freeze!"*

GRAMMAR RULES

Parts of Speech

In order to understand the agreement questions on the dSAT, we first need to make sure we're clear on certain parts of speech:

NOUNS = people, places, things, or ideas

- **Subject** nouns = the person/thing doing the verb

- **Object** nouns = the person/thing either
  - receiving the verb (or "being verb-ed")
    - ex. The <u>dog</u> (*subject noun*) chased the <u>cat</u> (*object noun*).
  - or
  - following the preposition
    - ex. That <u>dog</u> (*subject noun*) in the <u>house</u> (*object noun*) is tired.

Students may also commonly hear the term 'proper' noun, which refers to a noun that is automatically capitalized, like the name of a person, city, or country.

Noun Practice Questions:

Instructions: Circle all of the nouns in the following sentences.

1) Rose DeWitt Bukater loved Jack Dawson.

2) The ship hit the iceberg at night.

3) Molly Brown tried to save the others.

CHALLENGE:

Rose DeWitt Bukater took Jack Dawson's name in the end.

Answers on page 376

PRONOUNS = words that replace nouns

Examples: *I, you, he, she, it, we, they, y'all, their, these, that, this, those, his, them, etc.*

English uses many types of pronouns regularly. Pronouns help us to speak clearly and avoid repeating ourselves all the time.

Let's look at a comparison:

Without pronouns =

Molly went to the store, and then Molly went home. When Molly was cozy, Molly rented a few movies for the evening. Movies help Molly relax after after a long day.

With pronouns =

Molly went to the store, and then she went home. When she was cozy, Molly rented a few movies for the evening. They help her relax after after a long day.

Much less robotic and creepy with pronouns, right?

Let's look at a few of the most helpful types of pronouns to know:

Subject Pronouns = refer back to the subject of a sentence or clause

	Singular	Plural
1st Person	*I*	*we*
2nd Person	*you*	*you / you all / y'all*
3rd Person	*he / she / it*	*they*

Object Pronouns = refer back to the object of a sentence or clause

	Singular	Plural
1st Person	*me*	*us*
2nd Person	*you*	*you / you all / y'all*
3rd Person	*him / her / it*	*them*

Possessive Pronouns = indicate ownership / possession*

	Singular	Plural
1st Person	*my*	*our*
2nd Person	*your*	*your*
3rd Person	*his / her / its*	*their*

> *__STRATEGY__: Remember that possessive pronouns (like "my, your, its, his, her, & their") do not require an apostrophe to indicate possession, as this type of pronoun indicates possession by definition.*

As mentioned before, English uses many categories of pronoun, most of which don't make sense to cover here in much detail. In the exercise that follows, a few other types of pronouns are found and can be circled: **demonstrative** pronouns (ex. *this, that, these, those*) & **relative** pronouns (ex. *which, who, whom*).

WHO VS WHOM

Who and whom are two pronouns (in another category, called 'relative' pronouns, which relate things in a sentence or clause) that appear on the dSAT.

We can use our knowledge of subject vs object pronouns to help understand when to correctly use who and whom.

WHO
- subject pronoun
- refers back to the subject of the clause or sentence

WHOM
- object pronoun
- refers back to the object of the clause or sentence
- usually paired with a preposition (which we'll cover later this chapter)
   ex. *"to whom"* / *"for whom"* / *"by whom"* / *"with whom"*

Examples:
- *__I__ am the one **who** is typing this sentence.*
- *__You__ are the one **to whom** I am writing.*
*Note: the subject is the word "I" in both of these sentences.

Pronoun Exercise:

Instructions: Circle all of the pronouns in the passage below, which is adapted from Mark Twain's novel The Adventures of Tom Sawyer. Tom and his friend, Huck, are discussing going searching for buried treasure.

"But robbers don't do that way. They always hide it and leave it there."

"Don't they come after it any more?"

"No, they think they will, but they generally forget the marks, or else they die. Anyway, it lays there a long time and gets rusty; and by and by somebody finds an old yellow paper that tells how to find the marks—a paper that's got to be ciphered over about a week because it's mostly signs and hy'roglyphics."

"Hyro—which?"

"Hy'roglyphics—pictures and things, you know, that don't seem to mean anything."

"Have you got one of them papers, Tom?"

"No."

Answers on page 376

Pronoun Practice Questions:

1.
Aethelberht married Berhta, _____ brought over Bishop Liudhard as her private confessor.

Which choice completes the text so that it conforms to the conventions of standard English?

A) who
B) whom
C) whomever
D) whoever

2.
It is enclosed by a strongly fortified wall, _____ is flanked by thirteen towers.

Which choice completes the text so that it conforms to the conventions of standard English?

A) who
B) whom
C) when
D) which

3.
One legend represents the *aegis* as a fire-breathing monster like the Chimaera, which was slain by _____ afterward wore its skin as a cuirass.

Which choice completes the text so that it conforms to the conventions of standard English?

A) Athena who
B) Athena, who
C) Athena whom
D) Athena, whom

Answers on page 376

VERBS

There are <u>two types of verbs</u> it's helpful to be familiar with for the dSAT:

- **linking** verbs (aka helping verbs): *am, is, are, was, were, been, being*
- **action** verbs: *run, playing, kicked, will compete, had been challenged*

Students must also be familiar with six English <u>verb tenses</u>*:

- **PAST** tense = usually formed by adding an '-ed' to the end of a word to indicate that it happened in the past. *(ex. climbed)*

- **PRESENT** tense = usually the simple root form of the verb *(ex. climb)*

- **FUTURE** tense = usually formed by adding the word 'will' in front of the present tense verb to indicate that it has not yet happened *(ex. will climb)*

- **PAST PERFECT** tense = usually formed by adding the word 'had' or 'have' (singular and plural forms, respectively) in front of the past tense form of the verb to indicate that an action took place in the past and is complete / unlikely to repeat. *(ex. had climbed / have climbed)*

- **PRESENT PERFECT** tense = usually formed by adding the word 'has' or 'have' (singular and plural forms, respectively) in front of the past tense form of the verb to indicate that an action happened in the past and is likely to repeat in the future. *(ex. has climbed / have climbed)*

- **FUTURE PERFECT** tense = usually formed by adding the words 'will have' to the past tense form of the verb to indicate an action that will be complete before a specific time in the future. *(ex. will have climbed)*

One of the most common grammar question types is correcting verb tense.

> **STRATEGY**: Look at the other verbs in the sentence that aren't underlined for clues to which tense you need.

To easily identify dSAT 'verb tense' questions, look for answer options that are all different versions of the same verb.*

Speed Rating: *quick (usually)*

Here are some examples of what dSAT 'verb tense' questions look like:

1.

The spider suddenly let go its hold of the post and <u>was</u> quickly borne out of sight.

Which choice completes the text so that it conforms to the conventions of standard English?

A) is
B) was
C) were
D) being

*Wait, these answer options don't look like versions of the same verb! English has plenty of irregular verbs, and the linking verbs present in these answer choices are among the most commonly-used irregular English verb. Irregular just means that they don't follow the usual rules for indicating tense. For example, usually we add '-ed' to the end of a word to indicate past tense. Here, instead of writing "is+ed" as the past tense of is, it changes to "was."

2.

The river Darro, which runs through a deep ravine on the north, _____ the plateau from the Albaicin district of Granada.

Which choice completes the text so that it conforms to the conventions of standard English?

A) divide
B) divides
C) being divided
D) dividing

Answers on page 377

What are some strategies to use to approach verb tense questions?

When faced with an answer bank of all verb options, the first logical step is to **IDENTIFY THE SUBJECT of the sentence or clause where the verb is located.**

The subject is the noun (person/place/thing/idea) 'doing the action' or the verb of the sentence or clause. In some cases, sentences won't have an action verb (like *"swims"*) and instead will feature only linking verbs (like *"is"* or *"were,"* which function more as an equal sign between a subject and a modifier (descriptor) word or phrase. We will also need to correctly identify the subject for the agreement questions we see a few pages ahead.

> *STRATEGY: Be on the lookout for distracting prepositional phrases, interrupter clauses, and singular subjects that look plural (and vice versa) when finding the subject of a sentence or clause!*

Examples:

- *The top of the mountain is above the clouds.*
- subject = top
- interrupter prepositional phrase = "of the mountain"
- corresponding verb = is *(linking verb)*

- *The group of girls decided to hike to the highest peak.*
- subject = group
- interrupter prepositional phrase = "of girls"
- corresponding verb = decided *(action verb)*

- *The best in all of the league's divisions was a boy named Anthony.*
- subject = best
- interrupter prepositional phrase = "in all of the league's divisions"
- corresponding verb = was *(linking verb)*

In this sentence, the subject is where is usually is found: at the very beginning of the sentence. When this is the case, the sentence is generally in active voice. We'll cover active and passive voices in more depth on pages 197-199.

An "s" at the end of a verb doesn't make it plural!

A common trap students fall into is thinking that an 's' at the end of a verb makes it plural.

In fact, an "s" at the end of a verb usually means that it has a *singular* subject instead of a *plural* one! If you're ever unsure which verb is correct, replace the subject of a sentence with a pronoun and read each answer choice with the pronoun + verb combo to better tell which one is correct.

Consider this sentence and answer options:

An ambush of tigers _____ together every day.

A) hunt
B) hunts
C) hunting
D) had been hunt

Let's find the correct form of the verb to go with the tricky subject, "An ambush."

First, we need to determine whether the subject is singular or plural. The article 'an' gives a clear indication that we are dealing with a singular subject.

Singular subjects can be replaced with **singular** pronouns like *he, she, or it.*
Plural subjects can be replaced by **plural** pronouns like *we, you, or they.*

Usually, for this trick, the easiest replacement pronouns to use are "it" for singular subjects and "they" for plural subjects.

Let's try it out. Since the subject is singular, we'll replace it with the word "it" and test out the answer options.

A) it hunt
B) it hunts
C) it hunting
D) it had been hunt

This technique makes the correct answer, B, much easier to choose quickly.

Wait, isn't the subject "tigers?"

No, "of tigers" is one of those distractor phrases we were talking about earlier in the comma rules section. The test writers will commonly include these phrases (often prepositional phrases starting with the word "of" like we see here) in between the subject and verb of a sentence to try to trick students moving quickly.

Remember, the subject is usually at at the very beginning of the sentence and not used in a prepositional phrase (unless the sentence is in passive voice, which we'll cover later).

The word "ambush" is the subject because it's the collective term for a group of tigers. Animals get fantastic collective nouns (nouns that describe a group but are grammatically singular):

> Examples:
> - The *clowder* of kittens **plays** all day long.
> - The *fluffle* of rabbits **hops** around outside.
> - The *murder* of crows **lands** ominously.
> - The *wisdom* of owls **hoots** together at night.
> - The *herd* of wild horses **runs** freely across the plains.
> - The *crash* of rhinos* **thunders** toward the campsite.

Notice how all of these collective nouns, despite describing a multiple creatures, is still considered grammatically singular. This is true for non-animal collective nouns as well, like *group, family, community, committee, etc.*

> **STRATEGY**: If you're ever unsure which verb is correct, use the 'pronoun trick' and replace the subject of a sentence with a pronoun and read each answer choice with the pronoun + verb combo to better tell which one is correct.

*There are several correct plural forms of rhinoceros: *rhinoceri, rhinoceroses, rhinoceros,* and for the slang nickname, *rhino,* we have the plural word *rhinos.*

Practice Verb Tense Questions

1.

After pressure is applied, the mass _____ taken out, and it forms a compact coherent cylinder of tolerably clear ice, which has a perfectly sharp edge, and is an accurate copy of the mold.

Which choice completes the text so that it conforms to the conventions of standard English?

A) was
B) were
C) is
D) are

2.

One of the most attractive features of Brooklyn is Prospect _____ 516 acres of high ground in the west central part of the borough, on a site made memorable by the battle of Long Island.

Which choice completes the text so that it conforms to the conventions of standard English?

A) Park, occupying about
B) Park, occupied about
C) Park, which occupies about
D) Park, about

3.

Mosaic work _____ composed of small pieces of marble, stone, glass, or pottery, laid as paving or wall lining, usually in some ornamental pattern or design.

Which choice completes the text so that it conforms to the conventions of standard English?

A) is
B) are
C) were
D) being

4.

The name Alhambra, meaning in Arabic 'the red,' is probably derived from the color of the sun-dried *tapia*, or bricks, made of fine gravel and clay, of which the outer walls of the structure _____ built.

Which choice completes the text so that it conforms to the conventions of standard English?

A) are
B) is
C) was
D) being

5.

The *aegis* of legend appears to have actually been a goat's skin _____ as a belt to support a shield.

Which choice completes the text so that it conforms to the conventions of standard English?

A) use
B) used
C) uses
D) using

6.

In his writings, Abano _____ the medical and philosophical systems of Averroes and other Arabian writers.

Which choice completes the text so that it conforms to the conventions of standard English?

A) expounds and advocates
B) expound and advocates
C) expounds and advocate
D) expounding and advocating

7.

A million seconds _____ only eleven and a half days and nights. But a billion seconds will make actually more than thirty thousand years!

Which choice completes the text so that it conforms to the conventions of standard English?

    A) making
    B) makes
    C) made
    D) make

8.

In works of art, the *aegis* is sometimes depicted as an animal's skin _____ over the shoulders and arms and other times as a cuirass, with a border of snakes, usually with the Gorgon Medusa's head in the center.

Which choice completes the text so that it conforms to the conventions of standard English?

    A) having been thrown
    B) throwing
    C) throwed
    D) thrown

9.

Aasen continued to enlarge and improve his grammar and vocabulary. He lived very quietly in lodgings surrounded by his books and _____ from publicity, but his name grew into wide political favour as his ideas about the language of the peasants became more and more the watch-word of the popular party.

Which choice completes the text so that it conforms to the conventions of standard English?

A) shrank
B) has shrunk
C) shrinks
D) shrink

10.
Greenwood cemetery, one of the most beautiful cemeteries in the United States, occupies about 478 acres of Prospect Park. At the main entrance is a beautiful gateway of elaborately wrought brown stone 142 feet wide _____ a central tower 100 feet in height.

Which choice completes the text so that it conforms to the conventions of standard English?

A) and having
B) which had
C) with
D) and so

CHALLENGE:

Instead of the snow, I _____ irregular pieces of ice, _____ them together, _____ new pieces of ice, _____ them again, and so on, until the mold is full.

Which choice completes the text so that it conforms to the conventions of standard English?

A) Instead of the snow, I took irregular pieces of ice, press them together, add new pieces of ice, press them again, and so on, until the mold is full.

B) Instead of the snow, I took irregular pieces of ice, pressed them together, add new pieces of ice, pressed them again, and so on, until the mold is full.

C) Instead of the snow, I take irregular pieces of ice, press them together, add new pieces of ice, press them again, and so on, until the mold is full.

D) Instead of the snow, I take irregular pieces of ice, pressing them together, add new pieces of ice, pressing them again, and so on, until the mold is full.

Answers on page 377

MODIFIERS: ADJECTIVES & ADVERBS = words that describe

Adjectives
- describe nouns
- Examples: *big, zealous, ruffled, inflatable, relative, infrequent, noisy*

Adverbs
- Describe verbs, adjectives, or other adverbs
- Often end in *-ly*
- Tell <u>how</u> or <u>when</u> something was done
   Examples: *well, very, commonly, successfully, often, never, sometimes*

- Adverbs can also be stacked together for emphasis
   Examples: *"She trains so insanely diligently." "He is not feeling very well."*

CONJUNCTIONS = sentence joiners

It can be helpful to be familiar with three types of conjunctions:

Coordinating conjunctions = join 2 independent clauses when used with a comma. Examples: *and, but, yet, for, not, so, nor, or* (*Mnemonic: FANBOYS) These are the only seven coordinating conjunctions in English.

Subordinating conjunctions = join 1 independent and 1 dependent clause. Depending on the sentence, a comma may or may not be used. Examples: *as, because, before, in order that, how, since, that*, whereas, while, etc.*

Conjunctive adverbs = join 2 independent clauses with a particular purpose (ex. to show contrast, sequence, etc); these are often transition words. Examples: *again, besides, finally, for example, meanwhile, otherwise, etc.*

ARTICLES

Small words like *a, an,* and *the* are called articles and act as language facilitators to help us communicate clearly in English.

Wait, I thought you said before that "that" is a pronoun! It is. Isn't English grand? The word "that," depending on context, can function as both a demonstrative pronoun as well as a subordinating conjunction. Not to worry, the dSAT doesn't test the specific names of the types of conjunctions.

PREPOSITIONS & PREPOSITIONAL PHRASES

Prepositions have a clue to their purpose in the name: 'position.'

Prepositions are words that help us relate two objects or ideas in relative position (either literal position physically in space or figuratively in an abstract way.

Examples: *of, by, next to, around, between, in front of, about, at, on, near, with, up, into, toward, etc.*

Prepositions are usually short words or phrases that begin what we call prepositional phrases.

A prepositional phrase = **(preposition) + (object of the preposition)**

Examples:
- of waffles
  "of" = preposition
  "waffles" = object of the preposition
- in the spotlight
  "in" = preposition
  "the spotlight" = object of the preposition
- under pressure
  "under" = preposition
  "pressure = object of the preposition
- out of the ordinary
  "out of" = phrasal* preposition
  "the ordinary" = object of the preposition

These phrases, while usually grammatically removable, add on helpful, relevant information to add specificity to a sentence. They are also often used one right after the other to layer rich detail into clauses.

Example:
- (in front) + (of the whole school)
- (at the bus stop) + (down the street) + (next to the mini mart)

phrasal prepositions are made up of more than one word, like "next to" or "in front of"

Putting it all together, we can see that prepositions and prepositional phrases are common in everyday English. For the dSAT, being able to recognize prepositional phrases helps students identify distractor phrases.

Preposition Exercise:

Instructions circle all prepositional phrases in the sentences below.

> One day, when walking in her favorite park, a girl noticed a new trail leading into the woods. Curious, she and her dog decided to explore it together. It wasn't clear whether the narrow path through the trees had been created by a person or a creature. After a few minutes, the trail ended at the side of a beautiful creek that ran through the whole park.

Some of the dSAT's 'Words in Context' questions will include answer bank options with phrases that include idiomatic prepositions (or, certain prepositions that automatically go with certain words; for example, saying 'synonymous with' instead of 'synonymous to'). It's a subtle part of fluent speech that can be tricky to pick up on sometimes!

dSAT Example:

1.

The spider's threads were more than a yard _____ and diverged in an ascending direction from the spider.

Which choice completes the text so that it conforms to the conventions of standard English?

A) of length
B) to length
C) with length
D) in length

Answers on page 377

AGREEMENT

Words in sentences have to "agree" or relate to each other correctly and clearly in both number (singular vs plural) and case (subject, object, etc).

Subjects of sentence/clauses must agree with their corresponding verb(s).

Example: *Baile loves to learn about Palomino horses.*

subject = Baile
verb = loves

Pronouns must agree with their corresponding antecedent or referent word.

Example: *Renee is from Trinidad & Tobago. She visits with her family there annually.*

pronoun = She
antecedent/referent = Renee

Verbs in a sentence must agree in tense or make sense contextually when using different tenses.

Examples:
- *We want to <u>take</u> a long road trip, <u>swim</u> in the lake, and <u>enjoy</u> time together.*
- *When we <u>were</u> younger, going out <u>seemed</u> more fun, but now we <u>enjoy</u> the quiet life.*

Here are some examples of what dSAT 'agreement' questions look like:

Identifiers: *versions of the same verb in different tenses in the answer options*
Speed Rating: *quick (usually)*

Let's walk through one together:

1.
William Gilpin, who is so admirable in all that relates to landscapes, and usually so correct, _____ at the head of Loch Fyne, in Scotland, which he describes as "a bay of salt water, sixty or seventy fathoms deep, four miles in breadth," and about fifty miles long, surrounded by mountains.*

    A) stand
    B) stands
    C) standing
    D) had stood

There is a perfect example of not one but two "distractor" or "interrupter" clauses separating the subject from the blank in this sentence: a common trap on the test designed to distract the reader from the true subject of the sentence.

The subject of the sentence is William Gilpin. We can confirm this by double checking that he's the one doing the verb.

Try removing the interrupter phrases and testing the answer choices:

William Gilpin stand
William Gilpin stands
William Gilpin standing
William Gilpin had stood

Using this technique, we can much more easily see the necessary connection between the subject and the verb and eliminate answers down to the correct one: B.

*Does this passage look familiar? If so, you've seen this passage already in the WIC practice questions; however, the passage has been adjusted a bit to now test subject-verb agreement.

ACTIVE & PASSIVE VOICE

Active voice is how we usually speak:

subject + simple past/present/future verb + other stuff *(such as the direct/indirect object, prepositional phrase, etc.)*

Example: *The dog chases the ball.*

subject = the dog
simple verb = chases
other stuff (direct object, in this case) = the ball.

Passive voice changes the sentence's order to be less clear and more wordy:

other stuff + (participle verb) + subject in a prepositional phrase

Example: The ball was chased by the dog.

The dog is still the subject, still the one doing the chasing, but in passive voice, that is less apparent, since the subject isn't at the beginning of the sentence where we usually expect it to be.

The dSAT prefers active voice over passive voice, as active voice is more clear and concise.

Let's look at another example:

Active Voice: An ice climber scaled the dangerous, snowy mountain.
Passive Voice: The dangerous, snowy mountain was scaled by an ice climber.

Active vs Passive Example Questions:

1.

<u>To this cause the sailors attributed it;</u> at the time, however, I entertained some doubts, on account of the frequency and rapidity of the flashes.

Which choice completes the text so that it conforms to the conventions of standard English?

A) To this cause the sailors attributed it;
B) Sailors attributed it to this cause;
C) To this cause it attributed the sailors;
D) Sailors caused it to attribute;

2.

<u>The *aegis* is often represented on the statues of Roman emperors, heroes, and warriors, and on cameos and vases.</u>

Which choice completes the text so that it conforms to the conventions of standard English?

A) The *aegis* is often represented on cameos, vases, and the statues of Roman emperors, heroes, and warriors.

B) Roman emperors, heroes, and warriors often representing the *aegis* on and on cameos and vases.

C) The *aegis*, often represented on the statues of Roman emperors, heroes, and warriors, and on cameos and vases.

D) Cameos and vases often features representations of Roman emperors, heroes, and warriors.

3.

The individual larger pieces of ice which had been used in producing the ice blocks is recognized by experimenters, though they are somewhat changed and flattened.

Which choice completes the text so that it conforms to the conventions of standard English?

A) Experimenters would be able to recognize the individual larger pieces of ice which have been used producing the ice blocks, though they are somewhat changed and flattened.

B) The individual larger pieces of ice which have been used to produce the ice blocks are recognized, though they are somewhat changed and flattened.

C) Experimenters are able to recognize the individual larger pieces of ice which have been used to produce the ice blocks, though the ice pieces are somewhat changed and flattened.

D) The individual larger pieces of ice which had been used in producing the ice blocks is recognized by experimenters, though they are somewhat changed and flattened.

Answers on page 377

COMPARATIVES, COMPARISONS, & SPECIFICITY

COMPARATIVES & SUPERLATIVES = know the difference

comparative form = relates 2 things/people = use the -er ending

superlative form = relates 3+ things/people = use the -st or -est ending

> **STRATEGY**: Pay attention to number-related words in sentences like "both" or "couple" to determine whether comparative or superlative form is appropriate.

Examples:
- *She runs faster than he does.*
- *Of the three gymnasts, Ali is the tallest.*

dSAT Example Comparative / Superlative Questions:

1.
The spider's threads <u>were more</u> than a yard in length and diverged in an ascending direction from the spider.

Which choice completes the text so that it conforms to the conventions of standard English?

    A) was most
    B) was more
    C) were most
    D) were more

COMPARISONS = make sure they're balanced!

To correctly compare two things, we need to make it clear which two things are being related. We also often to use the word THAN (which creates a comparison) instead of THEN (which indicates a sequence of events); however, there are other words that can communicate a comparison: *like, similar to, as, compared to, etc.*

2.
The home team was more skilled _____ the away team.

A) then
B) than
C) and then
D) and than

3.
The appearance was very _____ might be expected from a large fish moving rapidly through a luminous fluid.

A) similar, to that
B) similar to that
C) similar, to that which
D) similar to that which

SPECIFICITY = if a pronoun option is ambiguous, be specific!

The dSAT prefers specificity and clarity over vagueness and ambiguity.

4.
Experimenters are able to recognize the individual larger pieces of ice which have been used to produce the ice blocks, though _____ are somewhat changed and flattened.

A) they
B) the experiments
C) the ice pieces
D) the ice blocks

Answers on page 377

EDITING
QUESTIONS

LOGICAL TRANSITION

Transition words help us link ideas logically.

Some common transition words include *additionally, but, however, for example, so, and yet.*

Here's the breakdown of what LearnCurious calls 'Logical Transition' questions on the four currently-released digital SAT exams:

	VM1	VM2a	VM2b
Test #1:	4/27 = 14.8%	3/27 = 11.1%	3/27 = 11.1%
Test #2:	1/27 = 3.7%	4/27 = 14.8%	3/27 = 11.1%
Test #3:	3/27 = 11.1%	2/27 = 7.4%	1/27 = 3.7%
Test #4:	1/27 = 3.7%	3/27 = 11.1%	3/27 = 11.1%

To summarize, there are
... between 1-4 logical transition (LT) questions on Verbal Module 1.
... between 2-4 logical transition (LT) questions on Verbal Module 2a.
... between 1-3 logical transition (LT) questions on Verbal Module 2b

LOGICAL TRANSITION questions appear toward the end of each Verbal Module, usually between questions #21-26. They ask students to connect ideas in a logical way, given the context. The transitions tested on the digital SAT can be helpfully grouped into three main categories: **support, contrast, and sequence/results transitions. If the transition word is found between two commas, it is likely used more emphatically and should be able to be removed.**

How do I identify Logical Transition questions?

Logical Transition questions can be identified using these specific question stems:
- 'Which choice completes the text with the most logical transition?'
- 'Which choice most logically completes the text?'

Here are several examples of what digital SAT Logical Transition questions look like:

1.

Under Tiberius the cake-eating fell into disuse, but the wheat ears survived. In the middle ages they were either worn or carried by the bride. Eventually it became the custom for the young girls to assemble outside the church porch and throw grains of wheat over the bride, and _____ a scramble for the grains took place.

Which choice completes the text with the most logical transition?

A) afterward
B) in other words
C) nevertheless
D) similarly

2.

An immense variety of ornamental paving and walling tiles is now manufactured of different colors, sizes and shapes, and the use of these for lining sculleries, lavatories, bathrooms, and provision shops, makes for cleanliness and improved sanitary conditions. _____ being put to these uses, tiles are often used in the ornamentation of buildings, externally as well as internally.

Which choice completes the text with the most logical transition?

A) actually
B) besides
C) however
D) secondly

3.

Few of the original causes of fear now exist. The original danger was from wild animals chiefly. Seldom are we now in such danger. But of course this has been the case for only a short time. Our bodies are the same sort of bodies that our ancestors had; _____, we are full of needless fears.

Which choice completes the text with the most logical transition?

A) alternatively
B) besides
C) likewise
D) therefore

4.

In a wild state the typical Indian buffalo, The large size and wide separation of the horns, as well as the less thickly fringed ears, and the more elongated and narrow head, form marked points of distinction between the Asiatic and South African species. _____, all Asiatic buffaloes are distinguished from the African forms by having the hair on the fore-part of the back directed forwards.

Which choice most logically completes the text?

A) Still
B) First
C) However
D) Moreover

5.

Kellogg stated that venom of cottonmouths contains more neurotoxin than that of rattlesnakes and not only breaks down the nuclei of ganglion cells but also produces granular disintegration of the myelin sheath and fragmentation of the conducting portions of nerve fibers. _____, venoms contain both toxic elements and non-toxic substances that promote rapid spreading of the venom through the body of the victim.

Which choice completes the text with the most logical transition?

A) Instead
B) Next
C) Still
D) Thus

6.

A seeming arrangement of two stars in this way is known as a "double," or double star; or, indeed, to be very precise, an "optical double." In a pair of stars, both bodies may be about the same distance from us, and _____ connected as a system like, for instance, the moon and the earth. A pairing of stars in this way, though often casually alluded to as a double star, is properly termed a "binary," or binary system.

Which choice completes the text with the most logical transition?

A) Actually
B) Consequently
C) Finally
D) Increasingly

Answers on page 377

What are some helpful Logical Transition question strategies?

It is key for students to both be familiar with what transition words look like and what they mean in context.

The transition words in the following list have all appeared on the currently-available official SAT exams; therefore, these are the words included in the most of the answer options seen on the practice questions in this book.

Due to the adaptive nature of the new digital SAT test, there is evidence that a database of questions is used to create unique versions of the SAT for test-takers. Questions and answer options have been seen already to repeat and have the potential to continue doing so in the future. It makes sense to make sure you're familiar with how these words in particular are used.

Check off the ones you're familiar with and annotate this pages with notes about the ones that are unfamiliar.

- ❏ *actually*
- ❏ *afterward*
- ❏ *alternatively*
- ❏ *as a result*
- ❏ *besides*
- ❏ *by contrast*
- ❏ *consequently*
- ❏ *currently*
- ❏ *finally*
- ❏ *for example*
- ❏ *for instance*
- ❏ *for this reason*
- ❏ *furthermore*
- ❏ *hence*
- ❏ *however*
- ❏ *in addition*
- ❏ *in comparison*
- ❏ *in contrast*
- ❏ *increasingly*
- ❏ *indeed*
- ❏ *in fact*
- ❏ *in other words*
- ❏ *instead*
- ❏ *in sum*
- ❏ *likewise*
- ❏ *meanwhile*
- ❏ *moreover*
- ❏ *nevertheless*
- ❏ *next*
- ❏ *previously*
- ❏ *second / secondly*
- ❏ *similarly*
- ❏ *specifically*
- ❏ *still*
- ❏ *subsequently*
- ❏ *therefore*
- ❏ *thus*

While there are many categories of transition words, the transitions tested on the digital SAT can be helpfully grouped into three main categories: **support, contrast, and sequence/results transitions.**

SUPPORT

Support transition words indicate agreement, addition, or continuation of the same idea that was communicated in the sentence prior to the transition word's placement.

Examples: *additionally, for example, in fact, likewise, moreover, similarly*

CONTRAST

Support transition words indicate contradiction and and oppose the idea iterated in the sentence before the transition word.

Examples: *alternatively, by contrast, however, instead, nevertheless, regardless*

SEQUENCE / RESULTS

Sequence / Results transition words indicate a sequence or summary of events or ideas.

Examples: *afterward, consequently, hence, next, subsequently, therefore*

Here are a few strategic questions to ask yourself when faced with Logical Transition questions:

"Does the context call for a SUPPORT, CONTRAST, or SEQUENCE / RESULTS transition word?"

Here are the currently-released dSAT transition words grouped into these three categories.*

SUPPORT

additionally
for example
for instance
for this reason
furthermore
in addition
increasingly
indeed
in fact
in other words
likewise
moreover
similarly
specifically

CONTRAST

alternatively
by contrast
however
in contrast
instead
nevertheless
regardless

SEQUENCE / RESULTS

afterward
as a result
consequently
currently
finally
hence
Meanwhile
in sum
next
previously
second / secondly
still
subsequently
therefore
thus

*There are a few transition words that can feasibly fit into multiple categories, depending on the context in which they are used: *actually, besides, & in comparison.*

"Is the blank nestled between two commas?"

If so, you're likely looking for a word used more for **emphasis** than for more direct transitional purposes.

There are two types of transitions to be on the lookout for on the digital SAT:

transitions **between** two complete sentences
&
transitions nested **within** sentences themselves (usually between two commas).

Transitions within sentences and between two commas are usually used more for emphasis and can be removed without impacting the meaning of the sentence overall.

Here are a few examples of what emphatic transitions look like:
- *He was, therefore, released from custody.*
- *It will be the third time, in fact, that she's seen a bear in the wild.*

STRATEGY: A good rule of thumb is to try removing the word(s) between the commas (or dashes) and reading the sentence again. If the meaning doesn't change without the transition word, the sentence doesn't require it to communicate its core message; therefore, the transition word is more emphatic than essential.

"Does this make sense both with the sentence *prior* to the transition word as well as the sentence *after* the transition word?"

The correct answer choice will work with the context surrounding the blank. Double checking the context of the sentence before and after the sentence with the blank can be a helpful way of narrowing down two remaining answers to one.

"Are there more transition words that could be tested?"

Since new editions of the test will be released, it is likely that other transition words not on the list above will be introduced. The list below consists of words that *may* appear on future editions of the Digital SAT.

Check off the ones you're familiar with and annotate these two pages with notes about the ones that are unfamiliar. *Next, assign each of the transition words above a category: SUPPORT, CONTRAST, or SEQUENCE/RESULTS*

<u>Category</u>

- ❑ *Accordingly*
- ❑ *Albeit*
- ❑ *Also*
- ❑ *Although*
- ❑ *And*
- ❑ *As well*
- ❑ *Because*
- ❑ *But*
- ❑ *By the same token*
- ❑ *By the time*
- ❑ *Comparatively*
- ❑ *Concurrently*
- ❑ *Conversely*
- ❑ *Correspondingly*
- ❑ *Despite*
- ❑ *Different from*
- ❑ *During*
- ❑ *Either*

- Equally
- Even more
- Even though
- For
- Further
- Immediately
- In order to
- In short
- In spite of
- In summary
- In the same way / fashion / vein
- Last(ly)
- Once
- Overall
- Presently
- Like
- Much less
- Namely
- Neither
- Nonetheless
- Nor
- Not only X but also Y
- Not to mention
- Of course
- On the contrary
- On the other hand
- Otherwise
- Or
- Rather
- Since
- So
- Soon
- Such as
- Suddenly
- That is
- Then
- Thereupon
- Though
- To summarize
- Too

- ❑ *Ultimately*
- ❑ *Unless*
- ❑ *Unlike*
- ❑ *Until*
- ❑ *Whenever*
- ❑ *While*
- ❑ *Whereas*
- ❑ *Yet*

Answers on page 377

Logical Transition Practice:

1.

Brooklyn is connected with Manhattan by three bridges across the East river—the lowest, known as the Brooklyn, opened in 1883; another, known as the Williamsburg or East River bridge, opened in 1903; and a _____, the Manhattan, was opened in 1909.

Which choice completes the text with the most logical transition?

A) meanwhile
B) third
C) second
D) thus

2.

The removal of limestone pebbles from the clay is of great importance, as during the firing they would be converted into quicklime, which has a tendency to shatter the brick on exposure to the weather. As before stated, these marls burn to a yellow colour which is quite distinctive, _____ in some cases, where the percentage of limestone is very high, over 40%, the colour is grey or a very pale buff.

Which choice most logically completes the text?

A) although
B) finally
C) in sum
D) meanwhile

3.

Cottonmouths generally migrate inland in autumn, usually to dry forested hill-sides, where they den along with other species of snakes. _____ a few warm days in spring they migrate back to the water's edge.

Which choice completes the text with the most logical transition?

A) After
B) Before
C) Since
D) Still

4.

First came ten soldiers carrying clubs; these were all shaped like the three gar-deners. _____, the ten courtiers: these were ornamented all over with dia-monds. After these came the royal children: they were all ornamented with hearts.

Which choice completes the text with the most logical transition?

A) Next
B) Last
C) Finally
D) Once

5.

A true "cow town" is worth seeing,—such a one as Miles City, _____, espe-cially at the time of the annual meeting of the great Montana Stock-raisers' As-sociation. It would be impossible to imagine a more typically American assem-blage, for although there are always a certain number of foreigners, usually English, Irish, or German, yet they have become completely Americanized.

Which choice most logically completes the text?

A) afterward
B) currently
C) for instance
D) likewise

6.

The outward appearance of glaciers is very characteristically described by comparing them, with Goethe, to currents of ice. They generally stretch from the snow fields along the depth of the valleys, filling them throughout their entire breadth, and often to a considerable height. They _____ follow all the curvatures, windings, contractions, and enlargements of the valley.

Which choice completes the text with the most logical transition?

A) for instance
B) nevertheless
C) regardless
D) thus

7.

The brighter star is yellowish, and the faint one white. This brighter star is found by means of the spectroscope to be _____ composed of three stars so very close together that they cannot be seen separately even with a telescope. It is thus a triple star, and the three bodies of which it is composed are in circulation about each other.

Which choice most logically completes the text?

A) actually
B) hence
C) likewise
D) meanwhile

8.

Cheese may be legitimately made from full-milk, milk that has been enriched by addition of cream, or from milk that has been more or less skimmed. It varies _____ very widely in composition, so-called cream cheese containing not less than 60% of fat; Stilton upwards of 40%; and Cheddar about 30%; Dutch, Parmesan and some Swiss and Danish less than 20%.

Which choice completes the text with the most logical transition?

A) consequently
B) furthermore
C) in sum
D) finally

9.

It is hard to imagine a more conspicuous bird than the silver-bill; but the next and last tyrant flycatcher of which I shall speak possesses on the whole the most advertising coloration of any small bird I have ever seen in the open country, and _____ this advertising coloration exists in both sexes and throughout the year.

Which choice most logically completes the text?

A) as a result
B) in contrast
C) moreover
D) thus

10.

Those first lessons were better certainly; by them I obtained, and still retain, the power of reading what I find written and myself writing what I will; _____ in the others, I was forced to learn the wanderings of one Aeneas, forgetful of my own, and to weep for dead Dido, because she killed herself for love; the while, with dry eyes, I endured my miserable self dying among these things.

Which choice completes the text with the most logical transition?

A) for instance
B) in fact
C) moreover
D) whereas

CHALLENGE:

Dissemination is effected by the agency of water, of air, of animals—and fruits and seeds are _____ grouped in respect of this as *hydrophilous, anemophilous* and *zooidiophilous.** The needs for these are obvious—buoyancy in water and re-sistance to wetting for the first, some form of parachute for the second, and some attaching mechanism or attractive structure for the third.

Which choice most logically completes the text?

A) indeed
B) in other words
C) still
D) therefore

HINT: use your word affix/root skills here!
Answers on page 377

NOTES

The digital SAT has introduced a new type of question which LearnCurious calls the "Notes" questions where we are given a bulleted list of notes and then asked a very specific question.

Here's the breakdown of what I call 'Notes' questions on the four currently-released digital SAT exams:

	VM1	VM2a	VM2b
Test #1:	2/27 = 7.4%	1/27 = 3.7%	2/27 = 7.4%
Test #2:	6/27 = 22.2%	0/27 = 0%	2/27 = 7.4%
Test #3:	4/27 = 14.8%	2/27 = 7.4%	4/27 = 14.8%
Test #4:	6/27 = 22.2%	1/27 = 3.7%	1/27 = 3.7%

To summarize, there are
... between 2-6 notes questions on Verbal Module 1.
... between 0-2 notes questions on Verbal Module 2a
... between 1-4 notes questions on Verbal Module 2b

NOTES questions appear toward the end of each Verbal Module, usually between questions #22-26. They ask students to use a set of bulleted notes to answer a specific question. Skip straight to the question on 'Notes' questions and use it to guide you through what information is relevant as eliminate answer choices. Avoid reading the notes themselves unless you absolutely have to!

How do I identify Notes questions?

Here are two examples of what digital SAT Notes questions look like:

1.
While researching a topic, a student took the following notes:

- The angler, also sometimes called fishing-frog, frog-fish, sea-devil (*Lophius piscatorius*).

- [It is] a fish well known off the coasts of Great Britain and Europe generally, the grotesque shape of its body.

- To the North Sea fishermen this fish is known as the "monk," a name which more properly belongs to *Rhina squatina*, a fish allied to the skates.

- Its head is of enormous size, broad, flat and depressed, the remainder of the body appearing merely like an appendage.

- The wide mouth extends all round the anterior circumference of the head; and both jaws are armed with bands of long pointed teeth, which are inclined inwards.

The student wants to summarize the nicknames of the angler fish. Which choice most effectively uses relevant information from the notes to accomplish this goal?

A) The angler fish, also known as the fishing-frog, frog-fish, sea-devil, or *Lophius piscatorius*, is common to the coasts of Europe.

B) All round its head and also along the body the skin bears fringed appendages resembling short fronds of sea-weed.

C) The angler fish is also known as the fishing-frog, frog-fish, sea-devil, *Lophius piscatorius*, or "monk" to some fishermen.

D) Combined with the extraordinary faculty of assimilating the color of the body to its surroundings, seaweed assists the angler fish greatly in concealing itself in places which it selects on account of the abundance of prey.

2.

While researching a topic, a student took the following notes:

- Fairley described the constituents of venom as:

  (1) neurotoxic elements that act on the bulbar and spinal ganglion cells of the central nervous system;
  (2) hemorrhagins that destroy the lining of the walls of blood vessels;
  (3) thrombose, producing clots within blood vessels;
  (4) hemolysins, destroying red blood corpuscles;
  (5) cytolysins that act on leucocytes and on cells of other tissues;
  (6) elements that slow coagulation of the blood;

- Elapid snakes tend to have more of elements 1, 4, and 6 in their venoms. Viperids and crotalids, of which the cottonmouth is one, have higher quantities of elements 2, 3, and 5.

- Venoms can contain both toxic elements and non-toxic substances that promote rapid spreading of the venom through the body of the victim.

- Jacques attributed this rapid spreading to the hyaluronidase content of venoms.

The student wants to specify a reason for the rapid spreading of venom. Which choice most effectively uses relevant information from the notes to accomplish this goal?

A) Elapid snakes tend to have more of 1, 4, and 6 in their venoms, while viperids and crotalids have higher quantities of elements 2, 3, and 5.

B) According to Fairley, snake venom consists of a combination of neurotoxic elements, hemorrhagins, and elements that slow the coagulation of the blood.

C) Kellogg postulated that cottonmouths' venom contains more neurotoxins than does that of rattlesnakes.

D) Jacques attributed this rapid spreading to the hyaluronidase content of venoms.

Answers on page 377

Notes questions can be identified using these specific question stems:

- While researching a topic, a student has taken the following notes:
- 4-6 bulleted points
- Specific request question stems
    'The student wants to _____
    - (introduce / describe) _____ to (a new audience / an audience unfamiliar / already familiar) with _____.
    - present the study and its (conclusions / methods)
    - present the significance of _____ to an audience (unfamiliar / already familiar) with _____
    - provide an explanation and example of _____
    - emphasize a (difference in / similarity between) _____
    - emphasize the (increase / decline) in _____ and why this occurred
    - emphasize the (role / aim / duration / purpose) of _____
    - emphasize the _____'s significance
    - make and support a generalization about _____
    - specify the reason the _____
    - compare the _____ of the _____
    - contrast _____ with _____
    - explain an (advantage / disadvantage) of _____
    - explain how _____
    - summarize the study
- Which choice most effectively uses relevant information from the notes to accomplish this goal?

What are some helpful Notes question strategies?

There is one main strategy to keep in mind for NOTES questions:

SKIP RIGHT TO THE QUESTION.

Notes questions can mostly be answered without even looking at the bulleted notes themselves. Instead, look first at the specific question being asked. Match the answer that best conveys the specific request referenced in the question stem. Ignore the notes unless you absolutely have to reference them; this will not usually be the case!
Instead, focus on what *exactly* the question is asking and look for the answer choice that best matches the specific request in the question.

For example. if the specific request in the question asks you to use the notes to introduce the idea to people who are unfamiliar with it, you are a part of that audience if you haven't yet read the notes!

In this case, reading the question then checking which answer introduces the topic most clearly to you is a strong approach.

Here are a few strategic questions to ask yourself when faced with NOTES questions:

"What is the question asking me to look for specifically?"

> **STRATEGY**: Skip straight to the question on 'Notes' questions and use it to guide you through what information is relevant as eliminate answer choices. Avoid reading the notes themselves unless you absolutely have to!

"Do I have time for this?"

Even using the strategy of skipping right to the question, notes questions can sometimes be time-consuming to answer confidently. Conveniently, they are already at the end of each Verbal Module, so there's no need to reorganize them to save them for last.

Practice Notes Questions

1.

While researching a topic, a student took the following notes:

- The Amazons appear in connexion with several Greek legends.

- They invaded Lycia, but were defeated by Bellerophon, who was sent out against them by Iobates, the king of that country, in the hope that he might meet his death at their hands.

- One of the tasks imposed upon Heracles by Eurystheus was to obtain possession of the girdle of the Amazonian queen Hippolyte.

- The origin of the story of the Amazons has been the subject of much discussion.

- While some regard them as a purely mythical people, others assume an historical foundation for them.

The student wants to contrast theories about the origins of the Amazons. Which choice most effectively uses relevant information from the notes to accomplish this goal?

A) While some regard the Amazons as a purely mythical people, others assume an historical foundation for them.

B) The Amazons are also said to have undertaken an expedition against the island of Leuke, at the mouth of the Danube, where the ashes of Achilles had been deposited by Thetis.

C) Hercules was accompanied by his friend Theseus, who carried off the princess Antiope, sister of Hippolyte.

D) Antiope perished fighting by the side of Theseus.

2.

While researching a topic, a student took the following notes:

- The glory of Agra, the most splendidly poetic building in the world, is the Taj Mahal, the mausoleum built in 1632 by the emperor Shah Jahan for the remains of his favorite wife, Mumtaz Manal, in which he himself also also lies buried.

- The building is of white marble throughout, crowned with a great white dome in the center, and with a smaller dome at each of its four corners.

- From the marble terrace which surrounds it rise four tall minarets of the same material, one at each corner.

- The Taj has been modeled and painted more frequently than any other building in the world, and the word pictures of it are numberless.

- The perfect symmetry of its exterior once seen can never be forgotten, nor the aerial grace of its domes, rising like marble bubbles into the azure sky.

The student wants to specify the reason the Taj Mahal was built. Which choice most effectively uses relevant information from the notes to accomplish this goal?

A) A marble masterpiece, the Taj and its magnificent, symmetric domed minarets have been a popular tourist destination in recent years.

B) The building is of white marble throughout, crowned with a great white dome in the center, and with a smaller dome at each of its four corners.

C) Mumtaz Manal commissioned the building of the Taj Mahal, which has continued to stun guests since being finished in 1632.

D) Emperor Shah Jahan built a white marble masterpiece, the Taj Mahal, as a mausoleum for both his wife, Mumtaz Manal, and himself.

3.

While researching a topic, a student took the following notes:

- Austin Edwin Abbey, an American painter, was born in Philadelphia, Pennsylvania, on the 1st of April 1852.

- He left the schools of the Pennsylvania Academy of Fine Arts at the age of nineteen to enter the art department of the publishing house of Harper & Brothers in New York.

- In company with such men as Howard Pyle, Charles Stanley Reinhart, Joseph Pennell and Alfred Parsons, he became very successful as an illustrator.

- In 1878 he was sent by the Harpers to England to gather material for illustrations of the poems of Robert Herrick.

- These, published in 1882, attracted much attention.

- They were followed by illustrations for Goldsmith's She Stoops to Conquer (1887), for a volume of Old Songs (1889), and for the comedies (and a few of the tragedies) of Shakespeare.

The student wants to introduce Austin Edwin Abbey to an audience unfamiliar with his artistic work.

A) Austin Edwin Abbey, an American painter, became very successful as a sculptor.

B) Austin Edwin Abbey was sent by the Harpers to England to gather material for illustrations of the poems of Robert Herrick.

C) Austin Edwin Abbey, an American painter, published illustrations of the poems of Robert Herrick and later for some of the comedies and tragedies of Shakespeare.

D) Austin Edwin Abbey attracted much attention when he left the schools of the Pennsylvania Academy of Fine Arts at the age of nineteen to enter the art department of the publishing house of Harper & Brothers in New York.

4.

While researching a topic, a student took the following notes:

- An anagram is the result of transposing the letters of a word or words in such a manner as to produce other words that possess meaning.

- A well-known anagram is the change *of Ave Maria, gratia plena, Dominus tecum* into *Virgo serena, pia, munda et immaculata.*

- Among others are the anagrammatic answer to Pilate's question, ``*Quid est veritas*''—namely, ``*Est vir qui adest*''; and the transposition of ``Horatio Nelson'' into ``*Honor est a* Nilo'';

- and of ``Florence Nightingale'' into ``Flit on, cheering angel.''

- James I.'s courtiers discovered in ``James Stuart'' ``A just master,'' and converted ``Charles James Stuart'' into ``Claimes Arthur's seat.'' ``

The student wants to introduce anagrams to an audience unfamiliar with them. Which choice most effectively uses relevant information from the notes to accomplish this goal?

A) A well-known anagram is the change of Ave Maria, *gratia plena, Dominus tecum* into *Virgo serena, pia, munda et immaculata.*

B) Among other well-known anagrams is the answer to Pilate's question, ``Quid est veritas?'' namely, ``Est vir qui adest.'' One can also create an anagram from the transposition of ``Horatio Nelson'' into ``Honor est a Nilo''

C) An anagram is the result of rearranging the letters of a word or words in such a manner as to produce other words that possess meaning.

D) James I.'s courtiers discovered an anagram in ``James Stuart'' ``A just master,'' and converted ``Charles James Stuart'' into ``Claimes Arthur's seat.'' ``

5.

While researching a topic, a student took the following notes:

- This experiment, which was first made by Tyndall, shows that a block of ice may be pressed into any mold just like a piece of wax.

- Instead of the snow, I take irregular pieces of ice, press them together, add new pieces of ice, press them again, and so on, until the mold is full.

- After pressure is applied, the mass is taken out, and it forms a compact coherent cylinder of tolerably clear ice, which has a perfectly sharp edge, and is an accurate copy of the mold.

- It might, perhaps, be thought that such a block had, by the pressure in the interior, been first reduced to powder so fine that it readily penetrated every crevice of the mold, and then that this powdered ice, like snow, was again combined by freezing.

- This suggests itself the more readily, since while the press is being worked a continual creaking and cracking is heard in the interior of the mold.

The student wants to emphasize the aim of the study. Which choice most effectively uses relevant information from the notes to accomplish this goal?

A) The resulting compressed block is most beautiful when clear pieces of ice are laid in the form and the rest of the space stuffed full of snow.

B) This experiment, which was first made by Tyndall, is designed to show that a block of ice may be pressed into any mold just like a piece of wax.

C) The cylinder is then seen to consist of alternate layers of clear and opaque ice, the former arising from the pieces of ice, and the latter from the snow.

D) This theory suggests itself the more readily, since while the press is being worked a continual creaking and cracking is heard in the interior of the mold.

6.

While researching a topic, a student took the following notes:

- A spider which was about three-tenths of an inch in length, while standing on the summit of a post, darted forth four or five threads from its spinners.

- They were more than a yard in length, and diverged in an ascending direction from the orifices.

- The spider then suddenly let go its hold of the post, and was quickly borne out of sight.

- The day was hot and apparently calm; yet under such circumstances, the atmosphere can never be so tranquil as not to affect a vane so delicate as the thread of a spider's web.

- If during a warm day we look either at the shadow of any object cast on a bank, or over a level plain at a distant landmark, the effect of an ascending current of heated air is almost always evident: such upward currents, it has been remarked, are also shown by the ascent of soap-bubbles, which will not rise in an in-doors room.

The student wants to present an observation about the spider seen by the researcher. Which choice most effectively uses relevant information from the notes to accomplish this goal?

A) A spider emitted four or five threads from its spinners. These threads traveled up and away from the spider, which suddenly let go its hold of the post and was quickly borne out of sight.

B) The day was hot and apparently calm; however, the atmosphere can never be so tranquil as not to affect a vane so delicate as the thread of a spider's web.

C) If we look either at the shadow of any object in the distance or at a distant landmark over a level plain on a hot day, the effect of an ascending current of heated air is almost always evident.

D) Scientists have noted that while soap-bubbles will no rise indoors, they are seen to ascend outdoors in these upward currents of warmer air.

7.

While researching a topic, a student took the following notes:

- Fairley described the constituents of venom as:
  (1) neurotoxic elements that act on the bulbar and spinal ganglion cells of the central nervous system;
  (2) hemorrhagins that destroy the lining of the walls of blood vessels;
  (3) thrombose, producing clots within blood vessels;
  (4) hemolysins, destroying red blood corpuscles;
  (5) cytolysins that act on leucocytes and on cells of other tissues;
  (6) elements that slow coagulation of the blood;

- Elapid snakes tend to have more of elements 1, 4, and 6 in their venoms.

- Viperids and crotalids, of which the cottonmouth is one, have higher quantities of elements 2, 3, and 5.

The student wants to contrast the composition of the venoms of elapids with viperids. Which choice most effectively uses relevant information from the notes to accomplish this goal?

A) Jacques attributed this rapid spreading to the hyaluronidase content of venoms.

B) Elapid snakes tend to have more of neurotoxic elements, hemolysins, and elements that slow blood coagulation in their venoms, while viperids and crotalids have higher quantities of hemorrhagins, thrombose, and cytolysins.

C) According to Fairley, snake venom consists of a combination of neurotoxic elements, hemorrhagins, thrombose, hemolysins, cytolysins, and elements that slow the coagulation of the blood.

D) Kellogg postulated that cottonmouths' venom contains more neurotoxins than does that of rattlesnakes.

CHALLENGE:

While researching a topic, a student took the following notes:

* [Austin Edwin Abbey's] water-colours and pastels were no less successful than the earlier illustrations in pen and ink.

* Abbey now became closely identified with the art life of England, and was elected to the Royal Institute of Painters in Water-Colours in 1883.

* Abbey became a member not only of the Royal Academy, but also of the National Academy of Design of New York, and honorary member of the Royal Bavarian Society, the Societe Nationale des Beaux Arts (Paris), the American Water-Colour Society, etc.

The student wants to provide examples of how internationally recognized Austin Edwin Abbey is in the art world to an audience already familiar with some of his illustrations. Which choice most effectively uses relevant information from the notes to accomplish this goal?

A) Austin Edwin Abbey became a member not only of the Royal Academy, but also of the National Academy of Design of New York, and honorary member of the Royal Bavarian Society, the Societe Nationale des Beaux Arts (Paris), the American Water-Colour Society, etc.

B) Austin Edwin Abbey became closely identified with the art life of England. Apart from his other paintings, special mention must be made of the large frescoes entitled ``The Quest of the Holy Grail.''

C) Austin Edwin Abbey's best known pastels are perhaps ``Beatrice,'' ``Phyllis,'' and ``Two Noble Kinsmen.'' The dramatic subjects, and the brilliant coloring of his on pictures, gave them pronounced individuality among the works of contemporary painters.

D) Austin Edwin Abbey was elected to the Royal Institute of Painters in Water-Colours in 1883. Possibly his best known pastels are ``Beatrice,'' ``Phyllis,'' and ``Two Noble Kinsmen.''

Answers on page 377

GRAMMAR AND PUNCTUATION DIAGNOSTIC QUIZ #1

Instructions: Choose the answer that best fits in the blank. When you have answered all of the questions, use the answer key to check your answers and refer to the recommendations for any questions you missed or felt unsure about (even if you got them right)!

1. "I see now that the circumstances of one's birth are _____ what you do with the gift of life that determines who you are." — *Mewtwo (Pokemon)*

    A) irrelevant, it is
    B) irrelevant it is
    C) irrelevant; it is
    D) irrelevant, it, is

2. "I knew exactly what to _____ in a much more real sense I had no idea what to do." — *Michael Scott, (The Office)*

    A) do but
    B) do; but
    C) do, but
    D) do. But

3. "Often when we guess at _____ motives, we reveal only our own." – *Mara Sov, (Destiny)*

    A) others'
    B) other's
    C) others's
    D) others

4. "I've given you weapons, taught you _____ you with knowledge. There's nothing more for me to give you." — *The Boss, (Metal Gear Solid 3)*

    A) techniques, and endowing
    B) techniques and endowed
    C) techniques, and endows
    D) techniques, and endowed

5. "_____ gonna completely ignore everything you just said." — *Jake Peralta, (Brooklyn Nine-Nine)*

    A) Sarge with all due respect, I am
    B) Sarge with all due respect I am
    C) Sarge to all due respect I am
    D) Sarge, with all due respect, I am

6. "I give myself very good _____ I very seldom follow it." — *Alice, (Alice in Wonderland)*

    A) advice, but,
    B) advice, but
    C) advice but
    D) advise but

7. "The surge of emotion that shot through me when I saved your life taught me an even more valuable _____ Caroline lives in my brain." — *GLaDOS, (Portal 2)*

    A) lesson; where
    B) lesson, wear
    C) lesson — where
    D) lesson where

8. "_____ a monster more dangerous than a lack of compassion." — *Master Splinter (Teenage Mutant Ninja Turtles)*

    A) There are not
    B) There will be not
    C) There were not
    D) There is not

9. That day, she was amazed to discover that when he was saying, _____. Even more amazing was the day she realized she truly loved him back. — *Grandfather, (The Princess Bride)*

    A) "As you wish" what he meant was, "I love you."
    B) "As you wish," what he meant was, "I love you."
    C) "As you wish", what he meant was, "I love you".
    D) "As you wish', what he meant was, "I love you."

10. "In the end what was your reward? You never said, but I think I _____" —*Brigid Tenenbaum, (BioShock)*

    A) know: a family.
    B) know a family.
    C) know; a family.
    D) know, — a family.

Recommendations:

If you missed…

#1 = review semicolon use
#2 = review independent vs dependent clause connection, coordinating conjunction, and comma rules
#3 = review apostrophe use
#4 = review parallel structure rules / using commas with lists
#5 = review comma use
#6 = review FANBOYS commas
#7 = review dash/colon use
#8 = review subject/verb agreement
#9 = review quotation mark use
#10 = review colon/dash use

Answers on page 377

GRAMMAR AND PUNCTUATION
QUIZ #2

Instructions: Choose the answer that best fits in the blank. When you have answered all of the questions, use the answer key to check your answers and refer to the recommendations for any questions you missed or felt unsure about (even if you got them right)!

1. "No, Jim, tell _____. *"Por que es muy rapido."* — *Darryl & Jim, (The Office)*

   A) us. Why is it called Señor Loadenstein"?
   B) us. Why is it called Señor Loadenstein."
   C) us why is it called Señor Loadenstein"?
   D) us. Why is it called Señor Loadenstein?"

2. "Not everyone can become a great _____ a great artist can come from anywhere." — *Anton Ego, (Ratatouille)*

   A) artist, but
   B) artist but
   C) artist; but
   D) artist but,

3. "It's not a man purse. _____ called a satchel. Indiana Jones wears one." — *Alan Garner, (The Hangover)*

   A) It's,
   B) It's
   C) Its
   D) Its'

4. "_____ braver than you believe, stronger than you seem, and smarter than you think." — *Christopher Robin, (Winnie The Pooh)*

   A) Your
   B) You're
   C) You're,
   D) Your,

5. "I walk around like everything's fine, but deep down, inside my shoe, my sock _____ sliding off." — *Anonymous*

    A) being
    B) were
    C) was
    D) is

6. "We've busted murderers; we've taken down cartels. But today we face the worst New York has to _____ Department." — *Jake Peralta, (Brooklyn Nine-Nine)*

    A) offer: the Fire
    B) offer' the Fire
    C) offer the Fire
    D) offer; the Fire

7. "Everything you _____ exists together in a delicate balance. As King, you need to understand that balance and respect all the creatures, from the crawling ant to the leaping antelope." — *Mufasa, (The Lion King)*

    A) see
    B) seeing
    C) seen
    D) sees

8. "They don't even ask _____ just assume that their wish is our command." — *Joey Gladstone, (Full House)*

    A) anymore they
    B) anymore, they
    C) anymore; they
    D) anymore and they

9. "There's nothing better than a beautiful day at the beach filled with _____ note-taking." — *Pam Beesly, (The Office)*

    A) sun surf, and uh diligent
    B) sun, surf, and uh, diligent
    C) sun, surf and uh diligent
    D) sun surf and uh diligent

10. "No need to seize the last _____ Baelish. I'll assume it was something clever." —*Sansa Stark, (Game of Thrones)*

    A) word; Lord
    B) word: Lord
    C) word Lord
    D) word, Lord

Recommendations:

If you missed…

#1 = review period / question mark / quotation mark use
#2 = review comma rules
#3 = review apostrophe use
#4 = review apostrophe use
#5 = review subject/verb agreement
#6 = review colon use
#7 = review subject/verb agreement
#8 = review semicolon use
#9 = review comma rules
#10 = review comma rules

Answers on page 377

Punctuation, Grammar, & Editing
Question Types Overview, Identification Phrases, & Strategies

PUNCTUATION questions appear toward the end of each Verbal Module, usually between questions #14-23. They ask students to choose the correct punctuation mark given certain sentence structures. To answer these questions efficiently, **say the sentences slowly in your head; try each answer; eliminate answers as you go; & review rules for apostrophe, comma, colon, dash, semicolon, and quotation use.**

Frequency: uncommon; *Speed rating:* quick (if you know all the rules)
Identifier(s): answer options with different punctuation mark options
Punctuation rules recap:

- COLONS must follow a complete sentence and link relevant information that answers the most logical question someone might ask about the sentence preceding the colon.

- SEMICOLONS separate related complete sentences and, on occasion, subgroups in complex lists that already contain commas.

- COMMAS have too many rules to list here and often require more practice than the other punctuation marks.

- APOSTROPHES create possessive words and contractions.

- SINGLE DASHES function exactly like colons -- they must follow a complete sentence and link relevant information that answers the most logical question someone might ask about the sentence preceding the colon.

- DASH PAIRS surround non-essential (but relevant) information that can be removed.

- QUOTATION MARKS used in pairs surrounding dialogue to indicate direct quotation. For the dSAT, other punctuation marks go INSIDE quotation marks.

GRAMMAR questions appear toward the end of each Verbal Module, usually between questions #14-23. They ask students to choose the word that fits in the blank with correct agreement, tense, and case. To complete these questions efficiently, **it is helpful to look at other verbs in the sentence and/or locate the subject in the sentence in question, determine whether it's singular or plural.**

Frequency: uncommon; *Speed rating:* quick / moderate
Identifier(s): noun, verb, or pronoun answer options
Strategies:
- <u>verb tense</u> = check & match the tense of other verbs in the sentence
- <u>subject-verb agreement</u> = check whether you need a singular or plural word to match with the subject of the sentence.

LOGICAL TRANSITION questions appear toward the end of each Verbal Module, usually between questions #21-26. They ask students to connect ideas in a logical way, given the context. The transitions tested on the digital SAT can be helpfully grouped into three main categories: **support, contrast, and sequence/results transitions. If the transition word is found between two commas, it is likely used more emphatically and should be able to be removed.**

Frequency: uncommon; *Speed rating:* moderate
Identifier(s): transition words in the answer options
Strategies:
- **support** transitions continue with same idea or emphasize
  - examples: *additionally, clearly, for example, indeed, in fact, furthermore, moreover*
- **contrast** transitions change ideas or emphasize
  - examples: *however, but, yet, although, nevertheless, nonetheless*
- **sequence/results** transitions provide a chronology/summary of events/ideas
  - examples: *because, in order to, since, thus*

NOTES questions appear toward the end of each Verbal Module, usually between questions #22-26. They ask students to use a set of bulleted notes to answer a specific question. **Skip straight to the question on 'Notes' questions, annotate the specific request, and use it to guide you through what information is relevant as you eliminate answer choices.**

Frequency: uncommon; *Speed rating:* moderate / time-consuming
Identifier(s): bulleted list of notes present in passage area
Strategies:
- Avoid reading the notes themselves unless you absolutely have to do so.
- Skip straight to the question & annotate the specific request.
- Eliminate answers as you go along.

Part III:

Test-Taking Tips
&
Appendices

Working with an Adaptive Test for the First Time

The digital SAT adapts in stages:
- **Module 1** of each section will contain a range of question difficulty.
- **Module 2** of each section will be adapted based on students' individual scores on Stage 1.

Those who score between 1-16 questions correct on Module 1 will be issued Module 2a, which will contain fewer advanced questions; however, students who take Module 2a will only have the opportunity to score a maximum of 1580 points.

Those who score between 17-27 questions correct on Module 1 will be issued Module 2b, which will contain more advanced questions; students who take Module 2b will have the chance to score a perfect 1600.

While the College Board reports that this adaptive staging helps to make the shorter length of the digital SAT more accurate, they have not yet revealed much about how exactly their scores are calculated. We do know that they are using Item Response Theory to scale questions, which will be weighted differently on the digital version of the test.

After official exams, students will not have access to test questions or be informed which specific questions they got (in)correct.

It's also key to note that **two questions per stage are experimental and unscored**. The paper version of the test often included a fifth 'experimental' section to allow the College Board to test out questions to potentially use on future versions of the exam. On the digital version of the test, the 'experimental' questions are automatically included in each test module.

> ***STRATEGY:*** *If a question seems unusually hard or difficult to understand, you may have come across an unscored question. Be willing to guess on, skip over, and come back to these questions later if there's time.*

The adaptive nature of the test also means that students who are testing in the same room won't be taking exactly the same test.

Creating Study Plans & Setting Goals

SELF-GUIDANCE TIPS

WHEN TO STUDY

- Study boring/difficult subjects first. Why? Harder stuff requires more energy. Reward yourself with the stuff you like later, when your brain doesn't need to work as hard.

- If something has been on your to-do list for more than a week, make it your first priority tomorrow morning.

- Learn what time(s) of day works best for you to study most effectively. Are you a early bird or a night owl? Or does it depend?

- Make creative use of pockets of available time. Listen to a subject-material-related podcast when you're driving or on the bus/train. Flip through note cards while you're waiting for class or practice to start. Every little bit helps.

WHAT TO STUDY

- What you're getting wrong.

- Error patterns show what you don't fully understand yet. Your challenge areas are your way forward. Absorb as much information about the areas you understand the <u>least</u>. Ask questions. Watch videos. Take notes. Repeat.

- High-quality study guides.
  If you could delegate the task of making a study guide to someone else, wouldn't you? Granted, the process of making a guide counts as studying. But if you're crunched for time, include "filetype:pdf" with your google search to find printable, well-formatted study guides for nearly any subject, any unit, any test. Enjoy.

SELF-AWARENESS TIPS

If you haven't already, develop the habit of noticing

- **Small gains.** Remember they often lead to big changes over time.

  Ask yourself: "Can I do just one more thing tonight?" (It's okay when the answer is 'no'! The point is to get in the habit of asking the questions and answering it honestly to be able to better predict your own thresholds in the future.

- **Noise level.**

  Ask yourself: "Is it too loud in here to focus well?" Study in silence or listening to instrumental music or white noise. Ambient noise website recommendations: noisly.com or asoftmurmur.com (apps also available)

- **Self-criticism.**

  Ask yourself, "Would I say these things to others?" Pay attention to the language you use toward yourself. Be kind to yourself and tell positive stories. Practice self-compassion and self-acceptance.

- **Mindset.**

  Ask yourself: "Is my thinking growth & process-focused or fixed & outcome-focused?" Don't strive for perfection; try your best to do better than yesterday.

- **Priorities.**

  Ask yourself: "Am I putting less-important things first?" Don't forget to take time for things that aren't urgent but are important to not feeling drained/frustrated. For example,

- **How others misuse your time.**

  Ask yourself: "Does it make more sense to say 'no'?" Protip: Don't stay up late to do something you wouldn't get up early to do.

- Your own perspective / bias.

Ask yourself: "How long has it been since my last reality check?" / "Would I pay myself for what I've done today?" / "What contribution have I made to my future today?"

- Your progress.

Ask yourself: Have I written down* the steps I need to take to reach my goal? Do I need to update them or change them based on what I've learned so far?

*The sooner you write down what you want and what you need to do to get it, the sooner your dreams will become goals and, eventually, reality. You must take action to make progress.

Understand the difference between a dream and a goal. We'll talk more about that next...

Goal-setting: How to Make Things Happen

Understand the difference between a dream and a goal.

> A **goal** is something you have to <u>plan</u> out and <u>work</u> toward to achieve.
> A **dream** is an <u>unplanned</u> goal.

To make things happen, structure your goals into small steps that make up an actionable plan, and then commit to it. It's not easy, but it gets easier once you learn what works for you. To do that, you must practice setting goals often and note what helps you achieve them.

A good goal is...

1. SPECIFIC, SMALL, & WITHIN YOUR CONTROL

Focus on what you can control: the process. We can't control the outcome in most events. We usually can't guarantee we'll win the game or get a certain grade on a test. We can control how we prepare for things.

2. WRITTEN DOWN & REWARD-DRIVEN

> Write down:
> - What you want
> - What exactly you need to do to get it
> - What you'll reward* yourself with for achieving it.
> > *(Tip: use the little things you crave throughout the day as micro-motivators to strengthen your discipline skills.*

3. PART OF YOUR BIGGER PICTURE

The smaller the steps you divide a project into, the better. We're more likely to start small tasks than big ones. <u>You</u> have to make it happen. Waiting & relying on others is putting luck in more control of your life than yourself. Feeling in-control makes our brains happy. Our minds are more likely to cooperate with us on reaching our goals if we work in a little practical psychology. We tend to see more progress when we feel like we have freedom of choice in matters relating to our lives and goals. What are some things you can control?

Step-by-step process to set a good goal:

Step 1:

Know what's required & when! Be clear on what's expected of you on homework or in-class assignments (especially writing exercises). Ask specific questions and clarify anything you don't understand. Take notes on what you learn. Enter deadlines in your planner or timeline checklist; work backwards from deadlines to design a plan of attack for big assignments. Cross off each checklist item as you complete it; it's encouraging to see progress toward your goal.

Step 2:

Choose what to work on* first & how to work on it. Break it down into smaller, more manageable tasks and keep track of them using a list or spreadsheet. Give yourself deadlines and actively work toward them.

> *Not sure what your goal should be? The obstacle is the way. Often the thing we find the most intimidating is a great thing to start breaking down into small, specific goals. Ask yourself what the biggest challenges you feel stand in your way of what you're trying to accomplish: getting to college.

Step 3:

Try what successful athletes and scholars do as part of the process of discovering what works for their unique skillset: keep what works; scrap what doesn't. Customize your effort to fit your style.

Comparisons

Others may come along and do something faster, better, differently than you ever could based on your set of experiences. Comparing yourself to them isn't fair to yourself or how it could result in you treating them. Learning from them instead, adapting their experiences to benefit you, results in growth. It's valuable to compare your present self to your past self. Have you grown in important ways? Are you able to handle your emotions in ways that result in you feeling good about yourself? Creating & prioritizing steps to making improvements in yourself that matter personally to you will result in you being able to better relate to and communicate with others around you. Looking at positives within ourselves creates a habit of seeing positives in those around us and in situations beyond our control. It creates a window for viewing life in a way that promotes good mental health and kindness.

"But I need to get _this_ score to get into _this_ school..."

Those are two outcome-based stories. Even if you get that score, it's not guaranteed you'll get into that school. Even if you get into that school, it's not going to only be due to your SAT score. Focusing on an outcome is a limiting (and often frustrating) way of thinking about goals. It closes your eyes to other opportunities that may be a better choice for you and can make you feel like a failure if everything doesn't go perfectly. Striving for perfection is exhausting. Making perfection your goal in everything is a way to burn out fast. Setting a focused, achievable goal (instead of striving for perfection) can help you direct your skills to develop deeper mastery in a certain area.

Anxiety-Reducing Techniques:
A Strategy Guide to Confidence

After reading this article you will be able to...

- ❏ *demonstrate understanding of what anxiety is*
- ❏ *use science-backed techniques to reduce anxiety and see a clear path to the answer*
- ❏ *make confident, informed choices about how to better learn academic concepts*
- ❏ *share your new knowledge to help others who suffer from anxiety*

Feeling Overwhelmed?

Try these simple, fast techniques when you feel anxious to feel calmer:

1. Choose two specific things to be grateful for.
   (Say to yourself, "I am grateful for...___ and ____ because they help me feel ___.")
2. Label your emotions.
   (Say to yourself, "I feel...frustrated, overloaded, numb, joyous, etc.")
3. Make a decision.
   (About anything. Just decide something and take some control. Say to yourself, "I'm going to...take a walk, text my friend. Then do that.)
4. Hug someone.
   (Our brains release oxytocin, a calm-inducing, bonding chemical when we give/receive good hugs, especially when they are longer than 20 seconds or so.)
5. Breathe meditatively.
   (5-second inhale, 5 second breath hold, 5 second exhale) (repeat)
6. Go outside and take a walk in nature. *(Even if only for a few minutes.)*
7. Listen to music.
8. Read a favorite book - a childhood throwback, maybe?
9. Do self-care activities (hair/skin/nail treatments, long showers, etc.)

How do you respond to pressure?

Knowing the answer to this question is not only important for a timed test like the dSAT but also for preparing to handle unexpected or challenging situations well in the future.

Know yourself and how you respond to pressure in different situations.

Classroom or academic pressure may feel different than gameday pressure. Know what to expect from yourself and prepare for it.

Here's a good way to start that process: Fill in the following blanks:

I feel under pressure when _____.

A recent time I felt pressure was _____,

and I responded by _____.

What is anxiety?

Most people report experiencing anxiety. Anxiety is very common, and feeling nervous about taking a test like the dSAT is a normal challenge to face with the knowledge that what you learn about yourself will be useful not only on the dSAT but also in everyday life.

Anxiety is a different story for each person, which involves a combination of physiologic factors and psychosomatic symptoms. In other words, anxiety may not look or feel exactly the same for all of us. The good news is that we can address anxiety using similar strategies because the symptoms are based in the same biologic processes.

In order to learn more about anxiety, for the rest of this chapter, despite this being the verbal companion book, we will deep dive math anxiety in particular; however, the concepts discussed can be applied more broadly to other categories of anxiety.

What is math anxiety?

Math anxiety is a particular subset of anxiety which prevents students from performing as well or as comfortably as they are capable on math assignments and tests.

How common is math anxiety?

Extremely common. Most of the adults I know have it; most of the students I know have it. I used to have it — bad. I was one of the students who internalized the idea that, "I'm just not good at math." Since learning that this negative, unhelpful idea wasn't true, I've heard it countless times in the classroom from students who were just like me.

"I'm just not good at math" really means, "I'm uncomfortable with math because I don't understand some key elements yet." The important word there is "yet." Not comprehending a certain topic in math simply means that a student hasn't heard that information in the correct way for their brain...yet. When it comes to learning, it's often just a matter of time and desire. A student has to want the knowledge badly enough to put in the time to figure out how to gain a better understanding—their way.

My particular way turned out to be a bit weird, but it helped me to understand the core of math anxiety from an insider's perspective. During the middle of my 8th grade school year, I moved from Orlando in central Florida to Jacksonville, up on the Atlantic coast up near the border with Georgia. Not too far distance-wise, but far enough for the school curriculum standards to be different. In Orlando, algebra was a 9th grade course. In Jacksonville, it was an 8th grade course. To get into high school on time in Jacksonville, I needed an algebra credit.

The solution was for me to take algebra online using a self-taught course program—during the summer before 9th grade began. Not what a recently-uprooted teenager wants to hear about summertime. Despite my initial resistance, teaching myself forced me to try to better understand what I needed to know, what I knew, and what I didn't even know I didn't know yet. The fact that it was summertime in Florida motivated me to be efficient in my efforts to get through the material. I wanted to play! So I made a plan and blocked out time so that I'd finish the course in a few weeks.

A week in, I was already so behind. The sudden appearance of letters as variables in my math problems was jarring, and I didn't understand my confusion well enough to articulate what I didn't get. This is such a common challenge for students, I've since come to realize. A big part of the battle of understanding difficult material is knowing what you need to know. Up to that point, my teachers had done a great job organizing and spacing out material for me. I'd never had to plan my learning schedule on my own before.

That I'd failed so miserably right from the get-go discouraged teenage me. For the next few hot summer weeks, I didn't make much progress and felt more and more frustrated with myself for not just "getting it" already. Not knowing any better, I was trying to brute-force my way to understanding by re-reading the same information and re-trying the problems I wasn't getting correct without much becoming clearer. I could do plenty of the step-by-step operations, but when given a real-world style word problem, I froze.

I didn't know what to do differently. Looking back, I can relate my experience to some key information I learned much later after leaving Florida and moving to northern regions of the US.

When someone falls through thin ice into freezing cold water, the body experiences what's called a "cold shock response." (It should really be called a reaction.) You may have experienced a mild version of this cold shock response by drinking something cold and getting a "brain freeze." This series of cardio-respiratory reactions is the most common way people succumb to icy water, but this frigid fate can be avoided by possessing the right knowledge beforehand. In this video, you'll learn how to save yourself in the event you find yourself on thin ice. After this video, I'll explain how it's connected to math. https://www.youtube.com/watch?v=0gd6QC2Emrc

Often, when students encounter a tough-looking problem, they experience a "freeze" response. The SAT and ACT exams for high school juniors and seniors are famous for disguising familiar concepts into confusing-seeming monsters.

In this moment of panic, anxiety often says, "Oh no, have I seen this before? Do I need to use all of this information? I don't know what that word means, and I'm running out of time! I don't know where to begin! What does this question want from me?"

This panic reaction is similar to what someone uninformed about the cold shock response may do: flail around in the cold water, wasting time and energy by panicking and moving too fast without understanding what needs to happen in that moment.

Even students who are stellar in math class can get stumped by intimidatingly long word problems, especially when they include a diagram. Not only are these questions lengthy, but the time it takes to interpret and solve them can be a good bit longer — and that isn't even counting the cold shock response time that must elapse before a path to the answer is clear.

What helps alleviate anxiety?

Jumping into the cold water often, in safe, risk-free circumstances. Similar to what we saw in the video, we can manage anxiety freezes by better understanding what our bodies are going through and allowing ourselves to relax. By doing this enough the relaxation becomes habitual, and your confidence increases as your anxiety starts to decrease. The more times you choose to encounter a difficult concept (and don't allow yourself to panic or get discouraged), the easier you're making life for your future self. Failing a lot usually means you're learning a lot. If you anticipate this and give yourself permission to make mistakes when it doesn't matter, you're much more likely to perform well when it does matter.

For academic test-taking, "jumping into the water" means taking as many practice tests as you can before you go in to sit for your real exam. It also means exposing yourself to sources of information about what is making you anxious. Talk to teachers, family, and friends about what you're studying. Use the results from your practice tests to guide your studies. If you don't know how to do that, seek out a tutor who can help you interpret them. Expert tutors are available to help students worldwide at www.learncurious.com/tutoring

If we expand our scope to any student experiencing anxiety (not just test-takers), the answer remains the same: develop a set of tools to fit the specific student that promote awareness and confidence. Create a study plan and develop strategies that will help fill in the conceptual grey areas and make you prouder of your grey matter. Others can help you by suggesting tools and providing you with resources or assistance, but you're the one who can really tell if it's clicking or not. Pay attention to what's happening when light bulb moments occur and to how you're solving problems. Learn how you learn!

If students understand the underlying reasons for their anxiety, it can vanish or show up much-reduced and more-manageable. With practice, results analysis, help from the community, students soon feel confidence and positivity where they once felt fear and dread. I know because I've lived it, and I've seen it often in the classroom.

What about math anxiety specifically? Any tools for that?

Seek information about new math concepts from as many sources as possible. LearnCurious' digital SAT math companion book is coming soon! The key is to receive the information a way your mind can interpret it well; the challenge is to find that way. It may happen the first time with some sources (bookmark those) or it may take listening to 20 less-helpful sources to find that 21st that leads you to the glorious light-bulb moment you seek.

I've said that the trouble with classroom learning is that when a teacher explains a topic, on a good day only maybe 80% of the students are on board with the given explanation. The other 20% are left feeling at least iffy on the subject, if not wholly confused. The 20%ers may feel like they "just don't get it" or even aren't "smart enough" to get it. This kind of feeling, if unaddressed, tends to compound when it comes to math. Many math concepts build upon each other, so if an early idea is unclear, it makes later ideas harder to learn.

To combat concept gaps and address math anxiety at its source, diagnostic screening and strategic conceptual assessment can be helpful for students of any age who would like to feel more confident in math.

My students are used to me reminding them when they're experiencing frustration that the SAT and ACT don't test your "math knowledge." They test your knowledge of what they test and how they test it. The SAT tests what the College Board deems representative of math skills and concepts, and these may differ greatly from the state standards or school curriculum guidelines in place at local schools. Many students go into the test without realizing this and succumb to their cold shock responses.

Getting SAT and ACT math questions correct is a matter of recognizing concepts when they've been cleverly and purposely disguised by the psychologists who design standardized tests. So you'll need to equip yourself with a psychological wet suit, so to speak (to keep the cold shock metaphor alive)

Here's a starter tool you can use to equip your wet suit: math vocab. Many students don't realize is that math, despite being separate from "verbal" parts on tests, includes SO MUCH VOCAB. Learning how to translate word problems is a wildly useful math skill. Many words have a direct mathematical equivalent. Here's a brief example:

"What is 175% of 29?"

"what" = x   *(substitute unknowns with variables)

"is" = equals   *("has" and "was" often mean equals, too)

175% = 1.75   *(conceptual knowledge of converting percents to decimals needed here)

"of" = multiply   *(one of the most-helpful math vocab terms; many wrongly think it means to divide)

29 = 29   *(numbers don't need translatin')

Put together, we get $x = (1.75)(29)$.

We've created a solvable equation from the given words, and in so doing we've also created a systematic path to the answer for percent word problems like this that we encounter in the future.

Now we can get to the answer confidently in seconds by solving the equation we created using math vocab translation:

$x = (1.75)(29)$

$x = 50.75$

Now let's ramp it up with a common type of "trick" question on the SAT and ACT, which is only a slight (but important!) variation on what we just translated.

29 is what percent of 175?

$29 = (x\%)(175)$

$x = 29/175$

$x = 0.166$
$x = 16.6\%$

Or, another similar version of this type of question may look like this:

175 is 29% of what value?

$175 = (0.29)(x)$

$175/0.29 = x$

$x = 603.45$

Despite these three questions using the same two numbers, they lead to different potential answers depending on the way the question is worded. These percent questions in particular are used to catch students off-guard, especially those who rely on mental math for speed. You can count on the most commonly-made error results to be an answer option on the SAT & ACT. Having a practiced system (like translating math vocabulary into a solvable equation) for solving these problems often leads to faster and more confident performance and improved results on tests.

If you spend your study time learning new solving strategies and testing them out to see if they work well for you, you're managing your study time efficiently. It may feel like it takes more time in the beginning — and it does! — because it's new. That's why starting early enough is important. You allow yourself the time it takes to adjust, figure out what you don't know, and design a system to learn it well.

Stray thoughts

Wet suits don't keep you dry. That's what a dry suit does. I learned this when I jumped into the water for the first time wearing a wet suit and was surprised when I got wet. Wet suits keep you warm.

For anyone curious, here's a non-animated demonstration of a cold shock response and self-rescue from icy water: https://www.youtube.com/watch?v=A3g-NTP6F3w

Appendices

Appendix A: Vocabulary

*Note: words in **bold** have already appeared more than once on currently-released official Digital SAT tests.*

ADJECTIVES

	Know it!	Need to study	Definition:	Synonym(s):	Example sentence(s):
abrupt					
acceptable					
advantageous					
aggressive					
appropriate					
approximate					
beneficial					
careful					
catastrophic					
common					
compelling					
complementary					
concealed					
concerning					
confident					
controversial					
critical					
deceptive					
decisive					
disconcerting					
disorienting					
disparate					

diverse					
dynamic					
dormant					
elusive					
evolving					
extensive					
fruitless					
haphazard					
healthy					
imminent					
indecipherable					
impartial					
impenetrable					
imperceptible					
important					
impractical					
inadequate					
indecipherable					
inexplicable					
infrequent					
innocuous					
inspirational					
interchangeable					
intricate					
intriguing					
inventive					
lacking					
latent					
legitimate					
localized					

mandatory					
mystifying					
novel					
nuanced					
obscure					
observant					
offhand					
operative					
ordinary					
ornamental					
peripheral					
persistent					
pragmatic					
predatory					
predetermined					
premeditated					
preventable					
recognizable					
replicable					
resilient					
restrained					
rudimentary					
satisfactory					
satisfying					
secretive					
simple					
skeptical					
significant					
struggling					
substantial					

tenuous					
undeniable					
unimportant					
unintended					
universal					
unobtrusive					
unknown					
unoriginal					
unpredictable					
useful					
variable					
widespread					

ADVERBS

	Know it!	Need to study	Definition:	Synonym(s):	Example sentence(s):
beneficially					
involuntarily					
smoothly					
strenuously					

IDIOMATIC PREPOSITION PHRASES
(verb + preposition pairs)

	Know it!	Need to study	Definition:	Synonym(s):	Example sentence(s):
adhere to					
ambivalence toward					

beneficiary of					
collected with					
comparable to					
concern about					
confined to					
conform to					
consistent with					
derived from					
distraction for					
enthusiasm for					
experiment with					
grapple with					
handmade from					
improve on					
independent of					
indicated by					
indifference to					
irrelevant to					
mastery over					
obtained from					
overshadowed by					
paucity of					
profusion of					
proponent of					
quarrel about					
react to					
recognized in					
renunciation of					
representative of					
represented by					

repressed by					
responsiveness to					
supplement to					
surpassed by					
surprise at					
verisimilitude in					

NOUNS

	Know it!	Need to study	Definition:	Synonym(s):	Example sentence(s):
hibernation					
moderation					
prediction					
synchronization					

VERBS

	Know it!	Need to study	Definition:	Synonym(s):	Example sentence(s):
accommodate					
acquired					
aggravate					
annotate					
acknowledged					
buttress					
challenged					
committed					
compose					

comprises					
concede					
conceptualize					
conditions					
contrived					
created					
deciding					
defends					
delegate					
demand					
deny					
deviate					
discourage					
disengage					
dispute					
diverge					
doubt					
eclipses					
encourages					
engulf					
enhance					
ensured					
establish					
evaluate					
exemplify					
explains					
fabricate					
foretell					
foster					
fulfill					

hinder					
illustrate					
imitated					
implement					
improvise					
inspecting					
interject					
interpret					
intersect					
invalidate					
mimic					
misrepresent					
neglect					
originates					
overcome					
overreact					
perceive					
persist					
predicted					
prescribe					
presume					
prevail					
proclaim					
produced					
provoke					
question					
rebuts					
recant					
receive					
reciprocate					

reflect					
refute					
regret					
relate					
remember					
renounce					
replenishes					
repudiates					
require					
restored					
retaliates					
selecting					
speculate					
succumb					
surmise					
tolerate					
underestimate					
underscore					
validate					
waive					
withdraw					
worry					

Appendix B: Practice Tests

Instructions:

Score Module 1 before deciding to complete Module 2a or Module 2b.

If your score is between 1 - 16 questions correct out of 27, you should complete Module 2a.

If you score between 17 - 27 out of 27 questions on Module 1, you should complete Module 2b.

- Score and scale your tests using the tables on pages 382-385.

Practice Test 1
Verbal Module 1 (VM1)

1.

Then Sun Tzŭ sent a messenger to the King saying: "Your soldiers, Sire, are now properly drilled and disciplined, and ready for your majesty's _____. They can be put to any use that their sovereign may desire; bid them go through fire and water, and they will not disobey."

Which choice completes the text with the most logical and precise word or phrase?

A) inspection
B) resentment
C) fabrication
D) overreaction

2.

"Side by side recordings of the effects of a medicine given simultaneously to a plant and an animal have shown astounding unanimity in result," he pointed out. "Everything in man has been <u>foreshadowed</u> in the plant. Experimentation on vegetation will contribute to lessening of human suffering."

As used in the text, what does the word "foreshadowed" most nearly mean?

A) hindered
B) predicted
C) enhanced
D) misrepresented

3.

The preparation of mantlets, movable shelters, and various <u>implements</u> of war, will take up three whole months.

As used in the text, what does the word "implements" most nearly mean?

A) provocations
B) commitments
C) fabrications
D) tools

4.

But Rajendra's little animal never permitted my oversized steed a moment's rest, even at the most perilous turns. On, on, untiringly came Rajendra's horse, oblivious to all but the joy of competition. Our <u>strenuous</u> race was rewarded by a breath-taking view. For the first time in this life, I gazed in all directions at sublime snow-capped Himalayas, lying tier upon tier like silhouettes of huge polar bears.

As used in the text, what does the word "strenuous" most nearly mean?

A) inventive
B) common
C) imperceptible
D) arduous

5.

Bride-favors, anciently called bride-lace, were at first pieces of gold, silk, or other lace, used to bind up the sprigs of rosemary formerly worn at weddings. <u>These took later the form of bunches of ribbons, which were at last metamorphosed into rosettes.</u>

Which choice best describes the function of the underlined portion in the text as a whole?

A) It provides examples of obsolete bride-favors that were replaced by 'bride-lace.'

B) It suggests that ribbons have remained the most popular choice for brides through the years.

C) It indicates that more brides of the past preferred rosettes to ribbons.

D) It shows the changes to traditional bride-favors over time.

6.

The following is adapted from Mark Twain's novel '*The Adventures of Tom Sawyer*," in which a young boy, Tom, experiences life in a small town along the Mississippi River.

Tom took up his brush and went tranquilly to work. Ben Rogers hove in sight presently—the very boy, of all boys, whose ridicule he had been dreading. Ben's gait was the hop-skip-and-jump — proof enough that his heart was light and his anticipations high. <u>He was eating an apple, and giving a long, melodious *whoop*, at intervals, followed by a deep-toned *ding-dong-dong, ding-dong-dong,* for he was personating [sic] a steamboat.</u>

Which choice best describes the function of the third sentence in the overall structure of the text?

A) It describes the actions of Ben Rogers as he approaches Tom Sawyer.
B) It explains why Tom doesn't want to whitewash the fence.
C) It describes the actions of Tom Sawyer as he approaches Ben Rogers.
D) It explains Ben's longtime fascination with steamboats.

7.
Amethyst is a very widely distributed mineral, but fine clear specimens fit for cutting as ornamental stones are confined to comparatively few localities. Such crystals occur either in cavities in mineral-veins and in granitic rocks, or as a lining in agate geodes.

What is the main idea of the text?

A) It gives details on the rarity, quality variation, and distribution of amethyst.

B) It describes the countries and geographic locations where amethyst is always found.

C) It provides evidence for amethyst appearing in more diverse locations than researchers had previously recorded.

D) It opposes a commonly-held idea and provides evidence to support the counterclaim.

8.
The following text is adapted from Lewis Carroll's *Alice in Wonderland*.

The Duchess said after a pause, "I'm doubtful about the temper of your flamingo. Shall I try the experiment?"
"He might bite," Alice cautiously replied, not feeling at all anxious to have the experiment tried.
"Very true," said the Duchess, "flamingos and mustard both bite. And the moral of that is—'Birds of a feather flock together.'"
"Only mustard isn't a bird," Alice remarked.
"Right, as usual," said the Duchess: "what a clear way you have of putting things!"
"It's a mineral, I think," said Alice.

Which choice best describes the overall structure of the text?

A) It emphasizes Alice's concern that the Duchess is growing more upset.
B) It details a conversation between Alice and the Duchess.
C) It critiques Alice's flamingo technique and then describes an argument with the Duchess.
D) It compares the flamingo technique of Alice to that of the Duchess.

9.

The following is adapted from William Butler Yeats's 1865 poem 'Where My Books Go.'

All the words that I utter,
  And all the words that I write,
Must spread out their wings untiring,
  And never rest in their flight,
Till they come where your sad, sad heart is,
  And sing to you in the night,
Beyond where the waters are moving,
  Storm-darken'd or starry bright.

Based on the text, where do the speaker's books go?

A) Into the homes and minds of his audience around the world

B) Into the stormy waters of the night

C) Into the hearts of those with untiring wings

D) Into the starry, bright night sky

10.
'On a Fly drinking out of his Cup' is a poem by William Oldys. The speaker draws a comparison between his life span and that of the fly.

Busy, curious, thirsty fly!
Drink with me and drink as I:
Freely welcome to my cup,
Couldst thou sip and sip it up:
Make the most of life you may,
Life is short and wears away.

Both alike are mine and thine
Hastening quick to their decline:
Thine 's a summer, mine 's no more,
Though repeated to threescore.
Threescore summers, when they're gone,
Will appear as short as one!

Which quotation from the poem most effectively illustrates the speaker's comparison?

A) "Drink with me and drink as I:
Freely welcome to my cup,"

B) "Make the most of life you may,
Life is short and wears away."

C) "Thine 's a summer, mine 's no more,
Though repeated to threescore."

D) "Threescore summers, when they're gone,
Will appear as short as one!"

11.

Name	Anagram
Bryan Waller Proctor	Barry Cornwall, poet*
Calvinus	Alcvinus
Dame Eleanor Davies	Never soe mad a ladie
Eleanor Audeley	Reveale, O Daniel
Francois Rabelais	Alcofribas Nasier
Henry Rogers	R. E. H. Greyson*

*It is to be noted that the two of these are impure anagrams, an ``r'' being left out in both cases.

An anagram is the result of rearranging the letters of a word or words in such a manner as to produce other words that possess meaning. The construction of anagrams is an amusement of great antiquity. The pseudonyms adopted by authors are often transposed forms, more or less exact, of their names; for example, _____.

Which choice most effectively uses data from the table to complete the example?

A) It is to be noted that the last two are impure anagrams, an ``r'' being left out in both cases.

B) Eleanor Audeley, wife of Sir John Davies, is said to have been brought before the High Commission in 1634 for extravagances, stimulated by the discovery that her name could be transposed to 'Reveale, O Daniel.'

C) Another species of anagram, called 'palindrome,' is a word or sentence which may be read backwards as well as forwards, letter by letter, while preserving the same meaning.

D) 'Calvinus' becomes 'Alcvinus;' ``Francois Rabelais' becomes 'Alcofribas Nasier;' 'Bryan Waller Proctor' becomes 'Barry Cornwall, poet;' 'Henry Rogers' becomes 'R. E. H. Greyson.'

12.

Navigable mileage (Alabama river)	2000 miles
Muscle shoals (in Tennessee river)	38 miles
Amount spent on removal of impediments (to river travel)	$12 million
Duration (of removal projects)	1870-1904; 34 years

The navigable mileage of the Alabama rivers is 2000 miles, but obstructions often prevent the formation of a continuous route, notably the ``Muscle Shoals'' of the Tennessee, extending from a point 10 m. below Decatur to Florence, a distance of 38 miles.

Which choice best describes data from the table that support the passage's claim that "obstructions often prevent the formation of a continuous route."

A) To remove or circumvent these impediments, and to improve the Mobile harbor, the United States government spent, between 1870 and 1904, approximately $12,000,000.

B) As the streams in the mineral region are not navigable, the railways are the carriers of its products.

C) Mobile, the only seaport of the state, has a channel 30 ft. deep, on which the national government spends large sums of money.

D) An increasing amount of Alabama cotton is sent to New Orleans for shipment, and Pensacola, Florida, receives much of the lumber.

13.

The following text is adapted from Lewis Carroll's *Alice in Wonderland*. Alice looked round, eager to see the Queen.

First came ten soldiers carrying clubs; these were all shaped like the three gardeners. Next, the ten courtiers: these were ornamented all over with diamonds, and walked two and two, as the soldiers did. After these came the royal children: they were all ornamented with hearts. Next came the guests, and among them Alice recognized the White Rabbit: it was talking in a hurried nervous manner. Then followed the Knave of Hearts, carrying the King's crown on a crimson velvet cushion; last of all this grand procession, came _____.

Which choice most logically completes the text?

A) oblong and flat, with their hands and feet at the corners.

B) the King and Queen of Hearts.

C) the little dears jumping merrily along hand in hand, in couples.

D) smiling at everything that was said, and went by without noticing her.

14.

The work of laying bricks or tiles as paving falls to the lot of the bricklayer. Paving formed of ordinary bricks laid flat or on their edges was once in general use, but is now almost abandoned in favor of floors of special tiles or cement paving, the latter being practically non-porous and therefore _____.

Which choice most logically completes the text?

A) cleaner and more sanitary.

B) have grooves worked on the face to assist drainage but afford worse footholds.

C) are placed on edge the concrete for external paving may be omitted and the bricks bedded in sand.

D) the side joints of the bricks are grouted in with lime or cement.

15.

The amethyst was used as a gem-stone by the ancient _____ was largely employed in antiquity for intaglios. Beads of amethyst are found in Anglo-Saxon graves in England.

Which choice completes the text so that it conforms to the conventions of standard English?

A) Egyptians, and
B) Egyptians; and
C) Egyptians and
D) Egyptians: and

16.

In time, the wheat-grains came to be cooked into thin dry biscuits, which were broken over the bride's head, as is the custom in Scotland today when an oatmeal cake _____ used. Every wedding guest had one at least, and the whole collection were thrown at the bride the instant she crossed the threshold.

Which choice completes the text so that it conforms to the conventions of standard English?

A) being
B) was
C) is
D) were

17.

Mosaic work is composed of small pieces of marble, stone, glass, or pottery, laid as paving or wall _____ some ornamental pattern or design.

Which choice completes the text so that it conforms to the conventions of standard English?

A) lining, usually in
B) lining usually in
C) lining; usually in
D) lining, usually, in

18.

For a considerable portion of its _____, their business interests being in the borough of Manhattan; hence, Brooklyn has been called the "city of homes" and the "dormitory of New York."

Which choice completes the text so that it conforms to the conventions of standard English?

A) inhabitants, Brooklyn is only a place of residence,

B) inhabitants, residences are available in Brooklyn,

C) inhabitants, a place of residence is found in Brooklyn,

D) inhabitants, the only place of residence is Brooklyn,

19.

The principal timber of commerce is the Douglas fir. The wood is tough and strong and highly valued for _____ as well as for building purposes.

Which choice completes the text so that it conforms to the conventions of standard English?

A) ship's spars

B) ships' spars

C) ships spars

D) ships' spar's

20.

Upon the death of Mrs Brontë her husband invited his _____ leave Penzance and to take up her residence with his family at Haworth. Miss Branwell accepted the trust and would seem to have watched over her nephew and five nieces with conscientious care.

Which choice completes the text so that it conforms to the conventions of standard English?

A) sister-in-law Elizabeth Branwell, to

B) sister-in-law Elizabeth Branwell to

C) sister-in-law, Elizabeth Branwell, to,

D) sister-in-law, Elizabeth Branwell, to

21.

_____. The western white spruce is also much employed for various purposes.

Which choice completes the text so that it conforms to the conventions of standard English?

A) Red or giant, cedar which rivals the Douglas fir in girth, is plentiful and is used for shingles, as well as for interior work.

B) Red, or giant cedar, which rivals the Douglas fir in girth, is plentiful, and is used for shingles as well as for interior work.

C) Red or giant cedar which rivals the Douglas fir in girth, is plentiful and is used for shingles as well as for interior work.

D) Red, or giant, cedar, which rivals the Douglas fir in girth, is plentiful and is used for shingles as well as for interior work.

22.

Several countries — Greenland and Mexico, _____ — contain in the soil much meteoric iron, often in masses so large as to baffle all attempts at removal. Blocks of this kind have been known to furnish the natives in their vicinity for many years with sources of workable iron.

Which choice completes the text with the most logical transition?

A) For this reason

B) For instance

C) Furthermore

D) Indeed

23.

Cottonmouths have been found on occasion when other snakes were inactive because of low temperatures, but minimal temperatures tolerated by this species are not known. The annual cycle of activity is dependent upon temperature and _____ varies from north to south.

Which choice completes the text with the most logical transition?

A) additionally

B) in comparison

C) in contrast

D) thus

24.
While researching a topic, a student took the following notes:

- But the glory of Agra, the most splendidly poetic building in the world, is the Taj Mahal, the mausoleum built in 1632 by the emperor Shah Jahan for the remains of his wife, Mumtaz Manal, in which he himself also also lies buried.

- The building is of white marble throughout, crowned with a great white dome in the centre, and with a smaller dome at each of its four corners.

- From the marble terrace which surrounds it rise four tall minarets of the same material, one at each corner.

- The Taj has been modeled and painted more frequently than any other building in the world, and the word pictures of it are numberless.

- The perfect symmetry of its exterior once seen can never be forgotten, nor the aerial grace of its domes, rising like marble bubbles into the azure sky.

The student wants to emphasize the beauty of the Taj Mahal to an audience already familiar with the Indian landmark. Which choice most effectively uses relevant information from the notes to accomplish this goal?

A) A white marble masterpiece, the Taj and its magnificent, symmetric domed minarets are unforgettable.

B) The building is of white marble throughout, crowned with a great white dome in the center, and with a smaller dome at each of its four corners.

C) Emperor Shah Jahan built a white marble masterpiece, the Taj Mahal, as a mausoleum for both his wife, Mumtaz Manal, and himself.

D) From the marble terrace which surrounds it rise four tall minarets of the same material, one at each corner.

25.

While researching a topic, a student took the following notes:

* Austin Edwin Abbey, an American painter, was born in Philadelphia, Pennsylvania, on the 1st of April 1852.

* He left the schools of the Pennsylvania Academy of Fine Arts at the age of nineteen to enter the art department of the publishing house of Harper & Brothers in New York.

* In company with such men as Howard Pyle, Charles Stanley Reinhart, Joseph Pennell and Alfred Parsons, he became very successful as an illustrator.

* In 1878 he was sent by the Harpers to England to gather material for illustrations of the poems of Robert Herrick.

* These, published in 1882, attracted much attention.

* They were followed by illustrations for Goldsmith's She Stoops to Conquer, for a volume of Old Songs, and for the comedies (and a few of the tragedies) of Shakespeare.

The student wants to present the significance of Abbey's illustrations of the poems of Robert Herrick to an audience unfamiliar with Austin Edwin Abbey.

A) Austin Edwin Abbey attracted much attention when he painted famous works based on the writings of Shakespeare.

B) Austin Edwin Abbey, an American painter, attracted much attention when his illustrations of the poems of Robert Herrick were published in 1882.

C) Austin Edwin Abbey attracted much attention when he left the schools of the Pennsylvania Academy of Fine Arts.

D) Austin Edwin Abbey, an American painter, attracted much attention when he entered the art department of the publishing house of Harper & Brothers in New York.

26.
While researching a topic, a student took the following notes:

- Some animals are wholly pigmented during the summer and autumn.

- Through the winter and spring, however, they are in the condition of extreme partial albinism and become almost complete albinos.

- In the case of the Norway hare, it has been stated that a general moult, including all the hairs and under fur, takes place and new white hairs are substituted.

- On the other hand, it has been stated that during the whole of the transformation in the fur no hairs fall from the animal, and it is attributed to an actual change in the color of the hair.

The student wants to contrast the theory of a general moult with the theory that creatures do not lose their hair while undergoing the transformation to the condition of extreme partial albinism. Which choice most effectively uses relevant information from the notes to accomplish this goal?

A) How the change from the autumnal to the winter condition takes place appears not to be definitely settled in all cases, and accurate observations are much to be desired.

B) The transformation known as extreme partial albinism is seen when the fur of creatures who live in snowy climates, such as the arctic fox, changes from pigmented to white.

C) Experts theorize that either a general moult takes place and new white hairs are substituted or that during the whole of the transformation in the fur no hairs fall from the animal, and it is attributed to an actual change in the color of the hair.

D) Such instances are found in the Scotch blue hare, in the Norway hare, in the North American hare, in the arctic fox, in the stoat and ermine, and among birds, in the ptarmigan, and some other species of Lagopus.

27.
While researching a topic, a student took the following notes:

* An anagram is the result of transposing the letters of a word or words in such a manner as to produce other words that possess meaning.

* The construction of anagrams is an amusement of great antiquity.

* Anagrams were known to the Greeks and also to the Romans, although the known Latin examples of words of more than one syllable are nearly all imperfect.

* They were popular throughout Europe during the middle ages and later, particularly in France, where a certain Thomas Billon was appointed ``anagrammatist to the king'' by Louis XIII.

* Dryden disdainfully called the pastime the ``torturing of one poor word ten thousand ways,'' but many men and women of note have found amusement in it.

The student wants to contrast the amusement of the ancients with the disdain of Dryden toward anagrams. Which choice most effectively uses relevant information from the notes to accomplish this goal?

A) Anagrams were known to the Greeks and also to the Romans, although the known Latin examples of words of more than one syllable are nearly all imperfect.

B) They were popular throughout Europe during the middle ages and later, particularly in France, where a certain Thomas Billon was appointed ``anagrammatist to the king'' by Louis XIII.

C) W. Camden defines ``Anagrammatisme'' as ``a dissolution of a name truly written into his letters, as his elements, and a new connection of it by artificial transposition, without addition, subtraction or change of any letter, into different words, making some perfect sence applyable to the person named.''

D) Dryden disdainfully called the pastime the ``torturing of one poor word ten thousand ways,'' but many men and women of note have found amusement in it.

END OF MODULE 1

Please check your answers on page 379 before proceeding past this page.

If you scored between 1 - 16 questions correct, please proceed to Verbal Module 2a, on page 286.

If you scored between 17 -27 questions correct, please proceed to Verbal Module 2b, on page 302.

If you choose to try both Verbal Module 2a and 2b, the more accurate score range for you will be that which is based on the score ranges detailed above.

So, if you score highly enough on Verbal Module 1 qualify for Module 2b, the score range you'd receive if you took Verbal Module 2a would not be representative of how the actual test would proceed.

To sum up, consider the Verbal Module that you don't qualify for as available extra practice, but the total score range information calculated from it won't reflect your skills or be a good predictor of an accurate Digital SAT score range.

Practice Test 1
Verbal Module 2a (VM2a)

1.

"Sir, how do you happen to come here?" I felt baffled resentment over his _____ presence. "Everything is mysterious today! Less than an hour ago I had just finished my bath in the Ganges when Swami Pranabananda approached me. I have no idea how he knew I was there at that time.

Which choice completes the text with the most logical and precise word or phrase?

A) diverse
B) legitimate
C) predatory
D) inexplicable

2.

The rising of birds in their flight is the sign of an ambuscade. Startled beasts _____ that a sudden attack is coming.

Which choice completes the text with the most logical and precise word or phrase?

A) tolerate
B) require
C) question
D) indicate

3.

"These exceptional stanzas cannot possibly be of aid in your Sanskrit test." The scholar dismissed them _____, but familiarity with that particular poem enabled me on the following day to pass the Sanskrit examination.

Which choice completes the text with the most logical and precise word or phrase?

A) interchangeably
B) carefully
C) unpredictably
D) skeptically

4.

Whatever the cause may be of each slight difference in the offspring from their parents — and a cause for each must exist — it is the steady accumulation, through natural selection, of such differences, when _____ the individual, that gives rise to all the more important modifications of structure, by which the innumerable beings on the face of this earth are enabled to struggle with each other, and the best adapted to survive.

Which choice completes the text with the most logical and precise word or phrase?

A) beneficial to
B) indifferent to
C) concerned about
D) surprised at

5.

Now let us suppose the mocking-thrush of Chatham Island to be blown to Charles Island, which has its own mocking-thrush: why should it succeed in establishing itself there?

As used in the text, what does the word "establishing" most nearly mean?

A) disputing
B) withdrawing
C) encouraging
D) instituting

6.

Residing in Paris during the spring and part of the summer of 18, I there became acquainted with a Monsieur C. Auguste Dupin. This young gentleman was of an excellent, indeed of an illustrious family, but, by a variety of untoward events, had been reduced to such poverty that the energy of his character _____ beneath it, and he ceased to bestir himself in the world, or to care for the retrieval of his fortunes.

Which choice completes the text with the most logical and precise word or phrase?

A) surpassed
B) succumbed
C) supplement
D) compare

7.

 He does not strive to ally himself with all and sundry, nor does he foster the power of other states. He carries out his own secret designs, keeping his antagonists in awe.

As used in the text, what does the word "foster" most nearly mean?

A) circumvent
B) promote
C) retaliate
D) reciprocate

8.

The following is adapted from Mark Twain's novel *The Adventures of Tom Sawyer*, in which a young boy, Tom, experiences life in a small town along the Mississippi River.

When they reached the haunted house there was something so weird and grisly about the dead silence that reigned there under the baking sun, and something so depressing about the loneliness and desolation of the place, that they were afraid, for a moment, to venture in.

According to the text, why was the silence significant?

A) It was normal in the busy neighborhood.

B) It was inviting and seemed to beckon them into the house.

C) It contributed to the eeriness of the house.

D) It was equally exciting and weird.

9.
The following is adapted from Frank L. Baum's novel *The Wonderful Wizard of Oz*, in which a young girl, Dorothy, is transported to a mysterious, colorful land called Oz where she faces a Wicked Witch.

Now the Wicked Witch had a great longing to have for her own the Silver Shoes which the girl always wore. Her bees and her crows and her wolves were lying in heaps and drying up, and she had used up all the power of the Golden Cap; but if she could only get hold of the Silver Shoes, they would give her more power than all the other things she had lost.

Which quotation from the story best illustrates the Wicked Witch's claim that the Silver shoes would give her power?

A) "The little girl, seeing she had lost one of her pretty shoes, grew angry, and said to the Witch, "Give me back my shoe!"

B) "I shall keep it, just the same," said the Witch, laughing at her, "and someday I shall get the other one from you, too."

C) "The wicked woman was greatly pleased with the success of her trick, for as long as she had one of the shoes she owned half the power of their charm.

D) "Didn't you know water would be the end of me?" asked the Witch, in a wailing, despairing voice.

10.

'The Rainbow' is a poem by William Wordsworth. The speaker claims he will feel the same level of delight as an old man as he did as a child upon seeing a rainbow.

My heart leaps up when I behold
A rainbow in the sky:
So was it when my life began;
So is it now I am a man;
So be it when I shall grow old,
    Or let me die!
The Child is father of the Man;
I could wish my days to be
Bound each to each by natural piety.

Which quotation from the poem most effectively illustrates the speaker's claim?

A) "My heart leaps up when I behold"

B) "So is it now I am a man;"

C) "So be it when I shall grow old,"

D) "Bound each to each by natural piety."

11.

The figures relating to temperature and precipitation are from a table prepared by Mr R.F. Stupart, director of the meteorological service. The station at Victoria may be taken as representing the conditions of the southern part of the coast of British Columbia, although the rainfall is much greater on exposed parts of the outer coast.

Location	Mean Temperature (in Fahrenheit)			Absolute Temperature		Rainfall (in inches)		
	Coldest Month	Warmest Month	Average Annual Temp.	Highest	Lowest	Wettest Month	Driest Month	Average Annual
Victoria	January 37.5°	July 60.3°	48.8°	90°	-1°	December 7.98	July .4	37.77
Agassiz	January 33.0°	Aug. 64.7°	48.9°	97°	-13°	December 9.43	July 1.55	66.85
Kamloops	January 24.2°	Aug. 68.5°	47.1°	101°	-27°	July 1.61	April .37	11.46
Port Simpson	January 34.9°	Aug. 56.9°	45.1°	88°	-10°	October 12.42	June 4.37	94.63

A researcher interprets the data and concludes that rainfall in Victoria _____ from December to July.

Which choice most effectively uses data from the table and text to complete the researcher's statement?

A) decreases

B) increases

C) stays the same

D) inclines

12.

Text 1

According to J. Vurtheim, the Amazons were of Greek origin: "all the Amazons were Dianas, as Diana herself was an Amazon." In works of art, combat between Amazons and Greeks is placed on the same level as and often associated with combat between Greeks and centaurs. Their occupation was hunting and war; their arms were the bow, spear, axe, and a half shield, nearly in the shape of a crescent, called a *pelta*.

Text 2

The history of Bohemia affords a parallel to the Greek Amazons. During the 8th century, a large band of women, under a certain Vlasta, carried on war against the duke of Bohemia and enslaved or put to death all men who fell into their hands. Additionally, the Spanish explorer Orellana asserted that he had come into conflict with fighting women in South America on the river Maranon. The existence of 'Amazons' (in the sense of fighting women) in the army of Dahomey is an undoubted fact, but they are said to have died out during the French protectorate.

Based on the texts, how would Vurtheim most likely respond to the claims made by Text 2 about non-Greek fighting women.

A) Vurtheim might suggest that the Greek Amazons were influenced by the groups of South American fighting women.

B) Vurtheim might suggest that since these other historic groups of fighting women were not Greek, then they were not Amazons.

C) Vurtheim might point out that the women described in Text 2 meet his definition and can be classified as Amazons.

D) Vurtheim might remind the author of Text 2 that reliefs from the frieze of the temple of Apollo at Bassae, vases, and sarcophagus reliefs all have been observed to feature depictions of Amazon women.

13.

The following is text is from William Dean Howells's 1837 poem 'Earliest Spring,' in which the speaker claims to perceive hints of springtime in the still-wintery month of March.

Tossing his mane of snows in wildest eddies and tangles,
  Lion-like March cometh in, hoarse, with tempestuous breath,
Through all the moaning chimneys, and 'thwart all the hollows and angles
  Round the shuddering house, threating of winter and death.

But in my heart I feel the life of the wood and the meadow
  Thrilling the pulses that own kindred with fibres that lift
Bud and blade to the sunward, within the inscrutable shadow,
  Deep in the oak's chill core, under the gathering drift.

Nay, to earth's life in mine some prescience, or dream, or desire
  (How shall I name it aright?) comes for a moment and goes—
Rapture of life ineffable, perfect—as if in the brier,
  Leafless there by my door, trembled a sense of the rose.

Which quotation from the poem most effectively illustrates the speaker's claim?

  A) "Lion-like March cometh in, hoarse, with tempestuous breath,"

  B) "Round the shuddering house, threating of winter and death."

  C) "But in my heart I feel the life of the wood and the meadow"

  D) "Rapture of life ineffable, perfect—as if in the brier,"

14.

Magnesia may replace lime to some extent in such marls, but the firing temperature must be higher when magnesia is present. Marls usually contract very little, if at all, in the burning, and generally produce a strong, square brick of fine texture and good color. When under-fired, marl bricks are very liable to disintegrate under the action of the weather, and great care must be exercised in burning them at a sufficiently high temperature.

According to the text, why was burning marl bricks at a sufficiently high temperature significant?

A) Burning marl bricks at a sufficiently high temperature ensures they will disintegrate.
B) Burning marl bricks at a sufficiently high temperature is important when magnesia is used to replace lime because otherwise the marl will contract excessively.
C) Burning marl bricks at a sufficiently high temperature is important in order to ensure that the bricks are not under-fired and fragile.
D) Burning marl bricks at a sufficiently high temperature is not required when magnesia is present.

15.

The color of the greater proportion of alpaca imported into the United Kingdom is black and brown, but there is also a fair proportion of white, gray, and fawn. It is customary to mix these colors together, thus _____.

Which choice most logically completes the text?

A) producing a curious ginger-colored yarn, which upon being dyed black in the piece takes a fuller and deeper shade than can be obtained by piece-dyeing a solid-colored wool.

B) the history of the manufacture of this wool into cloth is one of the romances of commerce.

C) alpaca is somewhat akin to hair, being very glossy, but its softness and fineness enable the spinner to produce satisfactory yarns with comparative ease.

D) alpaca yarn was spun in England for the first time about the year 1808. It does not appear to have made any headway, however, and alpaca wool was condemned as an unworkable material.

16.

Amber is extensively used for beads and other trivial ornaments, and for cigar-holders and the mouth-pieces of pipes. It is regarded by the Turks as specially valuable, inasmuch as it is said to be incapable of transmitting infection as the pipe passes from mouth to mouth. Thus, _____.

Which choice most logically completes the text?

A) The variety most valued in the East is the pale straw-coloured, slightly cloudy amber.

B) Divers have been employed to collect amber from the deeper waters.

C) Systematic dredging on a large scale was at one time carried on in the Kurisch-es Haff by the great amber merchants of Konigsberg.

D) Some of the best qualities are sent to Vienna for the manufacture of smoking appliances.

17.

The venture cost the sisters about £50 in all, but only two copies were sold. There were nineteen poems by _____ by Emily, and the same number by Anne. A consensus of criticism has accepted the fact that Emily's verse alone revealed true poetic genius.

Which choice completes the text so that it conforms to the conventions of standard English?

A) Charlotte twenty-one
B) Charlotte; twenty-one
C) Charlotte: twenty-one
D) Charlotte, twenty-one

18.
The *amanitas* include some of the most showy representatives of the *Agaricineae* or mushroom order of fungi. In the first stages of growth, _____ completely enveloped by an outer covering called the veil.

Which choice completes the text so that it conforms to the conventions of standard English?

A) it is
B) they are
C) they being
D) it was

19.
Much fine amethyst comes from Russia, especially from near Mursinka in the Ekaterinburg district, where it occurs in drusy cavities in granitic rocks. Many localities in India yield _____ is found also in Ceylon, chiefly as pebbles.

Which choice completes the text so that it conforms to the conventions of standard English?

A) amethyst; and it
B) amethyst; it
C) amethyst, it
D) amethyst it

20.
An immense variety of ornamental paving and walling tiles is now manufactured and used for lining sculleries, lavatories, bathrooms, provision shops. _____ to these uses, tiles are often used in the ornamentation of buildings, externally as well as internally.

Which choice completes the text so that it conforms to the conventions of standard English?

A) Besides, however, being put,
B) Besides being put
C) Besides, however being put
D) Besides however being put

21.

The crowning of the bride is still observed by the Russians and by the Calvinists of Holland and Switzerland. The wearing of orange blossoms is said to have started with the _____ regarded them as emblems of fecundity. It was introduced into Europe by the Crusaders.

Which choice completes the text so that it conforms to the conventions of standard English?

A) Saracens, who

B) Saracens who,

C) Saracens, whom

D) Saracens, whom,

22.

The haunts of the Indian buffalo are the grass-jungles near swamps, in which the grass exceeds 20 feet in height. Here the _____ covered pathways, in which they are completely concealed.

Which choice completes the text so that it conforms to the conventions of standard English?

A) buffaloes — like the Indian rhinoceros — form

B) buffaloes, like the Indian rhinoceros — form

C) buffaloes: like the Indian rhinoceros form

D) buffaloes — like, the Indian rhinoceros — from

23.

On Park Slope, immediately west of Prospect Park and St Mark's Avenue, in another part of the borough, are also attractive residential districts. The south shore of Brooklyn also has various summer pleasure resorts, of which Coney Island _____.

Which choice completes the text so that it conforms to the conventions of standard English?

A) is the more popular.
B) is the most popular.
C) is the much popular.
D) is the minor popular.

24.

Light travels at the tremendous speed of about 186,000 miles a second. It _____ takes only about a second and a quarter to come to us from the moon. It traverses the 93,000,000 of miles which separate us from the sun in about eight minutes.

Which choice completes the text with the most logical transition?

A) afterward
B) finally
C) instead
D) therefore

25.

On a former excursion I crossed the Lucia near its mouth, and I was surprised to observe how easily our horses, _____ not used to swimming, passed over a width of at least six hundred yards.

Which choice completes the text with the most logical transition?

A) although
B) hence
C) likewise
D) still

26.

He immediately raised his eyes to heaven, and with a pious appeal to the Deity, laid the monster dead at his feet. Such a prodigy was not likely to be passed over in the legends of the saints. _____ we find it recorded that a certain holy man going to a fountain in the desert suddenly beheld a basilisk.

Which choice completes the text with the most logical transition?

A) Accordingly
B) Increasingly
C) Nevertheless
D) Specifically

27.

While researching a topic, a student took the following notes:

- But the glory of Agra, the most splendidly poetic building in the world, is the Taj Mahal, the mausoleum built in 1632 by the emperor Shah Jahan for the remains of his favorite wife, Mumtaz Manal, in which he himself also also lies buried.

- The building is of white marble throughout, crowned with a great white dome in the centre, and with a smaller dome at each of its four corners.

- From the marble terrace which surrounds it rise four tall minarets of the same material, one at each corner.

- The Taj has been modeled and painted more frequently than any other building in the world, and the word pictures of it are numberless.

- The perfect symmetry of its exterior once seen can never be forgotten, nor the aerial grace of its domes, rising like marble bubbles into the azure sky.

The student wants to emphasize the purpose of the Taj Mahal to an audience already familiar with its appearance. Which choice most effectively uses relevant information from the notes to accomplish this goal?

A) The Taj Mahal, built by Emperor Shah Jahan in 1632, has been painted often and is one of the most-photographed buildings in the world.

B) The Taj Mahal, built by Emperor Shah Jahan in 1632, is constructed of white marble and boasts a large central dome.

C) The Taj Mahal, built by Emperor Shah Jahan in 1632, to honor his children with his wife, Mumtaz Manal.

D) The Taj Mahal, built by Emperor Shah Jahan in 1632, serves as a final resting place for both the Emperor and his wife, Mumtaz Manal.

Answers on page 379

Practice Test 1
Verbal Module 2b (VM2b)

1.

The physician stared at me incredulously. But he sought me out a fortnight later, with an apologetic air. "Dr. Roy has made a complete recovery!" he exclaimed. "It is the most amazing case in my experience. Never before have I seen a dying man show such an _____ comeback. Your guru must indeed be a healing prophet!"

Which choice completes the text with the most logical and precise word or phrase?

A) disconcerting
B) inexplicable
C) secretive
D) preventable

2.

This consideration led Sir George Cayley to think only of adapting a propeller to some machine having of itself an independent power of support—in a word, to a balloon; the idea, however, being _____, or original, with Sir George, only so far as regards the mode of its application to practice. He exhibited a model of his invention at the Polytechnic Institution.

Which choice completes the text with the most logical and precise word or phrase?

A) mystifying
B) novel
C) preventable
D) impenetrable

3.

Lord Byron was brought to trial for the murder before the House of Lords; and it appearing clearly that the duel was not _____, but fought at once, and in the heat of passion, he was found guilty of manslaughter only, and ordered to be discharged upon payment of his fees.

Which choice completes the text with the most logical and precise word or phrase?

A) tenuous
B) haphazard
C) premeditated
D) dynamic

4.

"I am fighting for nothing less than world peace," Gandhi has declared. Before the West dismisses Gandhi's program as one of an _____ dreamer, let it first reflect on a definition of Satyagraha by the Master of Galilee.

Which choice completes the text with the most logical and precise word or phrase?

A) concerning
B) ordinary
C) impractical
D) infrequent

5.

All payments were ordered to be made in paper, and between the 1st of February and the end of May, notes were _____ to the amount of upwards of 1500 millions of livres. But the alarm once sounded, no art could make the people feel the slightest confidence in paper which was not exchangeable into metal.

Which choice completes the text with the most logical and precise word or phrase?

A) fabricated
B) delegated
C) demanded
D) speculated

6.

The following is adapted from Frank L. Baum's novel 'The Wonderful Wizard of Oz,' in which a young girl, Dorothy, is transported to a mysterious, colorful land called Oz where she meets a Scarecrow who says he has no brain.

When Dorothy awoke, the sun was shining through the trees and Toto had long been out chasing birds around him and squirrels. She sat up and looked around her. There was the Scarecrow, still standing patiently in his corner, waiting for her.

"We must go and search for water," she said to him.

"Why do you want water?" he asked.

"To wash my face clean after the dust of the road, and to drink, so the dry bread will not stick in my throat."

"It must be inconvenient to be made of flesh," said the Scarecrow thoughtfully, "for you must sleep, and eat and drink. However, you have brains, and it is worth a lot of bother to be able to think properly."

Which choice best describes the function of the underlined sentence in the text as a whole?

A) To indicate that Dorothy is concerned that the Scarecrow not only doesn't have a brain but also seems to not need to wash, eat, or sleep.

B) To describe a human problem that Dorothy faces that is solved by the Scarecrow.

C) To examine the perspective of the Scarecrow with regard to human needs relative to the challenges he faces by believing he doesn't have brains.

D) To compare the perspectives of Dorothy and the Scarecrow with regard to human basic needs.

7.

Formerly, groomsmen and bridesmaids had important duties. The men were called bride-knights and represented a survival of the primitive days of marriage by capture, when a man called his friends in to assist to "lift" the bride.

Which finding, if true, would most directly support the author's claim that bridesmaids had important duties?

A) Bridesmaids were usual in Saxon England.

B) The making of the bridal wreath, the decoration of the tables for the wedding feast, the dressing of the bride, were among [the senior bridesmaid's] special tasks.

C) In the same way the senior groomsman (the best man) was the personal attendant of the husband.

D) These were called bidding-weddings, or bid-ales, which were in the nature of "benefit" feasts.

8.

Near Fernando Noronha, the sea gave out light in flashes. The appearance was very similar to that which might be expected from a large fish moving rapidly through a luminous fluid.

Which choice best states the main idea of the text?

A) It describes a natural oceanic phenomenon that occurs near Fernando Noronha.

B) It summarizes a study conducted in order to assess luminous fluid.

C) It introduces a theory of phosphorescence.

D) It compares theories about the causes of an observed phenomenon in Fernando Noronha.

9.

The following text is adapted from Lewis Carroll's *Alice in Wonderland*.

The Duchess said after a pause, "I'm doubtful about the temper of your flamingo. Shall I try the experiment?"

"He might bite," Alice cautiously replied, not feeling at all anxious to have the experiment tried.

"Very true," said the Duchess, "flamingos and mustard both bite. And the moral of that is—'Birds of a feather flock together.'"

"Only mustard isn't a bird," Alice remarked.

"Right, as usual," said the Duchess: "what a clear way you have of putting things!"

"It's a mineral, I think," said Alice.

Which quotation most effectively illustrates Alice's claim that mustard is a mineral?

A) "I think I should understand that better," Alice said very politely, "if I had it written down: but I can't quite follow it as you say it."

B) "There's a large mustard-mine near here."

C) "And the moral of that is—'The more there is of mine, the less there is of yours.'"

D) "Oh, I know!" exclaimed Alice, "it's a vegetable. It doesn't look like one, but it is."

10.

The figures relating to temperature and precipitation are from a table prepared by Mr R.F. Stupart, director of the meteorological service. The station at Victoria may be taken as representing the conditions of the southern part of the coast of British Columbia, although the rainfall is much greater on exposed parts of the outer coast.

Location	Mean Temperature (in Fahrenheit)			Absolute Temperature		Rainfall (in inches)		
	Coldest Month	Warmest Month	Average Annual Temp.	Highest	Lowest	Wettest Month	Driest Month	Average Annual
Victoria	January 37.5°	July 60.3°	48.8°	90°	-1°	December 7.98	July .4	37.77
Agassiz	January 33.0°	Aug. 64.7°	48.9°	97°	-13°	December 9.43	July 1.55	66.85
Kamloops	January 24.2°	Aug. 68.5°	47.1°	101°	-27°	July 1.61	April .37	11.46
Port Simpson	January 34.9°	Aug. 56.9°	45.1°	88°	-10°	October 12.42	June 4.37	94.63

A researcher interprets the data and concludes that _____.

A) the highest annual temperature in Agassiz is lower than the highest annual temperature in Victoria, while the average driest month in Agassiz is drier than the driest month in Kamloops.

B) the highest annual temperature in Port Simpson is lower than the highest annual temperature in Victoria, while the average driest month in Agassiz is drier than the driest month in Kamloops.

C) the highest annual temperature in Kamloops is higher than the highest annual temperature in Port Simpson, while the average driest month in Agassiz is drier than the driest month in Port Simpson.

D) the highest annual temperature in Victoria is higher than the highest annual temperature in Port Simpson, while the average driest month in Agassiz is drier than the driest month in Kamloops.

11.

Navigable mileage (Alabama river)	2000 miles
Muscle shoals (in Tennessee river)	38 miles
Amount spent on removal of impediments (to river travel)	$12 million
Duration (of removal projects)	1870-1904; 34 years

The navigable mileage of the Alabama rivers is 2000 miles, but obstructions often prevent the formation of a continuous route, notably the ``Muscle Shoals" of the Tennessee, extending from a point 10 m. below Decatur to Florence, a distance of 38 miles.

Which choice best describes data from the table that undermine the passage's claim about the navigable mileage of the Alabama rivers.

A) To remove or circumvent these impediments, and to improve the Mobile harbor, the United States government spent, between 1870 and 1904, approximately $12,000,000.

B) As the streams in the mineral region are not navigable, the railways are the carriers of its products.

C) The navigable mileage of the Alabama rivers is actually 2500 miles, and, to remove impediments, the United States government spent $18,000,000.

D) An increasing amount of Alabama cotton is sent to New Orleans for shipment, and Pensacola, Florida, receives much of the lumber.

12.

The day was hot and apparently calm; however, if we look either at the shadow of any object in the distance or at a distant landmark over a level plain on a hot day, the effect of an ascending current of heated air is almost always evident.

Which choice best describes the overall structure of the text?

A) It makes a general observation and then contrasts it with information about atmospheric air movement.

B) It provides detail about how the air in these currents sometimes appears to shimmer.

C) It draws a similarity between the fine lines projected from a spider's spinners and rays of light.

D) It specifies a reason why spiders are able to fly through the air.

13.

The literary life [of the Brontë family], however, opened bravely for the three girls during those years. In 1846, a volume of verse appeared from the shop of Aylott & Jones of Paternoster Row: "Poems, by Currer, Ellis, and Acton Bell," was on the title-page. These names disguised the identity of Charlotte, Emily and Anne Brontë.

Based on the text, what is the significance of the names Currer, Ellis, and Acton Bell?

A) The names were recommended by the shop Aylott & Jones in order to promote the Brontë sisters' surname's familiarity.

B) The names served as pennames that hid the true identities of the Brontë sisters as the authors of their work.

C) The names indicated a means of deception used by the Brontë sisters in order to hide from their enemies.

D) The names belong to the three authors with whom the Brontë sisters competed most in the 1840s.

14.

Buffaloes are heavily built oxen, with sparsely haired skin, large ears, long, tufted tails, broad muzzles and massive angulated horns. In the Cape buffalo, *Bos (Bubalus) caffer,* the horns do not attain an excessive length, but in old bulls are so expanded and thickened at the base as to form a helmet-like mass protecting the whole forehead.

According to the text, why is the thickening of the base of older buffaloes' horns significant?

A) It serves as a harder surface so that male buffaloes do more damage to opponents.

B) It provides more protection for the buffaloes' foreheads.

C) It is a genetic mutation that prevents the horns from growing longer.

D) It is currently theorized that buffaloes' thick horn base helps form the anatomic structure that allows for such a broad muzzle.

15.

The amanitas include some of the most showy representatives of the *Agaricineae* or 'mushroom' order of fungi. They are beautiful objects in the autumn woods. _____.

Which choice most logically completes the text?

A) In the first stages of growth, they are completely enveloped by an outer covering called the veil.

B) *Amanita muscaria,* the fly fungus, formerly known as *Agaricus muscarius,* is especially remarkable by its bright red cap covered with white warts.

C) There are sixteen British species of Amanita.

D) They grow on the ground in or near woods. Several of the species are very poisonous.

16.
Amethyst is a violet or purple variety of quartz often used as an ornamental stone. The name is generally said to be derived from the Greek *a*, "not," and *methbskein*, "to intoxicate," expressing the old belief that the stone protected its owner from strong drink. Thus, some believed that _____.

Which choice most logically completes the text?

A) wine drunk out of a cup of amethyst would not intoxicate.

B) the word 'amethyst' is probably be a corruption of an Eastern name for the stone.

C) The color purple is soothing to those with a hangover.

D) Amethyst protected its owner from the effects of snake venom.

17.
The first brick buildings in America were erected on Manhattan Island in the year 1633 by a governor of the Dutch West India Company. These bricks were made in Holland, where the industry had long reached great _____ many years bricks were imported into America from Holland and from England.

Which choice completes the text so that it conforms to the conventions of standard English?

A) excellence; for

B) Excellence. And

C) excellence; and for

D) Excellence, for

18.

The removal of limestone pebbles from the clay is of great importance, as during the firing they would be converted into quicklime, which has a tendency to shatter the brick on exposure to the weather. As before stated, these marls (which usually contain from 15 to 30% of calcium carbonate) burn to a yellow color which is quite _____.

Which choice completes the text so that it conforms to the conventions of standard English?

A) distinctive, although in some cases where the percentage of limestone is very high over 40%, the color is grey or a very pale buff.

B) distinctive, although in some cases, where the percentage of limestone is very high, over 40%, the color is grey or a very pale buff.

C) distinctive, although in some cases where the percentage of limestone is very high over 40% the color is grey or a very pale buff.

D) distinctive; although in some cases, where the percentage of limestone is very high, over 40%, the color is grey or a very pale buff.

19.

Small fragments, formerly thrown away or used only for varnish, are now utilized on a large scale in the formation of ``ambroid'' or ``pressed amber.'' _____.
This pressed amber yields brilliant interference colors in polarized light.

Which choice completes the text so that it conforms to the conventions of standard English?

A) The pieces are carefully heated with exclusion of air and then compressed into a uniform mass by intense hydraulic pressure; the softened amber is then forced through holes in a metal plate.

B) The pieces are carefully heated with exclusion of air and then compressed into a uniform mass by intense hydraulic pressure and softened amber is then forced through holes in a metal plate.

C) The pieces are carefully heated with exclusion of air and then compressed into a uniform mass by intense hydraulic pressure; the softened amber had been forced through holes in a metal plate.

D) The pieces are carefully heated with exclusion of air and then compressed into a uniform mass by intense hydraulic pressure — the softened amber being forced — through holes in a metal plate.

20.

Rolled pieces of amber, usually small but occasionally of very large size, may be picked up on the east coast of England, having probably been washed up from deposits under the North Sea. Cromer is the best-known locality, but it occurs also on other parts of the Norfolk coast, as well as at Yarmouth, Southwold, Aldeburgh and Felixstowe in Suffolk, and as far south as Walton-on-the-Naze in Essex, and northward it is <u>not unknown</u> in Yorkshire.

Which choice completes the text so that it conforms to the conventions of standard English?

A) Not known
B) Not familiar
C) not unknown
D) Unfamiliar

21.

Abano was found guilty, however, and his body was ordered to be exhumed and burned, but a friend had secretly removed <u>it, and the Inquisition had, therefore,</u> to content itself with the public proclamation of its sentence and the burning of Abano in effigy.

Which choice completes the text so that it conforms to the conventions of standard English?

A) it and the Inquisition had, therefore,

B) it, and the Inquisition had, therefore,

C) it, and the Inquisition had therefore

D) it and the Inquisition had therefore

22.

The province is rich in forest _____ there is a steady demand for its lumber in the other parts of Canada as well as in South America, Africa, Australia and China.

Which choice completes the text so that it conforms to the conventions of standard English?

A) growth, and
B) growth and
C) growth: and
D) growth, and,

23.

_____. Subway lines, begun in 1904, connect Brooklyn with the subway system of Manhattan.

Which choice completes the text so that it conforms to the conventions of standard English?

A) Brooklyn is served directly by the Long Island Railway; by about fifty regular coast-wise and trans-Atlantic steamship lines; and by elevated or surface car lines on a large number of its streets.

B) Brooklyn is served directly by the Long Island Railway — by about fifty regular coast-wise and trans-Atlantic steamship lines; and by elevated or surface car lines on a large number of its streets.

C) Brooklyn is served directly by the Long Island Railway, by about fifty regular coast-wise and trans-Atlantic steamship lines; and by elevated or surface car lines on a large number of its streets.

D) Brooklyn is served directly by the Long Island Railway; by about fifty regular coast-wise and trans-Atlantic steamship lines and by elevated or surface car lines on a large number of its streets.

24.

Abraxas, a word engraved on certain antique stones, called on that account Abraxas stones, which were used as amulets or charms. The Basilidians, a Gnostic sect, attached importance to the word, if, _____, they did not bring it into use.

Which choice completes the text with the most logical transition?

A) hence
B) however
C) indeed
D) when

25.

His hair was sea-green, and trailed behind him on the water; his shoulders grew broad, and what had been thighs and legs assumed the form of a fish's tail. The sea-gods complimented him on the change of his appearance, _____ he himself was pleased with his looks.

Which choice completes the text with the most logical transition?

A) and
B) but
C) instead
D) previously

26.

While researching a topic, a student took the following notes:

- The Amazons are a legendary nation of female warriors, who were ruled by a Queen.

- No men were permitted to reside in their country, but once a year, in order to prevent their race from dying out, they visited the Gargareans, a neighbouring tribe.

- It is said that their right breast was cut off or burnt out, in order that they might be able to use the bow more freely; hence the ancient derivation of 'Amaxones from mafos, ``without breast.''

- But there is no indication of this practice in works of art, in which the Amazons are always represented with both breasts, although the right is frequently covered.

- maza, a Circassian word said to signify ``moon,'' has suggested their connexion with the worship of a moon- goddess, perhaps the Asiatic representative of Artemis.

The student wants to briefly introduce the Amazons to an audience unfamiliar with their cultural norms. Which choice most effectively uses relevant information from the notes to accomplish this goal?

A) It is said that their right breast was cut off or burnt out, in order that they might be able to use the bow more freely; hence the ancient derivation of 'Amaxones from mafos, ``without breast.''

B) The Amazons are a legendary nation of warriors who formed an independent kingdom; their capital was Themiscyra on the banks of the river Thermodon.

C) The Amazons are a legendary nation of female warriors who formed an independent kingdom under the government of a queen, and no men were permitted to reside in their country.

D) maza, a Circassian word said to signify ``moon,'' has suggested their connexion with the worship of a moon- goddess, perhaps the Asiatic representative of Artemis.

27.
While researching a topic, a student took the following notes:

- This experiment shows that a block of ice may be pressed into any mold just like a piece of wax. After pressure is applied, the mass is taken out, and it forms a compact coherent cylinder of tolerably clear ice, which has a perfectly sharp edge, and is an accurate copy of the mold.

- It might be thought that such a block had, by the pressure in the interior, been first reduced to powder so fine that it readily penetrated every crevice of the mold, and then that this powdered ice, like snow, was again combined by freezing.

- Yet the mere aspect of the cylinders pressed from blocks of ice shows us that the it has not been formed in this manner; for they are generally clearer than ice which is produced from snow, and the individual larger pieces of ice which have been used to produce them are recognized.

The student wants to summarize a theory behind why the ice takes the shape of the mold and then offer a piece of contrasting evidence. Which choice most effectively uses relevant information from the notes to accomplish this goal?

A) The cylinder is then seen to consist of alternate layers of clear and opaque ice, the former arising from the pieces of ice, and the latter from the snow.

B) This is most beautiful when clear pieces of ice are laid in the form and the rest of the space stuffed full of snow.

C) After pressure is applied, the mass is taken out, and it forms a compact coherent cylinder of tolerably clear ice, which has a perfectly sharp edge, and is an accurate copy of the mold. While the press is being worked, a continual creaking and cracking is heard in the interior of the mold.

D) Some posit that the pressure in the mold first reduces the ice to powder so fine that it readily penetrates every crevice of the mold, and then that this snow-like ice is again combined by freezing. Others suggest that the ice block has not been formed in this manner, as the individual larger pieces of ice which have been used to produce them are still visible in the resulting block.

Answers on page 379

Practice
Test 2

Practice Test 2
Verbal Module 1 (VM1)

1.

"High Ground," says Mei Yao-ch'en, "is not only more agreeable and salubrious, but more convenient from a military point of view; low ground is not only damp and unhealthy, but also _____ for fighting."

Which choice completes the text with the most logical and precise word or phrase?

A) satisfactory
B) universal
C) disadvantageous
D) pragmatic

2.

This discovery was therefore seized upon by the Columbia workers as a means for taking slow motion pictures of the passage of the electrical impulses in nerves. The nitella plant thus may become a sort of Rosetta stone for <u>deciphering</u> the closely guarded secrets close to the very borderland of mind and matter.

As used in the text, what does the word "deciphering" most nearly mean?

A) discerning
B) illustrating
C) defending
D) selecting

3.

A large part of the art of instruction lies in making the difficulty of new problems large enough to challenge thought, and small enough so that, in addition to the confusion naturally attending the _____ elements, there shall be luminous familiar spots from which helpful suggestions may spring.

Which choice completes the text with the most logical and precise word or phrase?

A) novel
B) unimportant
C) lacking
D) dormant

4.

I had three pieces of limestone on my desk, but I was terrified to find that they _____ to be dusted daily, when the furniture of my mind was all undusted still, and I threw them out the window in disgust. How, then, could I have a furnished house? I would rather sit in the open air, for no dust gathers on the grass, unless where man has broken ground.

Which choice completes the text with the most logical and precise word or phrase?

A) required
B) presumed
C) prevailed
D) remembered

5.

The name Alhambra, signifying in Arabic ``the red,'' is probably derived from the color of the sun-dried *tapia,* or bricks made of fine gravel and clay, of which the outer walls are built. Some authorities, however, hold that it commemorates the red flare of the torches by whose light the work of construction was carried on nightly for many years; others associate it with the name of the founder, Mahomet Ibn Al Ahmar; others derive it from the Arabic *Dar al Amra,* ``House of the Master.''

Which choice best describes the function of the underlined portion in the text as a whole?

A) It introduces an alternate theory about the meaning and origin of the name Alhambra.

B) It lists theories about the meaning and origin of the name Alhambra.

C) It indicates a possible connection between the name Alhambra and the name of its founder, Mahomet Ibn Al Ahmar.

D) It suggests that the meaning of the word Alhambra could be from the Arabic for 'House of the Master.'

6.

The following is adapted from Mark Twain's novel 'The Adventures of Tom Sawyer," in which a young boy, Tom, experiences life in a small town along the Mississippi River.

Tom appeared on the sidewalk with a bucket of whitewash and a long-handled brush. He surveyed the fence, and all gladness left him and a deep melancholy settled down upon his spirit. Thirty yards of board fence nine feet high. Life to him seemed hollow, and existence but a burden.

Which choice best describes the function of the fourth sentence in the overall structure of the text?

A) It reiterates the joy Tom felt upon seeing the fence.

B) It underscores the painful memories associated with the paintbrush.

C) It creates a clear image for the reader of the dimensions and appearance of the fence that Tom saw.

D) It emphasizes a statement made earlier in the passage about Tom's attitude toward painting the fence.

7.

Amethyst is a very widely distributed mineral, but fine clear specimens fit for cutting as ornamental stones are confined to comparatively few localities. Such crystals occur either in cavities in mineral-veins and in granitic rocks, or as a lining in agate geodes.

What is the main idea of the text?

A) It gives details on the rarity, quality variation, and distribution of amethyst.
B) It describes the countries and geographic locations where amethyst is always found.
C) It provides evidence for amethyst appearing in more diverse locations than researchers had previously recorded.
D) It opposes a commonly-held idea and provides evidence to support the counterclaim.

8.
The following is adapted from Frank L. Baum's novel '*The Wonderful Wizard of Oz*,' in which a young girl, Dorothy, is transported to a mysterious, colorful land called Oz where she travels to The Emerald City.

The Guardian of the Gates found a pair of glasses that would just fit Dorothy and put them over her eyes. There were two golden bands fastened to them that passed around the back of her head, where they were locked together by a little key that was at the end of a chain the Guardian of the Gates wore around his neck. When they were on, Dorothy could not take them off had she wished, but of course she did not wish to be blinded by the glare of the Emerald City, so she said nothing.

Which choice best states the main idea of the text?

A) It reiterates the danger of sleeping in the giant field of poppies.
B) It informs the reader why Dorothy refused to wear her glasses.
C) It describes the glasses given to Dorothy that are worn by all in Emerald City.
D) It indicates that Dorothy's glasses cannot be removed.

9.

The following text is from the 1900 poem 'As I Watch'd the Ploughman Plough-ing' by Walt Whitman.

As I watch'd the ploughman ploughing,
Or the sower sowing in the fields—or the harvester harvesting,
I saw there too, O life and death, your analogies:
(Life, life is the tillage, and Death is the harvest according.)

Based on the text, in what way is life like tillage?

A) Whitman compares ploughing to sowing in order to elaborate on important aspects of farm life.

B) Whitman likens life to tillage to demonstrate how he sees an analogy between growth and life as well as between harvest and death.

C) Whitman observes similarities in tillage and harvest that he finds unimportant.

D) Whitman suggests that there is only a coincidental relationship between farm work and death.

10.

The following is text is from William Dean Howells's 1837 poem "Earliest Spring" in which the speaker claims to perceive hints of springtime in the still-wintery month of March.

Tossing his mane of snows in wildest eddies and tangles,
  Lion-like March cometh in, hoarse, with tempestuous breath,
Through all the moaning chimneys, and 'thwart all the hollows and angles
  Round the shuddering house, threating of winter and death.

But in my heart I feel the life of the wood and the meadow
  Thrilling the pulses that own kindred with fibres that lift
Bud and blade to the sunward, within the inscrutable shadow,
  Deep in the oak's chill core, under the gathering drift.

Nay, to earth's life in mine some prescience, or dream, or desire
  (How shall I name it aright?) comes for a moment and goes—
Rapture of life ineffable, perfect—as if in the brier,
  Leafless there by my door, trembled a sense of the rose.

Which quotation from "Earliest Spring" most effectively illustrates the speaker's claim?

A) "Through all the moaning chimneys, and 'thwart all the hollows and angles"

B) "Thrilling the pulses that own kindred with fibres that lift"

C) "Deep in the oak's chill core, under the gathering drift."

D) "Leafless there by my door, trembled a sense of the rose."

11.

Text 1

According to J. Vurtheim, the Amazons were of Greek origin: "all the Amazons were Dianas, as Diana herself was an Amazon." In works of art, combat between Amazons and Greeks is placed on the same level as and often associated with combat between Greeks and centaurs. Their occupation was hunting and war; their arms were the bow, spear, axe, and a half shield, nearly in the shape of a crescent, called a *pelta*.

Text 2

The history of Bohemia affords a parallel to the Greek Amazons. During the 8th century, a large band of women, under a certain Vlasta, carried on war against the duke of Bohemia and enslaved or put to death all men who fell into their hands. Additionally, the Spanish explorer Orellana asserted that he had come into conflict with fighting women in South America on the river Maranon. The existence of 'Amazons' (in the sense of fighting women) in the army of Dahomey is an undoubted fact, but they are said to have died out during the French protectorate.

Based on the texts, how would the author of Text 2 most likely respond to the claims made by the author of Text 1?

A) The author of Text 2 might point out that groups of fighting women have been documented in history not just in Greece but all around the world.

B) The author of Text 2 would perhaps remind the author of Text 1 that there was a battle between Theseus and the Amazons.

C) The author of Text 2 would perhaps accept that the battle between Theseus and the Amazons is a favorite subject on the friezes of temples.

D) The author of Text 2 would perhaps agree that Greek Amazons were heavily influenced by the groups of South American fighting women.

12.

Name	Anagram
Bryan Waller Proctor	Barry Cornwall, poet*
Calvinus	Alcvinus
Dame Eleanor Davies	Never soe mad a ladie
Eleanor Audeley	Reveale, O Daniel
Francois Rabelais	Alcofribas Nasier
Henry Rogers	R. E. H. Greyson*

It is to be noted that the two of these are impure anagrams, an ``r'' being left out in both cases.

An anagram is the result of transposing the letters of a word or words in such a manner as to produce other words that possess meaning. An anagram is considered to be impure if any letters are left out from the original word or phrase. For example, _____.

Which choice most effectively uses information from the table to complete the example?

A) Henry Rogers' pseudonym becomes 'Barry Cornwall, poet.'

B) Eleanor Audeley, wife of Sir John Davies, is said to have been brought before the High Commission in 1634 for extravagances.

C) A palindrome, which is a word or sentence which may be read backwards as well as forwards while preserving the same meaning.

D) The pseudonyms adopted by authors are often transposed forms, more or less exact, of their names.

13.
The following is adapted from Frank L. Baum's novel '*The Wonderful Wizard of Oz*,' in which a young girl, Dorothy, is transported by a cyclone from her home in rural Kansas to a mysterious, colorful land called Oz.

The little girl gave a cry of amazement and looked about her, her eyes growing bigger and bigger at the wonderful sights she saw. The cyclone had set the house down very gently — for a cyclone — in the midst of a country of marvelous beauty. There were lovely patches of greensward all about, with stately trees bearing rich and luscious fruits. _____.

Which choice most logically completes the text?

A) Banks of gorgeous flowers were on every hand, and birds with rare and brilliant plumage sang and fluttered in the trees and bushes.

B) It was Toto that made Dorothy laugh and saved her from growing as gray as her other surroundings.

C) Toto played all day long, and Dorothy played with him and loved him dearly. Today, however, they were not playing.

D) Uncle Henry sat upon the doorstep and looked anxiously at the sky, which was even grayer than usual. Dorothy stood in the door with Toto in her arms, and looked at the sky too.

14.

In ancient Greece the amaranth (also called *chrusanthemon* and *elichrusos*) was sacred to Ephesian Artemis. It was supposed to have special healing properties, and as a symbol of immortality was used to decorate images of the gods and tombs. In legend, _____.

Which choice most logically completes the text?

A) In a village of Amarynthus, of which he was the eponymous hero.

B) There was a famous temple of Artemis Amarynthia or Amarysia.

C) Amarynthus (a form of Amarantus) was a hunter of Artemis and king of Euboea.

D) 'Globe amaranth' belongs to an allied genus, *Gomphrena*, and is also a native of India.

15.

A huge geode, or "amethyst _____ from near Santa Cruz in southern Brazil, was exhibited at the Dusseldorf Exhibition of 1902. Many of the hollow agates of Brazil and Uruguay contain a crop of amethyst-crystals in the interior.

Which choice completes the text so that it conforms to the conventions of standard English?

A) Grotto,"

B) Grotto"

C) grotto:"

D) Grotto;"

16.

Dutch clinkers are small, hard paving bricks burned at a high temperature and of a light yellow color; they are 6 inches long, 3 inches wide, 1.5 inches thick. A variety of paving tile called "oven tiles" is of similar material to the ordinary red brick and in size _____ 10 or 12 inches square and 1 to 2 inches thick.

Which choice completes the text so that it conforms to the conventions of standard English?

A) is
B) are
C) were
D) being

17.

The first brick buildings in America were erected on Manhattan Island in the year 1633 by a governor of the Dutch West India Company. These bricks were made in _____ the industry had long reached great excellence; for many years bricks were imported into America from Holland and from England.

A) Holland where
B) Holland, where
C) Holland where
D) Holland where

18.

For a considerable portion of its inhabitants, Brooklyn is only a place of residence, their business interests being in the borough of _____ has been called the "city of homes" and the "dormitory of New York."

Which choice completes the text so that it conforms to the conventions of standard English?

A) Manhattan; hence, Brooklyn,
B) Manhattan; hence Brooklyn,
C) Manhattan, hence, Brooklyn,
D) Manhattan; hence, Brooklyn

19.

Small fragments, formerly thrown away or used only for varnish, are now utilized on a large scale in the formation of ``ambroid" or ``pressed amber." _____.
This pressed amber yields brilliant interference colors in polarized light.

Which choice completes the text so that it conforms to the conventions of standard English?

The pieces are carefully heated with exclusion of air and then compressed into a uniform mass by intense hydraulic pressure; the softened amber is then forced through holes in a metal plate.

The pieces are carefully heated with exclusion of air and then compressed into a uniform mass by intense hydraulic pressure and softened amber is then forced through holes in a metal plate.

The pieces are carefully heated with exclusion of air and then compressed into a uniform mass by intense hydraulic pressure; the softened amber had been forced through holes in a metal plate.

The pieces are carefully heated with exclusion of air and then compressed into a uniform mass by intense hydraulic pressure — the softened amber being forced — through holes in a metal plate.

20.

On Park Slope, immediately west of Prospect Park and St Mark's Avenue, in another part of the borough, are also attractive residential districts. The south shore of Brooklyn also has various summer pleasure resorts, of which Coney Island _____.

Which choice completes the text so that it conforms to the conventions of standard English?

A) is the more popular.
B) is the most popular.
C) is the much popular.
D) is the minor popular.

21.

_____. The western white spruce is also much employed for various purposes.

Which choice completes the text so that it conforms to the conventions of standard English?

A) Red or giant, cedar which rivals the Douglas fir in girth, is plentiful and is used for shingles, as well as for interior work.

B) Red, or giant cedar, which rivals the Douglas fir in girth, is plentiful, and is used for shingles as well as for interior work.

C) Red or giant cedar which rivals the Douglas fir in girth, is plentiful and is used for shingles as well as for interior work.

D) Red, or giant, cedar, which rivals the Douglas fir in girth, is plentiful and is used for shingles as well as for interior work.

22.

For as the ice is being constantly diminished at the lower end by melting, it would entirely disappear if fresh ice did not continually press forward from above, which, again, is made up by the snowfalls on the mountain tops. But by careful ocular observation we may convince ourselves that the glacier does _____ move.

A) actually

B) instead

C) previously

D) secondly

23.

If white light (that of the sun, _____) be passed through a glass prism, namely, a piece of glass of triangular shape, it will issue from it in rainbow-tinted colours. It is a common experience with any of us to notice this when the sunlight shines through cut-glass, as in the pendant of a chandelier, or in the stopper of a wine-decanter.

Which choice completes the text with the most logical transition?

A) consequently
B) for instance
C) meanwhile
D) secondly

24.

The work of laying bricks or tiles as paving falls to the lot of the bricklayer. Paving formed of ordinary bricks laid flat or on their edges was _____ in general use, but is now almost abandoned in favor of floors of special tiles or cement paving, the latter being practically non-porous and therefore more sanitary and cleaner.

Which choice completes the text with the most logical transition?

A) furthermore
B) instead
C) once
D) thus

25.

While researching a topic, a student took the following notes:

- The deities worshipped by [the Amazons] were Ares (who is consistently assigned to them as a god of war, and as a god of Thracian and generally northern origin) and Artemis, not the usual Greek goddess of that name, but an Asiatic deity in some respects her equivalent.

- It is conjectured that the Amazons were originally the temple-servants and priestesses (hierodulae) of this goddess and that the removal of the breast corresponded with the self-mutilation of the galli, or priests, of Rhea Cybele.

- Another theory is that, as the knowledge of geography extended, travellers brought back reports of tribes ruled entirely by women, who carried out the duties which elsewhere were regarded as peculiar to man, in whom alone the rights of nobility and inheritance were vested, and who had the supreme control of affairs.

- Hence arose the belief in the Amazons as a nation of female warriors, organized and governed entirely by women.

The student wants to compare the theories of the origins of the Amazons. Which choice most effectively uses relevant information from the notes to accomplish this goal?

A) The deities worshiped by [the Amazons] were Ares and Artemis.

B) Historians assigned to them a god of Thracian and generally northern origin, not the usual Greek goddess of that name, but an Asiatic deity in some respects her equivalent.

C) It is believed by some that the Amazons were originally the temple-servants and priestesses of Artemis, while others think that travelers brought back reports of tribes ruled entirely by women.

D) The Amazons carried out the duties which elsewhere were regarded as peculiar to man, in whom alone the rights of nobility and inheritance were vested, and who had the supreme control of affairs.

26.
While researching a topic, a student has taken the following notes:

- Near Fernando Noronha, the sea gave out light in flashes.

- The appearance was very similar to that which might be expected from a large fish moving rapidly through a luminous fluid.

- I have sometimes imagined that a disturbed electrical condition of the atmosphere was most favorable to its production.

- Certainly I think the sea is most luminous after a few days of more calm weather than ordinary, during which time it has swarmed with various animals.

- Observing that the water charged with gelatinous particles is in an impure state, and that the luminous appearance in all common cases is produced by the agitation of the fluid in contact with the atmosphere, I am inclined to consider that the phosphorescence is the result of the decomposition of the organic particles, by which process (one is tempted almost to call it a kind of respiration) the ocean becomes purified.

The student wants to compare the process of the oceanic decomposition of organic matter to a human bodily function. Which choice most effectively uses relevant information from the notes to accomplish this goal?

A) It could be said that the water charged with gelatinous particles is in an impure state.

B) The luminous appearance in all common cases is produced by the agitation of the fluid in contact with the atmosphere.

C) I am inclined to consider that the phosphorescence is the result of the decomposition of the organic particles

D) The decomposition process acts as a kind of respiration by which the ocean becomes purified.

27.
While researching a topic, a student took the following notes:

- But the glory of Agra, the most splendidly poetic building in the world, is the Taj Mahal, the mausoleum built in 1632 by the emperor Shah Jahan for the remains of his favorite wife, Mumtaz Manal, in which he himself also also lies buried.

- The building is of white marble throughout, crowned with a great white dome in the center, with a smaller dome at each of its four corners.

- From the marble terrace which surrounds it rise four tall minarets of the same material, one at each corner.

- The perfect symmetry of its exterior once seen can never be forgotten, nor the aerial grace of its domes, rising like marble bubbles into the azure sky.

The student wants to provide details about the Taj Mahal's composition to an audience already familiar with the reason that the famous structure was built. Which choice most effectively uses relevant information from the notes to accomplish this goal?

A) But the glory of Agra, the most splendidly poetic building in the world, is the Taj Mahal, the mausoleum built in 1632 by the emperor Shah Jahan for the remains of his favorite wife, Mumtaz Manal, in which he himself also also lies buried.

B) The building is of white marble throughout, crowned with a great white dome in the center, with a smaller dome at each of its four corners. From the marble terrace which surrounds it rise four tall minarets of the same material, one at each corner.

C) The perfect symmetry of its exterior once seen can never be forgotten, nor the aerial grace of its domes, rising like marble bubbles into the azure sky.

D) The Taj has been modeled and painted more frequently than any other building in the world, and the word pictures of it are numberless.

Answers on page 380

337

END OF MODULE 1

Please check your answers on page 380 before proceeding past this page.

If you scored between 1 - 16 questions correct, please proceed to Verbal Module 2a, on page 339.

If you scored between 17 -27 questions correct, please proceed to Verbal Module 2b, on page 354.

If you choose to try both Verbal Module 2a and 2b, the more accurate score range for you will be that which is based on the score ranges detailed above.

So, if you score highly enough on Verbal Module 1 qualify for Module 2b, the score range you'd receive if you took Verbal Module 2a would not be representative of how the actual test would proceed.

To sum up, consider the Verbal Module that you don't qualify for as available extra practice, but the total score range information calculated from it won't reflect your skills or be a good predictor of an accurate Digital SAT score range.

Practice Test 2
Verbal Module 2a (VM2a)

1.

In the wise leader's plans, considerations of advantage and of disadvantage will be blended together. "Whether in an _____ position or a disadvantageous one," says Ts'ao Kung, "the opposite state should be always present to your mind."

Which choice completes the text with the most logical and precise word or phrase?

A) advantageous
B) disorienting
C) inadequate
D) unknown

2.

Although the beaks and feet of birds are generally quite clean, I can show that earth sometimes _____ them: in one instance I removed twenty-two grains of dry argillaceous earth from one foot of a partridge, and in this earth there was a pebble quite as large as the seed of a vetch.

Which choice completes the text with the most logical and precise word or phrase?

A) responds to
B) adheres to
C) experiments with
D) improves on

3.

"Let us run away to the Himalayas." My suggestion one day to Dwarka Prasad, the young son of our landlord in Bareilly, fell on unsympathetic ears. He revealed my plan to my elder brother, who had just arrived to see Father. Instead of laughing lightly over this _____ scheme of a small boy, Ananta made it a definite point to ridicule me.

Which choice completes the text with the most logical and precise word or phrase?

A) impractical
B) replicable
C) acceptable
D) restrained

4.

If about a dozen genera of birds had become extinct or were unknown, who would have ventured to have <u>surmised</u> that birds might have existed which used their wings solely as flappers, like the logger-headed duck.

As used in the text, what does the word "surmised" most nearly mean?

A) succumbed
B) enhanced
C) guessed
D) selected

5.

This [path] is particularly distinct to one standing on the middle of the pond in winter, just after a light snow has fallen, appearing as a clear undulating white line, _____ by weeds and twigs, and very obvious a quarter of a mile off in many places where in summer it is hardly distinguishable close at hand.

Which choice completes the text with the most logical and precise word or phrase?

A) impenetrable
B) unobscured
C) inspected
D) compelled

6.

Before the city, in a beautifully fenced grove, the traveller came across a small group of servants, both male and female, carrying baskets. In their midst, carried by four servants in an <u>ornamental</u> sedan-chair, sat a woman, the mistress, on red pillows under a colorful canopy.

As used in the text, what does the word "ornamental" most nearly mean?

A) catastrophic
B) observant
C) significant
D) decorative

7.

The first settlement within the present limits of Brooklyn was made in 1636, when some Dutch farmers took up their residence along the shore of Gowanus Bay. About the same time other Dutch farmers founded Flatlands (at first called Amersfoort), on Jamaica Bay, and a few Walloons founded Wallabout, where the navy yard now is.

Which finding, if true, would most directly undermine the author's claim that "the first settlement within the present limits of Brooklyn was made in 1636."

A) In 1642, a ferry was established across East river from the present foot of Fulton Street.

B) A settlement formed which was known as The Ferry.

C) The next year, Lady Deborah Moody with some followers from New England founded Gravesend near the southern extremity of the borough.

D) Artifacts from a pre-1600s settlement were discovered within the present limits of Brooklyn.

8.

The following is adapted from Frank L. Baum's novel 'The Wonderful Wizard of Oz,' in which Dorothy, is transported to a mysterious, colorful land where she befriends Glinda, the Good Witch.

"The Silver Shoes," said the Good Witch, "have wonderful powers. And one of the most curious things about them is that they can carry you to any place in the world in three steps, and each step will be made in the wink of an eye. All you have to do is to knock the heels together three times and command the shoes to carry you wherever you wish to go."

"If that is so," said the child joyfully, "I will ask them to carry me back to Kansas at once."

According to the text, what is curious about the Silver Shoes?

A) They are made of pure silver and fit whomever puts them on.

B) They are magical but only recently have lost their powers.

C) They are able to carry their wearer anywhere.

D) They are indestructible unless the wearer winks.

9.

The following text is adapted from Lewis Carroll's *Alice in Wonderland*.

The Duchess said after a pause, "I'm doubtful about the temper of your flamingo. Shall I try the experiment?"

"He might bite," Alice cautiously replied, not feeling at all anxious to have the experiment tried.

"Very true," said the Duchess, "flamingos and mustard both bite. And the moral of that is—'Birds of a feather flock together.'"

"Only mustard isn't a bird," Alice remarked.

"Right, as usual," said the Duchess: "what a clear way you have of putting things!"

"It's a mineral, I think," said Alice.

Which quotation most effectively illustrates Alice's claim that mustard is a mineral?

A) "I think I should understand that better," Alice said very politely, "if I had it written down: but I can't quite follow it as you say it."

B) "There's a large mustard-mine near here."

C) "And the moral of that is—'The more there is of mine, the less there is of yours.'"

D) "Oh, I know!" exclaimed Alice, "it's a vegetable. It doesn't look like one, but it is."

10.
'Earliest Spring' is a 1837 poem by William Dean Howells.

Tossing his mane of snows in wildest eddies and tangles,
  Lion-like March cometh in, hoarse, with tempestuous breath,
Through all the moaning chimneys, and 'thwart all the hollows and angles
  Round the shuddering house, threating of winter and death.

But in my heart I feel the life of the wood and the meadow
  Thrilling the pulses that own kindred with fibres that lift
Bud and blade to the sunward, within the inscrutable shadow,
  Deep in the oak's chill core, under the gathering drift.

Nay, to earth's life in mine some prescience, or dream, or desire
  (How shall I name it aright?) comes for a moment and goes—
Rapture of life ineffable, perfect—as if in the brier,
  Leafless there by my door, trembled a sense of the rose.

Based on the text, to what does the speaker compare the month of March?

A) A snowy-maned lion

B) A moaning chimney

C) A shuddering house

D) A gathering drift

11.

The amount of timber cut on Dominion government lands in 1904 was 22,760,222 ft., and the amount cut on provincial lands was 325,271,568 ft., giving a total of 348,031,790 ft.

In 1905 the cut on Dominion lands exceeded that in 1904, while the amount cut on provincial lands reached 450,385,554 ft.

Cargo shipments of British Columbia lumber, in feet, for the years 1904 and 1905

Location	1904 feet	1905 feet
United Kingdom	7,498,301	13,690,869
South America	15,647,808	13.332,993
Australia	10,045,094	11,596,482
South Africa	2,517,154	7,093,681
China and Japan	4,802,426	4,787,784

This data has led the author to claim that there is less of a market for British Columbia lumber in ____.

Which choice most effectively uses information from the graph to complete the author's claim?

A) the United Kingdom in 1905 than in South America in 1905.

B) China and Japan in 1904 than in China and Japan in 1905.

C) Australia in 1904 than in South Africa in 1905

D) South America in 1905 than in the United Kingdom in 1905.

12.

Text 1

Charles V. (1516-1556) rebuilt portions of the Alhambra in the modern style of the period and destroyed the greater part of the winter palace to make room for a modern structure which has never been completed.

Text 2

Philip V. (1700-1746) 'Italianized' the rooms and completed the degradation by running up partitions which blocked up whole apartments.

Based on the texts, how would the author of Text 1 most likely respond to the changes made to the Alhambra by Philip V?

A) The author of Text 1 would perhaps respond to the changes made by Philip V by protesting the destruction of the winter palace.

B) The author of Text 2 would perhaps respond to the changes made by Charles V by rejecting them in favor of a more modern, French design.

C) The author of Text 1 would perhaps respond to the changes made by Philip V by suggesting that Philip complete the modern structure that Charles planned and started but never finished.

D) The author of Text 2 would perhaps respond to the changes made by Charles V by pointing out that Charles V's unfinished restoration projects are separate from those of his own that were still in progress.

13.

The following text is from the 1865 poem 'Where My Books Go' by William Butler Yeats. The speaker conveys hope that his words will comfort his readers.

All the words that I utter,
  And all the words that I write,
Must spread out their wings untiring,
  And never rest in their flight,
Till they come where your sad, sad heart is,
  And sing to you in the night,
Beyond where the waters are moving,
  Storm-darken'd or starry bright.

Which quotation from the poem most effectively illustrates the speaker's hope?

A) "And all the words that I write,"
B) "And never rest in their flight,"
C) "And sing to you in the night,"
D) "Storm-darken'd or starry bright."

14.

The venture cost the sisters about £50 in all, but only two copies were sold. There were nineteen poems by Charlotte, twenty-one by Emily, and the same number by Anne. A consensus of criticism has accepted the fact that Emily's verse alone revealed true poetic genius.

Which finding, if true, would most directly support the author's claim about Emily Brontë's talent?

A) This was unrecognized then except by her sister Charlotte. It is obvious now to all.

B) The author was further told that a longer novel would be gladly considered.

C) Emily Brontë's longer novel, Jane Eyre appeared in October 1847, and was wildly acclaimed on every hand.

D) These names disguised the identity of Charlotte, Emily and Anne Brontë.

15.

The color of amethyst is usually attributed to the presence of manganese, but as it is capable of being much altered and even discharged by heat it has been referred by some authorities to an organic source. On exposure to heat, amethyst generally becomes yellow, and much of the cairngorm or yellow quartz of jewelry is said to be merely "burnt amethyst." Therefore, _____.

Which choice most logically completes the text?

A) veins of amethystine quartz are unlikely to lose their color on the exposed outcrop.

B) veins of amethystine quartz are more likely to grow deeper purple in color when exposed to sunlight.

C) veins of amethystine quartz are less likely to grow deeper purple in color when exposed to sunlight.

D) veins of amethystine quartz are apt to become more yellow in color on the exposed outcrop.

16.

A remarkably fine cup turned in amber from a bronze-age barrow at Hove is now in the Brighton Museum. Beads of amber occur with Anglo-Saxon relics in the south of England; and up to a comparatively recent period the material was valued as an amulet with healing properties. Thus, _____

Which choice most logically completes the text?

A) it is still believed by some to possess certain medicinal virtue.

B) Amber was much valued as an ornamental material in very early times.

C) It has been found in Mycenaean tombs.

D) It is known from lake-dwellings in Switzerland, and it occurs with neolithic remains in Denmark, whilst in England it is found with interments of the bronze age.

17.
The spider's threads _____ than a yard in length and diverged in an ascending direction from the spider.

Which choice completes the text so that it conforms to the conventions of standard English?

A) Was most
B) was more
C) were most
D) were more

18.
The anaconda, an aquatic boa, _____ the swamps and rivers of the dense forests of tropical South America. It is the largest of all modern snakes, said to attain over 30 feet in length.

Which choice completes the text so that it conforms to the conventions of standard English?

A) Inhabiting
B) Inhabits
C) Inhabited
D) Inhabit

19.
Amber was much valued as an ornamental material in very early times. It has been found in Mycenaean _____ known from lake-dwellings in Switzerland, and it occurs with neolithic remains in Denmark, while in England it is found with interments of the bronze age.

Which choice completes the text so that it conforms to the conventions of standard English?

A) tombs; it is
B) tombs, it is
C) tombs - it is,
D) tombs, it is,

20.

Maria, Elizabeth, Charlotte, and Emily were all sent to _____ at Cowan Bridge in 1824, and Maria and Elizabeth returned home in the following year. How far the bad food and drastic discipline were responsible cannot be accurately demonstrated.

Which choice completes the text so that it conforms to the conventions of standard English?

A) the Clergy Daughters' school
B) the Clergy Daughters; school
C) the Clergy Daughters: school
D) the Clergy Daughters, school

21.

Keene Valley, in the center of Essex county, is another picturesque region, _____ a pleasing combination of peaceful valley and rugged hills.

Which choice completes the text so that it conforms to the conventions of standard English?

A) presenting
B) present
C) presents
D) being presented

22.

The principal timber of commerce is the Douglas fir. The wood is tough and strong and highly valued for _____ as well as for building purposes.

Which choice completes the text so that it conforms to the conventions of standard English?

A) ship's spars
B) ships' spars
C) ships spars
D) ships' spar's

23.

The pseudonyms adopted by authors are often transposed forms, more or less exact, of their names; thus 'Calvinus' becomes 'Alcvinus;' ``Francois Rabelais' becomes 'Alcofribas Nasier;' 'Bryan Waller Proctor' becomes 'Barry Cornwall, poet;' 'Henry Rogers' becomes 'R. E. H. Greyson.' It is to be noted that the last two are impure anagrams because an ``r'' _____ left out in both cases.

Which choice completes the text so that it conforms to the conventions of standard English?

A) being
B) were
C) has been
D) been

24.

It is calculated that, at her surface, this is only about one-sixth of what we experience. A man transported to the moon would _____ be able to jump six times as high as he can here.

Which choice completes the text with the most logical transition?

A) additionally
B) by coincidence
C) instead
D) thus

25.

Amongst the languages of ancient times Sanskrit and Greek both indicate by signs the position of the chief pitch accent in the word, and the same method has been employed in modern times for languages in which pitch accent is well marked, as it is, _____ in Lithuanian, the language still spoken by some two millions of people.

Which choice completes the text with the most logical transition?

A) afterward
B) besides
C) finally
D) for example

26.
While researching a topic, a student took the following notes:

- The Amazons are a legendary nation of female warriors.

- They were said to have lived in Pontus near the shore of the Euxine sea, where they formed an independent kingdom under the government of a queen, the capital being Themiscyra on the banks of the river Thermodon.

- No men were permitted to reside in their country, but once a year, in order to prevent their race from dying out, they visited the Gargareans, a neighbouring tribe.

- It is said that their right breast was cut off or burnt out, in order that they might be able to use the bow more freely; hence the ancient derivation of 'Amaxones from mafos, ``without breast.''

- But there is no indication of this practice in works of art, in which the Amazons are always represented with both breasts, although the right is frequently covered.

- *maza*, a Circassian word said to signify 'moon,' has suggested their connexion with the worship of a moon- goddess, perhaps the Asiatic representative of Artemis.

The student wants to explain how the Amazons may have been connected to an Asiatic version of the Greek moon goddess Artemis. Which choice most effectively uses relevant information from the notes to accomplish this goal?

A) *Maza*, a Circassian word said to signify ``moon,'' has been suggested as a potential origin for the modern word "Amazon"

B) The Amazons are a legendary nation of female warriors.

C) They were said to have lived in Pontus near the shore of the Euxine sea, where they formed an independent kingdom under the government of a queen.

D) No men were permitted to reside in their country, but once a year, in order to prevent their race from dying out, they visited the Gargareans, a neighbouring tribe.

27.
While researching a topic, a student took the following notes:

- Fairley described the constituents of venom as:

  (1) neurotoxic elements that act on the bulbar and spinal ganglion cells of the central nervous system;
  (2) hemorrhagins that destroy the lining of the walls of blood vessels;
  (3) thrombose, producing clots within blood vessels;
  (4) hemolysins, destroying red blood corpuscles;
  (5) cytolysins that act on leucocytes and on cells of other tissues;
  (6) elements that slow coagulation of the blood;

- Elapid snakes tend to have more of elements 1, 4, and 6 in their venoms.

- Viperids and crotalids, of which the cottonmouth is one, have higher quantities of elements 2, 3, and 5.

- Kellogg stated that venom of cottonmouths contains more neurotoxin than that of rattlesnakes and not only breaks down the nuclei of ganglion cells but also produces granular disintegration of the myelin sheath and fragmentation of the conducting portions of nerve fibers.

- Thus, venoms contain both toxic elements and non-toxic substances that promote rapid spreading of the venom through the body of the victim.

- Jacques attributed this rapid spreading to the hyaluronidase content of venoms.

The student wants to explain briefly how hemorrhagins act on the body. Which choice most effectively uses relevant information from the notes to accomplish this goal?

A) They produce clots within blood vessels.
B) They slow the coagulation of the blood.
C) They destroy red blood corpuscles and act on leucocytes and on cells of other tissues.
D) They destroy the lining of the walls of blood vessels.

Answers on page 380

Practice Test 2
Verbal Module 2b (VM2b)

1.

Ho Shih thus expounds the paradox: "In warfare, first lay plans which will _____ victory, and then lead your army to battle; if you will not begin with stratagem but rely on brute strength alone, victory will no longer be assured."

Which choice completes the text with the most logical and precise word or phrase?

A) doubt
B) inspect
C) interject
D) ensure

2.

Development is conceived not as continuous growing, but as the unfolding of <u>latent</u> powers toward a definite goal. The goal is conceived of as completion,—perfection. Life at any stage short of attainment of this goal is merely an unfolding toward it.

As used in the text, what does the word "latent" most nearly mean?

A) aggressive
B) overwhelming
C) hidden
D) elongated

3.

At the present day, and in this country, as I find by my own experience, a few _____, a knife, an axe, a spade, a wheelbarrow, and for the studious, lamp-light, stationery, and access to a few books, rank next to necessaries, and can all be obtained at a trifling cost.

Which choice completes the text with the most logical and precise word or phrase?

A) impediments
B) implements
C) unknowns
D) approximations

4.

Those who were called skillful leaders of old knew how to drive a wedge between the enemy's front and rear (more literally, to 'cause the front and rear to lose touch with each other') to prevent co-operation between his large and small divisions; to <u>hinder</u> the good troops from rescuing the bad, the officers from rallying their men.

As used in the text, what does the word "hinder" most nearly mean?

A) allow
B) condition
C) prevent
D) prescribe

5.

Drs. K. S. Cole and H. J. Curtis reported having discovered that the long single cells of the fresh-water plant nitella, used frequently in goldfish bowls, are virtually identical with those of single nerve fibers. Furthermore, they found that nitella fibers, on being excited, _____ electrical waves that are similar in every way, except velocity, to those of the nerve fibers in animals and man.

Which choice completes the text with the most logical and precise word or phrase?

A) propagate
B) presume
C) provoke
D) proclaim

6.

The following is adapted from Frank L. Baum's novel *The Wonderful Wizard of Oz*,' in which a young girl, Dorothy, is transported by a cyclone from her home in rural Kansas to a mysterious, colorful land called Oz.

When Dorothy awoke, the sun was shining through the trees and Toto had long been out chasing birds around him and squirrels. She sat up and looked around her. There was the Scarecrow, still standing patiently in his corner, waiting for her.

"We must go and search for water," she said to him.

"Why do you want water?" he asked.

"To wash my face clean after the dust of the road, and to drink, so the dry bread will not stick in my throat."

"It must be inconvenient to be made of flesh," said the Scarecrow thoughtfully, "for you must sleep, and eat and drink. However, you have brains, and it is worth a lot of bother to be able to think properly."

Which choice best states the main purpose of the text?

A) To indicate that Dorothy is concerned that the Scarecrow does not seem to need to wash, eat, or sleep.

B) To describe a human problem that Dorothy faces that is solved by the Scarecrow.

C) To examine the relationship between the Scarecrow and water.

D) To compare the perspectives of Dorothy and the Scarecrow with regard to human basic needs.

7.

Text 1

According to J. Vurtheim, the Amazons were of Greek origin: "all the Amazons were Dianas, as Diana herself was an Amazon." In works of art, combat between Amazons and Greeks is placed on the same level as and often associated with combat between Greeks and centaurs. Their occupation was hunting and war; their arms were the bow, spear, axe, and a half shield, nearly in the shape of a crescent, called a *pelta.*

Text 2

The history of Bohemia affords a parallel to the Greek Amazons. During the 8th century, a large band of women, under a certain Vlasta, carried on war against the duke of Bohemia and enslaved or put to death all men who fell into their hands. Additionally, the Spanish explorer Orellana asserted that he had come into conflict with fighting women in South America on the river Maranon. The existence of 'Amazons' (in the sense of fighting women) in the army of Dahomey is an undoubted fact, but they are said to have died out during the French protectorate.

Based on the texts, how would the author of Text 1 most likely respond to the groups of fighting women discussed in Text 2?

A) The author of Text 1 would certainly change their definition of 'Amazons' to include other groups of fighting women noted in the world.

B) The author of Text 2 would perhaps remind the author of Text 1 that the Amazons were usually on horseback but sometimes on foot.

C) The author of Text 1 would be unlikely to classify the women described in Text 2 as true Amazons.

D) The author of Text 2 would certainly change their definition of 'Amazons' to include other groups of fighting women noted in the world.

8.

A spider which was about three-tenths of an inch in length, while standing on the summit of a post, darted forth four or five threads from its spinners. Spiders' threads, when glittering in the sunshine, might be compared to diverging rays of light.

Which choice best states the main idea of the text?

A) To specify a reason why spiders are able to travel through the air.
B) To compare spider travel to that of soap-bubbles.
C) To describe a spider and compare its threads to rays of light.
D) To contrast the researcher's theory with that of Mr. Murray.

9.

The following is adapted from Frank L. Baum's novel 'The Wonderful Wizard of Oz,' in which a young girl, Dorothy, is transported to a mysterious, colorful land called Oz where she faces a Wicked Witch.

The wicked creature was very cunning, and she finally thought of a trick that would give her what she wanted. She placed a bar of iron in the middle of the kitchen floor, and then by her magic arts made the iron invisible to human eyes. So that when Dorothy walked across the floor she stumbled over the bar, not being able to see it, and fell at full length. She was not much hurt, but in her fall one of the Silver Shoes came off; and before she could reach it, the Witch had snatched it away and put it on her own skinny foot.

Which choice best describes the overall structure of the text?

A) The text compares Dorothy's treatment of the shoes to that of the Wicked Witch.

B) The text describes an event planned by the Wicked Witch and goes on to list who attended it.

C) The text introduces a scheme and then details how the Wicked Witch executed her ploy.

D) The text raises a question and indicates how the Wicked Witch answered it.

10.

The figures relating to temperature and precipitation are from a table prepared by Mr R.F. Stupart, director of the meteorological service. The station at Victoria may be taken as representing the conditions of the southern part of the coast of British Columbia.

Location	Mean Temperature (in Fahrenheit)			Absolute Temperature		Rainfall (in inches)		
	Coldest Month	Warmest Month	Average Annual Temp.	Highest	Lowest	Wettest Month	Driest Month	Average Annual
Victoria	January 37.5°	July 60.3°	48.8°	90°	-1°	December 7.98	July .4	37.77
Agassiz	January 33.0°	Aug. 64.7°	48.9°	97°	-13°	December 9.43	July 1.55	66.85
Kamloops	January 24.2°	Aug. 68.5°	47.1°	101°	-27°	July 1.61	April .37	11.46
Port Simpson	January 34.9°	Aug. 56.9°	45.1°	88°	-10°	October 12.42	June 4.37	94.63

A researcher interprets the data and concludes that _____.

A) the highest annual temperature in Agassiz is higher than the highest annual temperature in Kamloops, while the average annual precipitation in Agassiz is higher than the average annual precipitation in Port Simpson.

B) the highest annual temperature in Agassiz is higher than the highest annual temperature in Port Simpson, while the average annual precipitation in Agassiz is lower than the average annual precipitation in Port Simpson.

C) the highest annual temperature in Agassiz is lower than the highest annual temperature in Kamloops, while the average annual precipitation in Victoria is lower than the average annual precipitation in Agassiz.

D) the highest annual temperature in Agassiz is lower than the highest annual temperature in Victoria, while the average annual precipitation in Agassiz is higher than the average annual precipitation in Kamloops.

11.

Year	Event
560	Aethelbert took the throne and became King of Kent.
568	Aethelbert married Berhta.
597	The mission of Augustine landed in Thanet and was received at first with some hesitation by the King.
603	Christ Church was consecrated.
604	Justus became first bishop of Rochester.
616	Aethelberht died and was succeeded by his son Eadbald.

Aethelberht exercised a stricter sway over Essex, where his nephew Saberht was King. He seems to have acted with prudence and moderation during the conversion of his kingdom and did not countenance compulsory proselytism.

Which choice most effectively uses information from the table to illustrate the claim that King Aethelberht often acted with "prudence and moderation?"

A) In 597 CE, the mission of Augustine landed in Thanet and was received at first with some hesitation by the king.

B) He also made grants to found the see of Rochester, of which Justus became first bishop in 604, and his influence established Mellitus at London in the same year.

C) A code of laws issued by Aethelberht, king of Kent, which is still extant, is probably the oldest document in the English language and contains a list of money fines for various crimes.

D) Towards the close of his reign his pre-eminence as Bretwalda was disturbed by the increasing power of Raedwald of East Anglia. He died probably in 616, and was succeeded by his son Eadbald.

12.

Observing that the water charged with gelatinous particles is in an impure state, and that the luminous appearance in all common cases is produced by the agitation of the fluid in contact with the atmosphere, I am inclined to consider that the phosphorescence is the result of the decomposition of the organic particles, by which process (one is tempted almost to call it a kind of respiration) the ocean becomes purified.

Which choice best describes the overall structure of the text?

A) It compares decomposition to respiration.

B) It indicates a contrast between gelatinous particles and decomposing particles.

C) It compares theories about the causes of an observed phenomenon in Fernando Noronha.

D) It states an observation followed by a conclusion.

13.

The first settlement within the present limits of Brooklyn was made in 1636, when some Dutch farmers took up their residence along the shore of Gowanus Bay. About the same time other Dutch farmers founded Flatlands (at first called Amersfoort), on Jamaica Bay, and a few Walloons founded Wallabout, where the navy yard now is.

Which finding, if true, would most directly undermine the author's claim that "the first settlement within the present limits of Brooklyn was made in 1636."

A) In 1642, a ferry was established across East river from the present foot of Fulton Street.

B) A settlement formed which was known as The Ferry.

C) The next year, Lady Deborah Moody with some followers from New England founded Gravesend near the southern extremity of the borough.

D) Artifacts from a pre-1600s settlement were discovered within the present limits of Brooklyn.

14.

Amethyst is a violet or purple variety of quartz often used as an ornamental stone. The name is generally said to be derived from the Greek *a*, "not," and *methbskein*, "to intoxicate," expressing the old belief that the stone protected its owner from strong drink.

According to the text, why was amethyst significant to the ancient Greek people?

A) Amethyst was said to be highly valuable and prized for jewelry.

B) Amethyst was said to cause its owner to feel intoxicated.

C) Amethyst was said to resemble quartz enough to pass for it at the Greek markets.

D) Amethyst was said to protect its owner from the effects of alcohol intoxication.

15.

Amazon-stone, or amazonite, is a green variety of microcline-felspar. The name is taken from that of the river Amazon, whence certain green stones were obtained, but it is doubtful whether green felspar occurs in the Amazon district. Thus, _____.

Which choice most logically completes the text?

A) Some other localities in the United States yield amazon-stone, and it is also found in pegmatite in Madagascar.

B) The stone is so named due to it originally being discovered in the Amazon region of South America.

C) The stone gets its name only from the name of the Amazon river and not from originating in the Amazon region of South America.

D) It is unknown why amazonite was given the nickname 'amazon stone.'

16.

The following is adapted from Lewis Carroll's novel 'Alice's Adventures in Wonderland,' in which a young girl, Alice, falls down a rabbit hole into a confusing world of colorful characters.

The chief difficulty Alice found at first was in managing her flamingo: she succeeded in getting its body tucked away, comfortably enough, under her arm, with its legs hanging down, but generally, just as she had got its neck nicely straightened out, it would twist itself round and look up in her face with such a puzzled expression _____.

Which choice most logically completes the text?

A) that she could not help bursting out laughing.

B) that she tried to continue baking the tarts.

C) that she couldn't understand the Duchess.

D) that she followed the path through the woods.

17.

The action of lime in bleaching the ferric oxide and producing a yellow instead of a red brick has not been thoroughly _____ seems probable that some compound is produced between the lime and the oxide of iron entirely different from that produced by oxide of iron in the absence of lime. Such marls require a harder fire than the ordinary brick-clays in order to bring about the reaction between the lime and the other ingredients.

Which choice completes the text so that it conforms to the conventions of standard English?

A) investigated, but

B) investigated but it

C) investigated, but it

D) investigated;

18.

The Canadian Pacific Railway Company has two lines of mail steamer running from Vancouver and _____ line, which runs to Japan and China once in three weeks and the Australian line to Honolulu, Fiji and Sydney, once a month.

Which choice completes the text so that it conforms to the conventions of standard English?

A) Victoria: the Empress

B) Victoria; the Empress

C) Victoria, the Empress,

D) Victoria the Empress

19.

In the spaces beyond the solar system we _____ a new order of distance. From sun to planets is measured in millions of miles, but from sun to sun is measured in billions.

Which choice completes the text so that it conforms to the conventions of standard English?

A) are faced to

B) were faced by

C) were faced to

D) are faced with

20.

Finally, the cave became a resort of bears; the remains of 334 specimens, in all stages of growth, including even sucking cubs, _____ discovered.

Which choice completes the text so that it conforms to the conventions of standard English?

A) being
B) were
C) are
D) was

21.

One legend represents the *aegis* as a fire-breathing monster like the Chimaera, which was slain by _____ afterward wore its skin as a cuirass.

Which choice completes the text so that it conforms to the conventions of standard English?

A) Athena who
B) Athena: who
C) Athena, who
D) Athena — who

22.

In the early days of the 19th century, the usual length of alpaca staples appears to have been about 12 inches, this being a three years' growth; today the length is little more than about half this, i.e., a _____ growth, although from time to time longer staples are to be found.

Which choice completes the text so that it conforms to the conventions of standard English?

A) one to two years
B) one to two years'
C) one to two year's
D) one' to two year's

23.

Though the climate in Keene Valley during the winter months is very <u>severe —
the temperature sometimes falling as low as -42 degrees Fahrenheit — the</u> region
is heavily forested with spruce, pine and broad-leaved trees.

Which choice completes the text so that it conforms to the conventions of standard English?

A) Severe; the temperature sometimes falling as low as -42 degrees Fahrenheit
the

B) Severe, the temperature sometimes falling as low as -42 degrees Fahrenheit —
the

C) severe — the temperature sometimes falling as low as -42 degrees Fahrenheit
— the

D) severe — the temperature sometimes falling as low as -42 degrees Fahrenheit,
the

24.

In Gymnosperms we have seeds, and the carpels may become modified and
close around these, as in Pinus, during the process of ripening to form an imitation of a box-like fruit which _____ opening allows the seeds to escape.

Which choice completes the text with the most logical transition?

A) actually
B) currently
C) subsequently
D) finally

25.

Brooklyn is connected with Manhattan by three bridges across the East river—the lowest, known as the Brooklyn, opened in 1883; _____, known as the Williamsburg or East River bridge, opened in 1903; and a third, the Manhattan, was opened in 1909.

Which choice completes the text with the most logical transition?

A) another
B) for this reason
C) in fact
D) specifically

26.
While researching a topic, a student took the following notes:

- [Austin Edwin Abbey's] water-colors and pastels were no less successful than the earlier illustrations in pen and ink.

- Possibly his best known pastels are ``Beatrice,'' ``Phyllis,'' and ``Two Noble Kinsmen.''

- In 1890 he made his first appearance with an oil painting, ``A May Day Morn,'' at the Royal Academy in London.

- Apart from his other paintings, special mention must be made of the large frescoes entitled ``The Quest of the Holy Grail,'' in the Boston Public Library, on which he was occupied for some years.

- The dramatic subjects, and the brilliant coloring of his on pictures, gave them pronounced individuality among the works of contemporary painters.

The student wants to introduce Austin Edwin Abbey to an audience already familiar with Royal Academy in London. Which choice most effectively uses relevant information from the notes to accomplish this goal?

A) Abbey now became closely identified with the art life of England, and was elected to the Royal Institute of Painters in Water-Colours in 1883.

B) Austin Edwin Abbey, a painter known for his dramatic subjects and brilliant coloring, debuted his piece, 'A May Day Morn,' at the Royal Academy in 1890.

C) Apart from Austin Edwin Abbey's other paintings, special mention must be made of the large frescoes entitled ``The Quest of the Holy Grail,'' in the Boston Public Library

D) Abbey became a member not only of the Royal Academy, but also of the National Academy of Design of New York, and honorary member of the Royal Bavarian Society, the Societe Nationale des Beaux Arts (Paris), the American Water-Colour Society, etc.

27.

While researching a topic, a student took the following notes:

- Some animals are wholly pigmented during the summer and autumn, but through the winter and spring they are in the condition of extreme partial albinism and become almost complete albinos.

- Such instances are found in the Scotch blue hare (Lepus timidus), in the Norway hare, in the North American hare, in the arctic fox, in the stoat and ermine, and among birds, in the ptarmigan, and some other species of Lagopus.

- How the change from the autumnal to the winter condition takes place appears not to be definitely settled in all cases, and accurate observations are much to be desired.

- In the case of the Norway hare, it has been stated that a general moult, including the hairs and under fur, takes place and new white hairs are substituted.

- On the other hand, it has been stated that during the whole of the transformation in the fur no hairs fall from the animal, and it is attributed to an actual change in the color of the hair.

The student wants to present a reason for scientists' uncertainty about how extreme partial albinism occurs. Which choice most effectively uses relevant information from the notes to accomplish this goal?

A) In the case of the Norway hare, it has been stated that a general moult, including all the hairs and under fur, takes place and new white hairs are substituted.

B) The transformation known as extreme partial albinism occurs in a variety of creatures who live in snowy climates.

C) Due to a paucity of accurate observations, scientists have not been able to collect the data necessary to draw definitive conclusions about how extreme partial albinism occurs.

D) In order to find out why extreme partial albinism occurs in so many creatures, scientists have conducted longitudinal studies and discovered that moulting cycles are common in the majority of the creatures who have been observed with extreme partial albinism.

Answers on page 380

Appendix C:

Answer Keys
&
Scoring Tables

Words in Context Example Question Answer (pages 27-28)

1. A; *difficulty level: basic*
2. C; *difficulty level: medium*
3. C; *difficulty level: advanced*
4. A; *difficulty level: medium*

Words in Context (WIC) Practice Question Answers (pages 34-37)

1. D; *difficulty level: basic*
2. A; *difficulty level: basic*
3. A; *difficulty level: medium*
4. D; *difficulty level: medium*
5. C; *difficulty level: medium*
6. A; *difficulty level: medium*
7. B; *difficulty level: advanced*
8. D; *difficulty level: medium*
9. A; *difficulty level: advanced*
10. B; *difficulty level: advanced*
CHALLENGE: D; *difficulty level: advanced*

Evidence Example Question Answers (pages 41-45)

1. A; *difficulty level: basic*
2. C; *difficulty level: medium*
3. B; *difficulty level: basic*
4. C; *difficulty level: advanced*
5. A; *difficulty level: basic*
6. A; *difficulty level: medium*
7. C; *difficulty level: advanced*
8. B; *difficulty level: advanced*

Evidence Practice Question Answers (pages 47-54)

1. B; *difficulty level: basic*
2. B; *difficulty level: basic*
3. B; *difficulty level: medium*
4. B; *difficulty level: medium*
5. C; *difficulty level: basic*
6. C; *difficulty level: medium*
7. D; *difficulty level: basic*
8. D; *difficulty level: advanced*
9. B; *difficulty level: medium*
10. D; *difficulty level: advanced*
Challenge: A; *difficulty level: advanced*

Logical Completion Example Question Answers (pages 57-58)

1. B; *difficulty level: basic*
2. D; *difficulty level: medium*
3. A; *difficulty level: advanced*

Logical Completion Practice Questions (pages 60-65)

1. B; *difficulty level: basic*
2. A; *difficulty level: medium*
3. A; *difficulty level: basic*
4. B; *difficulty level: basic*
5. A; *difficulty level: medium*
6. D; *difficulty level: advanced*
7. A; *difficulty level: medium*
8. C; *difficulty level: medium*
9. A; *difficulty level: advanced*
10. A; *difficulty level: advanced*
Challenge: C; *difficulty level: advanced*

Chart / Graph Interpretation Example Questions (pages 68-69)

1. B; *difficulty level: basic*
2. A; *difficulty level: medium*
3. C; *difficulty level: advanced*

Chart / Graph Interpretation Practice Questions (pages 71-81)

1. C; *difficulty level: basic*
2. D; *difficulty level: basic*
3. C; *difficulty level: medium*
4. A; *difficulty level: medium*
5. A; *difficulty level: medium*
6. D; *difficulty level: basic*
7. C; *difficulty level: basic*
8. A; *difficulty level: medium*
9. A; *difficulty level: advanced*
10. A; *difficulty level: advanced*
Challenge: C; *difficulty level: advanced*

Support Quotation Example Questions (pages 84-85)

1. C; *difficulty level: medium*
2. B; *difficulty level: medium*

Support Quotation Practice Questions (pages 87-96)

1. C; *difficulty level: basic*
2. B; *difficulty level: medium*
3. C; *difficulty level: basic*
4. B; *difficulty level: medium*
5. C; *difficulty level: basic*
6. A; *difficulty level: medium*
7. D; *difficulty level: medium*
8. B; *difficulty level: advanced*
9. C; *difficulty level: advanced*
10. D; *difficulty level: medium*
Challenge: D; *difficulty level: advanced*

Purpose Example Questions (pages 99-101)

1. B; *difficulty level: medium*
2. A; *difficulty level: basic*
3. D; *difficulty level: medium*
4. D; *difficulty level: advanced*

Purpose Practice Questions (pages 103-110)

1. D; *difficulty level: basic*
2. D *difficulty level: medium*
3. C; *difficulty level: basic*
4. A; *difficulty level: medium*
5. B; *difficulty level: basic*
6. A; *difficulty level: medium*
7. A; *difficulty level: medium*
8. A; *difficulty level: advanced*
9. B; *difficulty level: medium*
10. A; *difficulty level: advanced*
Challenge: D; *difficulty level: advanced*

Main Idea Example Questions (pages 113-114)

1. C; *difficulty level: basic*
2. C; *difficulty level: medium*
3. D; *difficulty level: advanced*

Main Idea Practice Questions (pages 116-122)

1. C; *difficulty level: basic*
2. C *difficulty level: medium*
3. C; *difficulty level: basic*
4. C; *difficulty level: medium*
5. C; *difficulty level: basic*
6. C; *difficulty level: medium*
7. C; *difficulty level: medium*
8. C; *difficulty level: advanced*
9. B; *difficulty level: medium*
10. C; *difficulty level: advanced*
Challenge: C; *difficulty level: advanced*

Passage Comparison Example Questions (pages 126-127)

1. A; *difficulty level: medium*
2. D; *difficulty level: advanced*

Passage Comparison Practice Questions (pages 129-131)

1. C; *difficulty level: basic*
2. A *difficulty level: medium/advanced*
Challenge: D; *difficulty level: advanced*

(Poetic) Structure Example Questions (pages 134-136)

1. C; *difficulty level: basic*
2. B; *difficulty level: advanced*
3. C; *difficulty level: medium*

(Poetic) Structure Practice Questions (pages 139-145)

1. A; *difficulty level: basic*
2. A; *difficulty level: basic*
3. C; *difficulty level: medium*
4. B; *difficulty level: advanced*
5. A; *difficulty level: medium*
6. D; *difficulty level: basic*
7. C; *difficulty level: medium*
8. C; *difficulty level: advanced*
9. B; *difficulty level: medium*
10. A; *difficulty level: advanced*
Challenge: A; *difficulty level: advanced*

Colon Practice Questions (page 157)

1. CORRECT. She wanted to visit three places.
2. She wanted to visit three places: Greece, Italy, and Spain.
3. They had a family rule: always clear your place after dinner.
4. He played two sports: volleyball and lacrosse
5. The team had three main goals: have fun, work hard, and win.
6. Twenty things happened today: 19 good and 1 bad.
7. I want to learn to play many instruments: piano, in particular.
8. "Worrying is like a rocking chair: it gives you something to do, but it doesn't get you anywhere." - National Lampoon's Van Wilder
9. He only had one thing on his mind after Thanksgiving dinner: a nap.
10. They wanted to get a few things from the store: camping supplies, a new broom, and heated gloves.

Semicolon Practice Questions (page 159)

1. This half starts with a capital letter; this half doesn't.
2. This part of the year can be stressful; ask for help when you need it.
3. They wanted to visit three places: Jackson Hole, Wyoming; Park City, Utah; and Aspen, Colorado.
4. They hired the crew: Alex, the videographer; Calvin, the producer; and Ernie, the chef. CHALLENGE: D; *difficulty level: advanced*

Practice Comma Questions (page 168)

1. "I award you no points, and may God have mercy on your soul." - *Billy Madison*, FANBOYS connection
2. Gentlemen, I wash my hands of this weirdness." - *Pirates of the Caribbean*, direct address
3. "Keep the change, ya filthy animal." - *Home Alone*, direct address
4. "Whatever I feel like I wanna do, gosh!" - *Napoleon Dynamite* - interjection
5. "Yeah, well, that's just like, your opinion, man."* - *The Big Lebowski* - interrupters
There are other options here that are technically correct: "Yeah, well, that's just, like, your opinion, man" is also correct.

6. "So you see, my son, there is a very fine line between love and nausea." - *Coming to America* - appositive / address
7. "Fish are friends, not food." - *Finding Nemo* - idea reversal
8. "Facts can be so misleading, whereas rumors, true or false, are always revealing." - *Inglorious Bast*rds* - appositive
9. She wanted to go to the fair, for she enjoyed eating funnel cakes. - FANBOYS connection
10. They wanted to go to the festival because they enjoyed the atmosphere. - CORRECT AS IS
11. Cookie dough is delicious; therefore, I want to eat it all. - introductory words
12. I do not, however, like the stomach ache or salmonella risk. - emphatic transition
13. Sometimes I take the risk, y'all, not gonna lie. - direct address
14. She was born on September 18th, 1959 in Austin, Texas. - date/year & city/state
15. "He looks, you know, like a man." - *Miss Swan, MAD TV* - interrupter clause
16. "Stop looking at me swan!" - *Billy Madison* - direct address

Practice Apostrophe Questions (page 172)

1. "**It's** not a man purse. It's a satchel. Indiana Jones wears one." - *The Hangover*
2. CORRECT - "I'll be back." - *The Terminator*
3. "**I'm** your **father's brother's nephew's cousin's** former roommate." - *Spaceballs*
4. "Yeah, **you're** a legend in your own mind." - *Dirty Harry*
5. "Sounds like **somebody's** got a case of the Mondays." - *Office Space*
6. "What did one shepherd say to the other? **Let's** get the flock outta here." - *Lethal Weapon*
CHALLENGE: "So you're tellin' me there's a chance." - *Dumb & Dumber*

Practice Dash Questions (page 174)

1. Everyone showed up to the party — except Dave.
2. Joey and Cal — the heads of student government — were liked by the majority of the students at the school.
3. Siobhan couldn't believe the judge's sentence — life in prison.
4. The pair of friends — Dan and Noah — had known each other since childhood.
5. CORRECT
6. Finally — after studying and training for years — Ben officially became a licensed physical therapist.

Noun Practice Questions (page 178)

1) **Rose DeWitt Bukater** loved **Jack Dawson**.
2) The **ship** hit the **iceberg** at **night**.
3) **Molly Brow**n tried to save the **others**.
CHALLENGE: **Rose DeWitt Bukater** took Jack Dawson's* **name** in the **end**.
Since it is made possessive by the apostrophe, Jack Dawson's name (which would usually count as a noun) is instead functioning as an adjective (a type of "modifier") describing whose name she took. Tricky!

Pronoun Exercise (page 181)

"But robbers don't do **that** way. **They** always hide **it** and leave **it** there."
"Don't **they** come after **it** any more?"
"No, **they** think **they** will, but **they** generally forget the marks, or else **they** die. Anyway, **it** lays there a long time and gets rusty; and by and by somebody finds an old yellow paper **that** tells how to find the marks—a paper **that's** got to be ciphered over about a week because **it's** mostly signs and hy'roglyphics."
"Hyro—**which**?"
"Hy'roglyphics—pictures and things, **you** know, **that** don't seem to mean anything."
"Have **you** got one of **them** papers, Tom?"
"No."

Pronoun Practice Questions (page 182)

1. A; *difficulty level: basic*
2. D; *difficulty level: medium*
3. B; *difficulty level: advanced*

Verb Tense Example Questions (page 184)

1. B; *difficulty level: basic*
2. B; *difficulty level: medium*

Verb Tense Practice Questions (page 188-191)

1. C; *difficulty level: basic*
2. C; *difficulty level: medium*
3. A; *difficulty level: basic*
4. A; *difficulty level: advanced*
5. B; *difficulty level: basic*
6. A; *difficulty level: medium*
7. D; *difficulty level: medium*
8. D; *difficulty level: advanced*
9. A; *difficulty level: medium*
10. C; *difficulty level: advanced*
CHALLENGE: C; *difficulty level: advanced*

Preposition Exercise (page 194)

One day, when walking **in her favorite park**, a girl noticed a new trail leading **into the woods.** Curious, she and her dog decided to explore it together. It wasn't clear whether the narrow path **through the trees** had been created **by a person** or **by a creature. After a few minutes,** the trail ended **at the side of a beautiful creek** that ran **through the whole park.**

dSAT example: D; *difficulty level: medium*

Active vs Passive Example Questions (pages 198-199)

1. B; *difficulty level: basic*
2. A; *difficulty level: medium*
3. C; *difficulty level: advanced*

Comparatives, Comparisons, & Specificity (pages 200-201)

1. D; *difficulty level: medium*
2. B; *difficulty level: basic*
3. D; *difficulty level: advanced*
4. C; *difficulty level: medium*

Logical Transition Example Questions (pages 204-206)

1. A; *difficulty level: basic*
2. B; *difficulty level: medium*
3. D; *difficulty level: medium*
4. D; *difficulty level: advanced*
5. D; *difficulty level: medium*
6. A; *difficulty level: advanced*

Logical Transition Practice (pages 213-217)

1. B; *difficulty level: basic*
2. A; *difficulty level: medium*
3. A; *difficulty level: basic*
4. A; *difficulty level: basic*
5. C; *difficulty level: medium*
6. D; *difficulty level: advanced*
7. A; *difficulty level: medium*
8. A; *difficulty level: advanced*
9. C; *difficulty level: advanced*
10. D; *difficulty level: advanced*
CHALLENGE: D; *difficulty level: advanced*

Example Notes Questions (pages 220-221)

1. C; *difficulty level: basic*
2. D; *difficulty level: medium*

Practice Notes Questions (pages 223-230)

1. A; *difficulty level: basic*
2. D; *difficulty level: medium*
3. C; *difficulty level: medium*
4. C; *difficulty level: medium*
5. B; *difficulty level: advanced*
6. A; *difficulty level: medium*
7. B; *difficulty level: advanced*
CHALLENGE: A; *difficulty level: advanced*

Grammar & Punctuation Diagnostic Quiz #1 (pages 231-233)

1) C; *difficulty level: medium*
2) C; *difficulty level: basic*
3) A; *difficulty level: advanced*
4) D; *difficulty level: medium*
5) D; *difficulty level: medium*
6) B; *difficulty level: basic*
7) C; *difficulty level: advanced*
8) D; *difficulty level: medium*
9) B; *difficulty level: advanced*
10) A; *difficulty level: advanced*

Grammar & Punctuation Diagnostic Quiz #2 (pages 234-236)

1. D; *difficulty level: basic*
2. A; *difficulty level: medium*
3. B; *difficulty level: advanced*
4. B; *difficulty level: basic*
5. D; *difficulty level: basic*
6. A; *difficulty level: advanced*
7. A; *difficulty level: medium*
8. C; *difficulty level: medium*
9. B; *difficulty level: advanced*
10. D; *difficulty level: medium*

Transition Word
Exercise (pages 211-213)

Support / Agreement

And
Also
As well
By the same token
Comparatively
Correspondingly
Equally
Even more
Further
In the same way / fashion / vein
Like
Much less
Namely
Not only X but also Y
Not to mention
Of course
Such as
That is
Too

Contrast

Albeit
Although
But
Comparatively
Conversely
Despite
Different from
Either / Or
Even though
In spite of
Neither / Nor
Nonetheless
On the contrary
On the other hand
Otherwise
Rather
Though
Unlike
While
Whereas
Yet

Sequence / Results

Accordingly
Because
By the time
Concurrently
During
For
Immediately
In order to
In short
In summary
Last(ly)
Once
Overall
Presently
Since
So
Soon
Suddenly
Then
Thereupon
To summarize
Ultimately
Unless
Until
When(ever)

Practice Test 1 Verbal Module 1	Practice Test 1 Verbal Module 2a	Practice Test 1 Verbal Module 2b
1. A	1. D	1. B
2. B	2. D	2. B
3. D	3. D	3. C
4. D	4. A	4. C
5. D	5. D	5. A
6. A	6. B	6. C
7. A	7. B	7. B
8. B	8. C	8. A
9. A	9. C	9. B
10. C	10. C	10. C
11. D	11. A	11. C
12. A	12. B	12. A
13. B	13. C	13. B
14. A	14. C	14. B
15. C	15. A	15. B
16. C	16. D	16. A
17. A	17. D	17. A
18. A	18. B	18. D
19. B	19. B	19. A
20. D	20. B	20. C
21. D	21. A	21. B
22. B	22. A	22. A
23. D	23. B	23. A
24. A	24. D	24. C
25. B	25. A	25. A
26. C	26. A	26. C
27. D	27. D	27. D

Practice Test 2
Verbal Module 1

1. C
2. A
3. A
4. A
5. B
6. D
7. A
8. C
9. B
10. D
11. A
12. A
13. A
14. C
15. A
16. A
17. B
18. D
19. A
20. B
21. D
22. A
23. B
24. C
25. C
26. D
27. B

Practice Test 2
Verbal Module 2a

1. A
2. B
3. A
4. C
5. B
6. D
7. D
8. C
9. B
10. A
11. D
12. C
13. C
14. C
15. D
16. A
17. D
18. B
19. A
20. A
21. A
22. B
23. C
24. D
25. D
26. A
27. D

Practice Test 2
Verbal Module 2b

1. D
2. C
3. B
4. C
5. A
6. D
7. C
8. C
9. C
10. B
11. A
12. D
13. D
14. D
15. C
16. A
17. C
18. A
19. D
20. B
21. C
22. B
23. C
24. C
25. A
26. B
27. C

SCORING TABLES

How to use these tables

Add the number of correct responses from VM1 and VM2a or VM2b together and find that value in the leftmost column of the tables below.

For example, if a student gets 18 questions correct on VM1 and 20 questions correct on VM2, their raw score would be 38. According to this table, if they took VM2a, their score would be 600. If they took VM2b, their score would be 580.

Disclaimers & Scoring Notes:

It may strike some as a bit silly to have a paper-based prep book for a digital test, and it's certainly something I considered when starting to write this book. While there is a Kindle digital copy available for those who prefer to read or annotate this document on a device, LearnCurious recommends that students use this (and our upcoming math prep) book as a supplement to digital prep materials.

The aim of this book is to help students gain more in-depth familiarity with the types of passages and questions they will encounter on the Digital SAT (dSAT) in order to better design a study plan that will target the categories of questions that are the most challenging for them.

It's important to note that the question type labels/categories specified in this book do not precisely match those designated by The College Board. This is intentional, and equivalencies have been noted where applicable. Please also note that many of the example and practice passages, questions, and answer choices in this book are slightly longer than they'll be on the official dSAT. This is also intentional and is meant to both offset the inferences we've had to make about the score ranges on our equivalence tables as well as to hopefully make the official test seem that much easier, since you've been prepping with somewhat tougher material. This book is designed to let you know the areas that make the most sense to focus on as well as your specific strengths / weaknesses.

Practice Test 1 - Score Conversion Table

score from VM1 + score from VM2a or VM2b	VERBAL SCORE RANGES	
	VM2a	VM2b
0	200	200
1	200	200
2	200	200
3	200	200
4	200	200
5	200	200
6	210	200
7	210	200
8	220	210
9	240	220
10	240	230
11	260	240
12	280	260
13	290	280
14	310	290
15	330	310
16	350	330
17	360	350
18	370	370
19	390	390
20	410	400
21	420	420
22	440	430
23	450	450
24	460	470
25	460	460

26	470	470
27	480	470
28	490	480
29	490	490
30	520	510
31	530	520
32	540	530
33	550	540
34	560	550
35	570	560
36	580	560
37	580	570
38	600	580
39	600	590
40	610	610
41	620	630
42	630	640
43	640	660
44	660	670
45	670	680
46	680	690
47	700	700
48	710	720
49	720	740
50	730	750
51	740	760
52	750	770
53	770	790
54	790	800

Practice Test 2 - Score Conversion Table

score from VM1 + score from VM2a or VM2b	VERBAL SCORE RANGES	
	LOWER	UPPER
0	200	200
1	200	200
2	200	200
3	200	200
4	210	200
5	210	200
6	220	210
7	240	220
8	240	230
9	260	240
10	280	260
11	290	280
12	300	290
13	310	310
14	320	320
15	330	330
16	350	350
17	360	370
18	370	390
19	390	400
20	410	410
21	420	420
22	440	430
23	450	450
24	460	460

25	460	470
26	470	480
27	480	490
28	490	510
29	490	520
30	500	530
31	510	540
32	520	550
33	530	560
34	540	560
35	550	570
36	560	580
37	570	600
38	590	610
39	610	630
40	630	650
41	650	660
42	660	680
43	670	690
44	680	690
45	680	700
46	690	710
47	700	720
48	710	730
49	720	740
50	730	750
51	740	760
52	750	770
53	770	790
54	790	800

Appendix D: Strategy Note Review

Test-Taking Strategies
Reading Skills

- Words in Context questions ask students to choose fitting words based on the specific context of a passage. Keep in mind that the words chosen for these questions can often be used in multiple ways, depending on the context; therefore, it's key to **always read the passage to answer these questions correctly.**

- Evidence questions require looking back at the passage, identifying connecting evidence, and matching it to the correct answer choice. There will be direct evidence for these types of questions, meaning the correct answer will contain verbatim or paraphrased evidence directly from the given passage.

- Logical Completion questions ask students to note the context of the passage and complete a paragraph or sentence with the most logical answer option. Students must pay attention to what is happening in the passage, make inferences, and anticipate answer choices having less direct evidence to support correct answer choices than the more direct evidence which is seen in other types of questions.

- Chart/Graph Interpretation (and Support Quotation) questions usually refer to a "claim" or "hypothesis" stated in the passage. Usually, the passage will directly use the those exact words, so it can be helpful to get in the habit of annotating the words "claim" and "hypothesis" as soon as you see them in a passage. Chances are, you'll need to spot them easily later.

- Support Quotation questions ask students to support a specific claim from the passage, often fiction or poetry; these questions usually refer to a "claim" or "hypothesis" stated in the passage. Usually, the passage will directly use the those exact words, so it can be helpful to **get in the habit of annotating the words "claim" and "hypothesis" as soon as you see them in a passage. Chances are, you'll need to spot them easily later.**

- If you're not already doing so, develop the habit of reading and annotating the citation information that is found at the very beginning of every fiction and poetry passage on the dSAT.

- If *__even one part__* of the answer choice is incorrect or doesn't match what you read in the passage, eliminate it.

Reading Comprehension
Question Types Overview, Identification Phrases, & Strategies

WORDS IN CONTEXT questions appear at the very beginning of each Verbal Module, usually between questions #1-6. They ask students to choose fitting words based on the specific context of a passage.

Frequency: common; *Speed rating:* quick (usually)
Identifier(s): 'most nearly means,' & 'logical and precise word or phrase,'
Strategies:
- come up with a synonym and match it to the answer choices
- look out for words which can be used multiple ways; consider other connotations
- use word positivity / negativity & roots/prefixes/suffixes to help break down unfamiliar vocab

EVIDENCE questions appear in the early-middle part of Verbal Modules, usually between questions #6 - 16. They ask about specific details from the passage, and students can expect there to be (verbatim or paraphrased) direct evidence from the passage to support the correct answer.

Frequency: uncommon; *Speed rating:* moderate
Identifier(s): - 'according to the passage / text,' 'based on the passage / text,' 'as presented in the text,' 'what is true about,' or 'the passage states / asserts / makes the claim / indicates'
Strategies:
- look back at the passage to find directly-stated or paraphrased evidence to support your answer

LOGICAL COMPLETION questions appear toward the late-middle of Verbal Modules, usually between questions #13-16. They ask students to note the context of the passage and complete a paragraph or sentence with the most logical answer option.

Frequency: uncommon; *Speed rating:* moderate
Identifier(s): "most logically completes"
Strategies:
- pay attention to what is happening in the passage; read closely.
- anticipate answer having less direct evidence to support correct answers
- use context clues to make an inference about what comes next.
    (inference: an idea based on clues or hints instead of direct (explicit) statements)

CHART / GRAPH INTERPRETATION questions appear in the early-middle part of Verbal Modules, usually between questions #6 - 16. They ask students to interpret a chart, table, or graph and complete a statement or example.
Frequency: uncommon/rare; *Speed rating:* **time-consuming**
Identifier(s): 'information from the table/graph,' or 'data from the table'
Strategies:
- annotate the "claim" or "hypothesis" in the passage text!
- pay attention to how the graph is titled and how axes or tables are labeled
- ask yourself whether the answer choices are true or false
- eliminate any false statements that conflict with the data from the chart or passage.

SUPPORT QUOTATION questions appear in the early-middle part of Verbal Modules, usually between questions #6 - 16. They ask students to support a specific claim from the passage, often fiction or poetry; the College Board refers to these as 'Textual Evidence' questions.

Frequency: rare; *Speed rating:* moderate/time-consuming
Identifier(s): 'which quotation'
Strategies:
- note whether the passage is poetry or prose (non-poetry, either fiction or non-fiction)
- read and annotate the citation (title, author, date info) at the beginning of fiction/poetry passages.
- annotate the "claim" or "hypothesis" in the passage text!
- use context clues to make an inference *(an educated guess based on indirect / implicit evidence)*about what comes next for questions that have a blank; anticipate having less direct evidence to support correct answers

PURPOSE questions appear in the early-middle part of Verbal Modules, usually between questions #6 - 16. They ask students to assess how a piece of text is functioning within the passage.

Frequency: rare; *Speed rating:* moderate
Identifier(s): 'purpose,' 'function' / 'function as,' 'in order to,' 'to illustrate,' 'serves to,' 'so that,' 'because.'
Strategies:
- remember to distinguish whether you're looking for the main purpose (ask "why") or the main idea (ask "what?") of the passage
- put yourself in the author's shoes & ask yourself "If I were the author of this text, why would I have bothered writing it?" and "What would be the goal I'd be hoping to achieve in writing this piece?"

MAIN IDEA questions appear in the early-middle part of Verbal Modules, usually between questions #6 - 16. They ask students to identify the primary claim or focus of the passage.

Frequency: rare; *Speed rating:* moderate
Identifier(s): 'main idea,' or 'primary claim'
Strategies:
- ask yourself what the majority of the paragraph is about or what the majority of the sentences have in common.
- write a mini summary by briefly (in one sentence) answering the questions **who? what? where? when? how?**

PASSAGE COMPARISON questions appear in the early-middle part of Verbal Modules, usually between questions #6 - 16. They ask students to compare and contrast authors' or passage characters' views on a claim or topic. Since Passage Comparison questions are so rare, it's often a good time-management strategy to guess on them, flag them for review, and come back to them if you have time.

Frequency: mythic; *Speed rating:* time-consuming
Identifier(s): 'most likely,' 'the author of Text 1 / 2'
Strategies:
- remember that PC questions require students to make inferences: guesses based on clues or hints instead of direct (explicit) statements; anticipate answer having less direct evidence to support correct answers.
- save for last

(POETIC) STRUCTURE questions appear in the early-middle part of Verbal Modules, usually between questions #6 - 16. They ask students to assess the how the passage is structured; these are similar to purpose questions.

Frequency: mythic; *Speed rating:* moderate
Identifiers: 'overall structure'
Strategies:
- read the passage / citation information carefully
- annotate transition words
- turn answer choices into TRUE / FALSE questions; eliminate any answers that are FALSE.

Writing & Editing Skills

- If you feel iffy on punctuation, circle any uncommon marks you notice in the passages in the verbal section. You can use these as examples to help remind yourself of the rules surrounding punctuation marks like colons, semicolons, dashes, and apostrophes.

- In order to use colons well, what follows a colon usually answers the most logical question someone might ask about the complete sentence that precedes the colon (before that question even needs to be asked).

- A comma can separate two complete sentences if you pair it with a FANBOYS (for, and, nor, but, or, yet, & so) coordinating conjunction. Watch out for the word because! It's not the "B" in FANBOYS. For example, there is no comma needed in the sentence, "I'm indoors because it is cold outside."

- Words between appositive commas can be removed, and the sentence will still make sense. Try removing the appositive phrase that is between the commas (or dashes / parentheses) and reading the sentence again. Many questions on the digital SAT (and ACT) exams contain examples of interrupter or appositive clauses. Remember, Interrupter clauses can be surrounded by pairs of commas, dashes, or parentheses. These must be balanced pairs — no mixing and matching!

- Remember, you can identify a mid-sentence interrupter when you can remove it completely and are left with a sentence that makes sense and is grammatically correct.

- Keep in mind that possessive pronouns (*mine, yours, hers, his, its, ours, & theirs*) & adjectives (*my, your, her, his, its, our, their*) don't require an apostrophe. They by definition are possessive and do not, therefore, require an apostrophe to denote it.

- Know the difference between its and it's.
  its = possessive pronoun (like your, my, our, his, hers, etc == doesn't need an apostrophe because the definition is possessive already)
  it's = contraction of 'it is,' 'it was,' or 'it has'
  its' = never correct on dSAT

- If you see a single dash or a single quotation mark in the answer options, look for non-underlined partners farther back or ahead in the sentence.

- Remember that possessive pronouns (like "my, your, its, his, her, & their") do not require an apostrophe to indicate possession, as this type of pronoun indicates possession by definition.

- Look at the other verbs in the sentence that aren't underlined for clues to which tense you need.

- Be on the lookout for distracting prepositional phrases, interrupter clauses, and singular subjects that look plural (and vice versa) when finding the subject of a sentence or clause!

- If you're ever unsure which verb is correct, use the 'pronoun trick' and replace the subject of a sentence with a pronoun and read each answer choice with the pronoun + verb combo to better tell which one is correct.

- Pay attention to number-related words in sentences like "both" or "couple" to determine whether comparative or superlative form is appropriate.

- A good rule of thumb is to try removing the word(s) between the commas (or dashes) and reading the sentence again. If the meaning doesn't change without the transition word, the sentence doesn't require it to communicate its core message; therefore, the transition word is more emphatic than essential.

- Skip straight to the question on 'Notes' questions and use it to guide you through what information is relevant as eliminate answer choices. Avoid reading the notes themselves unless you absolutely have to!

Punctuation, Grammar, & Editing
Question Types Overview, Identification Phrases, & Strategies

PUNCTUATION questions appear toward the end of each Verbal Module, usually between questions #14-23. They ask students to choose the correct punctuation mark given certain sentence structures. To answer these questions efficiently, **say the sentences slowly in your head; try each answer; eliminate answers as you go; & review rules for apostrophe, comma, colon, dash, semicolon, and quotation use.**

Frequency: uncommon; *Speed rating:* quick (if you know all the rules)
Identifier(s): answer options with different punctuation mark options
Punctuation rules recap:

- COLONS must follow a complete sentence and link relevant information that answers the most logical question someone might ask about the sentence preceding the colon.

- SEMICOLONS separate related complete sentences and, on occasion, subgroups in complex lists that already contain commas.

- COMMAS have too many rules to list here and often require more practice than the other punctuation marks.

- APOSTROPHES create possessive words and contractions.

- SINGLE DASHES function exactly like colons -- they must follow a complete sentence and link relevant information that answers the most logical question someone might ask about the sentence preceding the colon.

- DASH PAIRS surround non-essential (but relevant) information that can be removed.

- QUOTATION MARKS used in pairs surrounding dialogue to indicate direct quotation. For the dSAT, other punctuation marks go INSIDE quotation marks.

GRAMMAR questions appear toward the end of each Verbal Module, usually between questions #14-23. They ask students to choose the word that fits in the blank with correct agreement, tense, and case. To complete these questions efficiently, **it is helpful to look at other verbs in the sentence and/or locate the subject in the sentence in question, determine whether it's singular or plural.**

Frequency: uncommon; *Speed rating:* quick / moderate
Identifier(s): noun, verb, or pronoun answer options
Strategies:
- <u>verb tense</u> = check & match the tense of other verbs in the sentence
- <u>subject-verb agreement</u> = check whether you need a singular or plural word to match with the subject of the sentence.

LOGICAL TRANSITION questions appear toward the end of each Verbal Module, usually between questions #21-26. They ask students to connect ideas in a logical way, given the context. The transitions tested on the digital SAT can be helpfully grouped into three main categories: **support, contrast, and sequence/results transitions. If the transition word is found between two commas, it is likely used more emphatically and should be able to be removed.**

Frequency: uncommon; *Speed rating:* moderate
Identifier(s): transition words in the answer options
Strategies:
- **support** transitions continue with same idea or emphasize
        examples: *additionally, clearly, for example, indeed, in fact, furthermore, moreover*
- **contrast** transitions change ideas or emphasize
        examples: *however, but, yet, although, nevertheless, nonetheless*
- **sequence/results** transitions provide a chronology/summary of events/ideas
        examples: *because, in order to, since, thus*

NOTES questions appear toward the end of each Verbal Module, usually between questions #22-26. They ask students to use a set of bulleted notes to answer a specific question. **Skip straight to the question on 'Notes' questions, annotate the specific request, and use it to guide you through what information is relevant as you eliminate answer choices.**

Frequency: uncommon; *Speed rating:* moderate / time-consuming
Identifier(s): bulleted list of notes present in passage area
Strategies:
- Avoid reading the notes themselves unless you absolutely have to do so.
- Skip straight to the question & annotate the specific request.
- Eliminate answers as you go along.

Test-Taking Skills

Leave nothing blank.

Be willing to guess and skip over difficult questions and come back to them later.

If a question seems unusually hard or difficult to understand, you may have come across an unscored question. Be willing to guess on, skip over, and come back to these questions later if there's time.

GUESSING

If you don't have time to eliminate any answer options and need to make a guess on a question, have a consistent guess letter in mind. There is no truth to the common myth that "C" is the best guess to make. Pick your favorite letter and choose that for any guesses you need to make. By choosing one letter consistently, you are slightly more likely to earn free points by guessing correctly.

Approach each question as though there's been no discernable answer letter pattern. Don't try to game the test!

MATH*

Familiarize yourself with how to use **Desmos**, the free online graphing calculator tool that will be included in the resources provided for students to use on the digital SAT.

If math makes you nervous (like it does many of us), check out the math anxiety chapter on pages 249-255.

*more math strategies will be covered in our upcoming LearnCurious Companion to the Digital SAT MATH book.

Appendix E:
Checklists

Pre-Test To-Do & Checklists

TIMELINE TO TEST DAY
WHAT TO DO & WHEN TO DO IT

MONTH OF THE TEST

- Spend 20-30 minutes per night looking up different explanations (watch videos, listen to lecture recordings, find powerpoints online from other teachers, etc) of the concepts that seem most challenging to you.

- Write down questions as they come to mind. Re-write and reorganize the notes from the sections that are hardest for you. Ask your teachers and friends for clarification in any areas that still seem hazy.

- Time yourself through one full practice test and analyze the questions you get wrong. Practice more of that type of problem.

WEEK OF THE TEST

- **Monday & Tuesday** - Review strategy & math vocab notes. Read through your notes a few times.
- **Wednesday** - Run a timed practice drill of the section that's hardest for you, and ask someone for an explanation of the questions you missed; get a good night's sleep.
- **Thursday** - Review all strategy sheets & notes. Get good sleep.
- **Friday** - TREAT YO SELF. **<u>Don't study; definitely don't cram</u>**. Focus on relaxing as much as possible and getting a full night's rest. Charge your computer fully. Prep your outfit (layers!) and a bag with all you'll need for test day. Keep the big picture in mind. College = amazing. Congratulate yourself on the time you've dedicated to preparing for this test.

Here's a handy packing list:

- test ticket & photo ID (for those taking weekend SAT exams),
- **fully charged laptop computer or tablet device with the Bluebook app already downloaded and ready to go.**
- pencils/pens for scratch work
- low-sugar snacks *(ex. nuts, protein bar, trail mix, etc.)*
- water bottle
- clothing layers in case it is too hot/cold
- watch *(that doesn't beep or connect to the Internet!)*

DAY OF THE TEST

• Leave early & arrive early. It's stressful to feel rushed or to be late. Give yourself the time you need to be as calm as possible.

• EAT BREAKFAST. Even if you usually don't. Seriously. Eat something 'cause your brain's about to run a marathon, and it'll need more energy than usual.
   Example: spinach omelet + banana, oatmeal, not sugar-loaded

• Remember: worrying won't change things. Either you've done all you can to prepare, or you haven't. At this point, what matters is that you use what you've learned to do your best. You've got this!

Test-Taking Timeline & Checklists

Plan when you're taking the digital SAT exam far ahead of time, if possible. A few other important dates to keep in mind when making this kind of plan are the dates of finals and APs. Space out exams to balance your schedule.

JUNIOR YEAR ~ All Test Options

- August: SAT
- September: ACT
- October: ACT / SAT
- November: SAT
- December: ACT / SAT
- February: ACT (*sometimes out of state only)
- March: SAT
- April: ACT
- May: SAT
- June: ACT / SAT
- July: ACT (*sometimes out of state only)

SENIOR YEAR ~ Summer / Autumn Test Options

- August: SAT
- September: ACT
- October: ACT / SAT
    *Last accepted SAT date for some Early Action/Decision applications.
- November: SAT
    *Last accepted SAT date for some Early Action/Decision applications.
- December: ACT / SAT
    *Last accepted SAT date for some Regular Decision applications.

12th Grade Timeline & Checklist

JULY (before senior year)
- ❑ Sign up for Naviance (if you haven't already), and research/compare schools you're interested in
- ❑ Register on the Common App's website
- ❑ Begin application essay drafts (Tip: start with the Common App's prompts)
- ❑ Athletes - check to make sure you're meeting all NCAA division requirements for your chosen colleges and universities. Reach out with specific questions to schools you're interested in!

AUGUST (before senior year)
- ❑ Take the digital SAT if you haven't already
- ❑ Make a list of schools you want to apply to (keep application rates in mind!)
- ❑ Choose an Early Decision (*can only pick one) and/or Early Action schools.
- ❑ Make a list of all of the non-academic activities you've participated in during high school (sports, clubs, teams, religious/political groups, volunteer services, community outreach, etc.) Be specific and include anything you can think of that might count.

SEPTEMBER
- ❑ Take the ACT if you have studied for that exam as well.
- ❑ Request letters of recommendation from recent teachers, coaches, or counselors
- ❑ Make a list of essay questions for each school you're applying to; some you're interested in may not accept the Common App.
- ❑ Meet with your school's guidance or college counselor to talk about applications

OCTOBER
- ❑ Take dSAT / ACT
- ❑ Finish and send early applications by Nov 1 (the Early Action / Early Decision deadline)

NOVEMBER
- ❑ Take dSAT
- ❑ Revise and improve college essays and supplemental material.

DECEMBER
- ❑ (*emergency option) Take dSAT / ACT
- ❑ Fill out applications & send supplemental information to your chosen colleges.
- ❑ Send all applications by Jan 1 (the Regular Decision deadline for most* schools)

Appendix F: Resources Cited

Baum, Frank L. Adapted from The Wonderful Wizard of Oz," published as an ebook 1993. Accessed via Project Gutenberg, https://www.gutenberg.org/cache/epub/55/pg55-images.html

"Beach Games." The Office, created by Greg Daniels, season 3, episode 23, NBC, 10 May, 2007.

BioShock. Windows version, 2K, 2007.

Carroll, Lewis. Adapted from "Alice's Adventures in Wonderland," The Millenium Fulcrum Edition 3.0, cred. Dibianca, Arthur & Widger, David, published 2008. Accessed via Project Gutenberg, https://www.gutenberg.org/cache/epub/11/pg11-images.html

Darwin, Charles. From "On the Origin of Species By Means of Natural Selection," originally published 1859. Accessed via Project Gutenberg, https://www.gutenberg.org/cache/epub/1228/pg1228-images.html

Darwin, Charles. From "The Voyage of the Beagle," 1997. Accessed via Project Gutenberg, https://www.gutenberg.org/cache/epub/944/pg944-images.html

Destiny. XBox version, Bungie, 2014.

Dewey, John. Adapted from "Democracy and Education," published online, 1997; trans. David Reed & David Widger. Accessed via Project Gutenberg, https://www.gutenberg.org/cache/epub/852/pg852-images.html

"Dragonstone." Game of Thrones, created by David Benioff & D.B. Weiss, season 7, episode 1, HBO, 17 July, 2017.

Gutenberg, Project. Adapted from "The Project Gutenberg Encyclopedia, Volume 1 of 28," 1995, most text originally published 1911. Accessed via Project Gutenberg, https://www.gutenberg.org/cache/epub/200/pg200.html

Hesse, Herman. Adapted from "Siddhartha," published online, 2001. Accessed via Project Gutenberg, https://www.gutenberg.org/cache/epub/2500/pg2500-images.html#chap06

"Hostages." Brooklyn Nine-Nine, written by Dan Goor & Michael Schur, season 2, episode 15, Fox, 8 February, 2015.

"How To Survive Cold Water Shock." Youtube.com, uploaded by RLNI, 24 May, 2017, https://www.youtube.com/watch?v=0gd6QC2Emrc

Howells, William Dean. From "Oxford Book of English Verse," Oxford: Clarendon, 1919. Accessed via Bartleby.com, https://www.bartleby.com/lit-hub/the-oxford-book-of-english-verse/812-earliest-spring

"Lotto." The Office, created by Greg Daniels, season 8, episode 3, NBC, 6 October, 2011.

Mackay, Charles. Adapted from "Memoirs of Extraordinary Popular Delusions and the Madness of Crowds," originally published: Office of the National Illustrated Library, 1852; published online, 2008. Accessed via Project Gutenberg, https://www.gutenberg.org/cache/epub/24518/pg24518-images.html

"Man Demonstrates How To Self-Rescue When You Fall Through Ice." Youtube.com, uploaded by Rollie1313, 20 Oct. 2019, https://www.youtube.com/watch?v=A3g-NTP6F3w

Metal Gear Solid 3. PlayStation 2 version, Konami, 2004.

Milne, A. A. Quoted from, "Winnie the Pooh," originally published by E.P. Dutton & Co, [New York], 1926.

Oldys, William. From "Oxford Book of English Verse," Oxford: Clarendon, 1919. Accessed via Bartleby.com, https://www.bartleby.com/lit-hub/the-oxford-book-of-english-verse/438-on-a-fly-drinking-out-of-his-cup

"Operation: Broken Feather." Brooklyn Nine-Nine, written by Dan Goor & Michael Schur, season 1, episode 15, Fox, 2 February, 2014.

Poe, Edgar Allen. From "The Works of Edgar Allen Poe — Volume 1," 2000. Accessed via Project Gutenberg, https://www.gutenberg.org/cache/epub/7452/pg7452-images.html

Portal 2. Windows version, Valve, 2011.

Ratatouille. Directed by Brad Bird, Walt Disney Pictures & Pixar Animation Studios, 2007.

Shudo, Takeshi. Quoted from "The Art of Pokemon, The First Movie: Mewtwo Strikes Back!" published by VIZ Media LLC; 1st edition, December 1, 1999.

"Stress Relief." The Office, created by Greg Daniels, season 5, episode 13, NBC, 1 February, 2009.

"Teenage Mutant Ninja Turtles." Quoted from Master Splinter, written by Michael Reaves, 1987.

The Hangover. Directed by Todd Phillips, Warner Bro. Pictures, 2009.

The Lion King. Directed by Roger Allen & Rob Minkoff, Walt Disney Studios, 1994.

The Princess Bride. Directed by Rob Reiner, 20th Century Fox & Interaccess Film Distribution, 1987.

Thoreau, Henry David. Adapted from "Walden, and On The Duty Of Civil Disobedience," published online, 1995. Accessed via Project Gutenberg, https://www.gutenberg.org/cache/epub/205/pg205-images.html#chap16

"**Those Better Not Be The Days.**" Full House, written by Dennis Rinsler & Marc Warren, season 3, episode 063, 23 February, 1990.

Twain, Mark. Adapted from "The Adventures of Tom Sawyer, Complete," originally published by the American Publishing Company, 1884, released online 2004. Accessed via Project Gutenberg, https://www.gutenberg.org/cache/epub/74/pg74-images.html

Tzu, Sun. From "The Art of War," originally published 1910, trans. Lionel Giles. Accessed via Project Gutenberg, https://www.gutenberg.org/cache/epub/132/pg132-images.html

Various. Adapted from "The Project Gutenberg eBook of Encyclopaedia Britannica, 11th Edition, "Bréquigny, Louis Georges Oudard Feudrix de" to 'Bulgaria,'" originally published 2006. Accessed via Project Gutenberg,
https://www.gutenberg.org/cache/epub/19699/pg19699-images.html

Wordsworth, William. From "Oxford Book of English Verse," Oxford: Clarendon, 1919. Accessed via Bartleby.com, https://www.bartleby.com/lit-hub/the-oxford-book-of-english-verse/532-the-rainbow

Yeats, William Butler. From "Oxford Book of English Verse," Oxford: Clarendon, 1919. Accessed via Bartleby.com, https://www.bartleby.com/lit-hub/the-oxford-book-of-english-verse/862-where-my-books-go

Yogananda, Paramahansa. From "Autobiography of a Yogi," originally published 1946. Accessed via Project Gutenberg, https://www.gutenberg.org/cache/epub/7452/pg7452-images.html